District Gazetteers of India Series 13

BENGAL DISTRICT GAZETTEERS

BAKARGANJ

District Gazetteers of India Series 13

BENGAL DISTRICT GAZETTEERS

BAKARGANJ

J. C. JACK

52 VOLUMES

(VOL. 2nd)

GYAN

Published by

Gyan Publishing House
5, Ansari Road
Daryaganj, New Delhi-110002
Phone: 011-47034999, 9811692060
E-mail: books@gyanbooks.com

Distribution Network
gyanbooks.com
India, USA, Canada, UK, Australia, France

ISBN: 978-93-6208-915-1 (Set) 52 Volumes
978-81-212-5963-7 (PB)
First Published, 1918

2nd Impression 2024

Printed at: Gyan Press, Delhi.

BENGAL DISTRICT GAZETTEERS (VOL. 2nd)
Author: J. C. JACK

LIST OF VOLUMES

S. NO.	ISBN NO.	VOLUME	TITLE	AUTHOR	PRICE	PAGES
			ASSAM DISTRICT GAZETTEERS			
1	9788121285926	1st	Cachar	B. C. Allen	600	300
2	9788121285919	2nd	Sylhet	B. C. Allen	750	378
3	9788121285902	3rd	Goalpara	B. C. Allen	400	203
4	9788121285896	4th	Kamrup	B. C. Allen	675	344
5	9788121285889	5th	Darrang	B. C. Allen	725	364
6	9788121285872	6th	Nowgong	B. C. Allen	560	280
7	9788121285865	7th	Sibsagar	B. C. Allen	675	343
8	9788121285858	8th	Lakhimpur	B. C. Allen	690	347
9	9788121285841	9th	Naga Hills and Manipur	B. C. Allen	580	294
10	9788121285834	10th	The Khasi And Jaintia Hills, The Garo Hills And The Lushai Hills	B. C. Allen	675	363
11	9788121285827	11th	The Sadiya and Balipara Frontier Tract	B. C. Allen	375	190
			BENGAL DISTRICT GAZETTEERS			
12	9788121218672	1st	Angul	L. S. S. O'Malley	340	168
13	9788121259637	2nd	Bakarganj	J. C. JACK	970	194
14	9788121218696	3rd	Balasore	L. S. S. O'Malley	450	228
15	9788121259590	4th	Bankura	L. S. S. O'Malley	1000	199
16	9788121218375	5th	Bhagalpur	J. Byrne	390	194
17	9788121218290	6th	Birbhum	L. S. S. O'Malley	300	150
18	9788121259651	7th	Eastern Bengal and Assam - Bogra	J. N. Gupta	940	188
19	9788121218351	8th	Burdwan	J. C. K. Peterson	450	227
20	9788121259538	9th	Calcutta District Gazetteer - Statistics, 1901 - 02		340	68
21	9788121218313	10th	Champaran	L. S. S. O'Malley	410	205
22	9788121259613	11th	Eastern Bengal District Gazetters - Chittagong	L. S. S. O'Malley	1080	216
23	9788121259552	12th	Chota Nagpur Tributary		130	26
24	9788121259415	13th	The Cooch Behar Gazette: Statistics		1460	292
25	9788121218412	14th	Cuttack	L. S. S. O'Malley	490	248
26	9788121261357	15th	Eastern Bengal District Gazetteers Dacca	B. C. Allen	400	207
27	9788121218436	16th	Darbhanga	L. S. S. O'Malley	360	180
28	9789362089335	17th	Darjeeling	L. S. S. O'Malley	500	248
29	9788121259453	18th	Eastern Bengal District Gazetteers - Dinajpur	F. W. Strong	890	178
30	9788121259392	19th	Faridpur	L. S. S. O'Malley	700	140
31	9788121218474	20th	Gaya	L. S. S. O'Malley	540	270
32	9788121214032	21st	Bihar and Orissa District Gazetteer: Hazaribagh	E. Lister	715	234
33	9788121218337	22nd	Hooghly	L. S. S. O'Malley	680	340
34	9788121218191	23rd	Bengal District Gazetteer Howrah	L. S. S. O'Malley	390	199
35	9788121259293	24th	Eastern Bengal and Assam - Jalpaiguri	John F. Gruning	890	178
36	9788121259279	25th	Jessore	L. S. S. O'Malley	960	192
37	9788121259231	26th	Khulna	L. S. S. O'Malley	1100	220
38	9788121259217	27th	Malda	G. E. Lambourn	670	134
39	9788121267854	28th	Manbhum	H. Coupland	600	313
40	9788121218498	29th	Midnapore	L. S. S. O'Malley	500	252
41	9788121218597	30th	Monghyr	L. S. S. O'Malley	560	280
42	9788121259156	31st	Murshidabad	L. S. S. O'Malley	1250	250
43	9788121259576	32nd	Bengal District Gazetteers - Muzaffarpur	L. S. S. O'Malley	940	188
44	9788121259132	33rd	Mymensingh	F. A. Sachse	960	192
45	9788121259118	34th	Nadia	J. H. E. Garrett	1070	214
46	9788121259095	35th	Eastern Bengal and Assam - Noakhali	J. E. Webster	580	115
47	9788121218450	36th	Feudatory States of Orissa	L. E. B. Cobdenramsay	790	395
48	9788121259071	37th	Pabna	L. S. S. O'Malley	710	142
49	9788121218511	38th	Palamau	L. S. S. O'Malley	380	190
50	9788121218634	39th	Patna	L. S. S. O'Malley	500	250
51	9788121218535	40th	Puri	L. S. S. O'Malley	650	328
52	9788121218757	41st	Purnea	L. S. S. O'Malley	440	220
53	9788121258937	42nd	Rajshahi	L. S. S. O'Malley	1080	216
54	9788121256681	43rd	Bihar and Orissa District Gazetteers: Ranchi	M. G. Hallett	1350	278
55	9788121258913	44th	Eastern Bengal and assam - Rangpur	J. A. Vas	890	178
56	9788121218559	45th	Sambalpur	L. S. S. O'Malley	480	242
57	9788121214056	46th	Santal Parganas	L. S. S. O'Malley	940	308
58	9788121218610	47th	Saran	L. S. S. O'Malley	380	190
59	9788121218658	48th	Shahabad	L. S. S. O'Malley	380	190
60	9788121256704	49th	The Gazetteer of Sikhim	H. H. Risley	960	481
61	9788121218573	50th	Singhbhum, Saraikela And Kharsawan	L. S. S. O'Malley	560	280
62	9788121259439	51st	Eastern Bengal District Gazetteers - Tippera	J. E. Webster	730	146
63	9788121259033	52nd	24 Parganas	L. S. S. O'Malley	1420	284

S. NO.	ISBN NO.	VOLUME	TITLE	AUTHOR	PRICE	PAGES
			CENTRAL PROVINCES DISTRICT GAZETTEERS			
64	9789362081728	1st, Vol. A	Akola (Descriptive)	A. E. Nelson, C. Brown	870	436
65	9789362085481	2nd, Vol. A	Amraoti (Descriptive)	S. V. Fitzgerald, A. E. Nelson	1050	524
66	9789362089267	3rd,Vol. A	Balaghat (Descriptive)	R. V. RUSSELL	430	216
67	9789362083494	4th, Vol. A	Betul (Descriptive)	R. V. RUSSELL	610	306
68	9789362085146	5th, Vol. A	Bhandara (Descriptive)	R. V. RUSSELL	580	292
69	9789362088390	6th, Vol. A	Bilaspur (Descriptive)	R. V. RUSSELL	870	434
70	9789362086044	7th, Vol. A	Buldana (Descriptive)	A. E. Nelson	1090	543
71	9789362089014	8th, Vol. B	Chanda (Descriptive)	R. V. RUSSELL	470	234
72	9789362086938	9th	Chhattisgarch Feudatory State	E. A. De Brett	880	440
73	9789362082961	10th	Chhindwara (Descriptive)	R. V. RUSSELL	550	274
74	9789362089342	11th, Vol. A & B	Damoh (Descriptive and Statistical Tables 1891-1901)	R. V. RUSSELL	830	414
75	9789362081230	12th, Vol. A	Durg (Descriptive)	A. E. Nelson	460	232
76	9789362086037	13th, Vol. A	Hoshangabad (Descriptive)	R. V. RUSSELL	860	430
77	9789362086792	14th, Vol. A	Jubbulpore (Descriptive)	A. E. Nelson	950	474
78	9789362089663	15th, Vol. A & B	Mandla (Descriptive and Statistical Tables 1891-1901)	R. V. RUSSELL	370	186
79	9789362086419	16th, Vol. A	Nagpur (Descriptive)	R. V. RUSSELL	790	394
80	9789362080646	17th, Vol. A	Narsinghpur (Descriptive)	R. V. RUSSELL	510	257
81	9789362084835	18th, Vol. A	Nimar (Descriptive)	R. V. RUSSELL	600	299
82	9789362087737	19th, Vol. A	Raipur (Descriptive)	A. E. Nelson	790	396
83	9789362080264	20th, Vol. A	Saugor (Descriptive)	R. V. RUSSELL	570	285
84	9789362081117	21st, Vol. A	Seoni (Descriptive)	R. V. RUSSELL	460	232
85	9789362084965	22nd, Vol. A	Wardha (Descriptive)	R. V. RUSSELL	600	302
86	9789362083401	23rd, Vol. A	Yeotmal (Descriptive)	R. V. RUSSELL	550	277
87	9789362080325	24th, Vol. I, Pt. I	Gwalior (Text and Tables)	R. V. RUSSELL	980	489
88	9789362087133	24th, Vol. I, Pt. II	Gwalior (Maps)	R. V. RUSSELL	400	198
89	9789362086341	24th, Vol. I, Pt. III	Gwalior (Village List)	R. V. RUSSELL	810	406
90	9789362085467	24th, Vol. I, Pt. IV	Gwalior (Photos)	R. V. RUSSELL	1400	698
91	9789362087393	25th, Vol. II	Indore (Text and Tables)	C. E. Luard	1050	524
92	9789362084422	26th, Vol. III	Bhopal (Text and Tables)	C. E. Luard	540	272
93	9789362086815	27th, Vol. IV	Rewah (Text and Tables)	C. E. Luard	500	250
94	9789362087584	28th, Vol. V, Pt. A	Western States - Malwa (Text)	C. E. Luard	1520	762
95	9789362087300	29th, Vol. VI, Pt. A	Eastern States - Bundelkhand (Text)	C. E. Luard	930	463
96	9789362082169	30th, Vol. VI, Pt. B	Eastern States - Bundelkhand (Tables)	C. E. Luard	830	417
			GAZETTEER OF THE BOMBAY PRESIDENCY:			
97	9788121283441	1st, Part I	History of Gujarat	Ed.: James M. Campbell	3220	644
98	9788121285582	1st, Part II	History of the Konkan Dakhan and Southern Maratha Country	Ed.: James M. Campbell	4200	840
99	9788121285568	2nd	Gujarat, Surat and Broach	Ed.: James M. Campbell	2990	598
100	9788121285544	3rd	Kaira and Panch Mahals	Ed.: James M. Campbell	1690	339
101	9788121285520	4th	Ahmedabad	Ed.: James M. Campbell	1860	372
102	9788121285506	5th	Cutch, Palanpur, and Mahi Kantha	Ed.: James M. Campbell	2390	478
103	9788121285483	6th	Rewa Kantha, Narukot, Cambay, and Surat States	Ed.: James M. Campbell	1450	290
104	9788121285469	7th	Baroda	Ed.: James M. Campbell	3260	652
105	9788121285445	8th	Kathiawar	Ed.: James M. Campbell	3790	758
106	9788121285421	9th, Part I	Gujarat Population - Hindus	Ed.: James M. Campbell	3170	636
107	9788121285407	9th, Part II	Gujarat Population - Musalmans and Parsis	Ed.: James M. Campbell	1520	304
108	9788121285384	10th	Ratnagiri and Savantvadi	Ed.: James M. Campbell	2500	501
109	9788121285360	11th	Kolaba and Janjira	Ed.: James M. Campbell	2550	513
110	9788121285346	12th	Khandesh	Ed.: James M. Campbell	3190	638
111	9788121285322	13th Part I	Thana	Ed.: James M. Campbell	2050	413
112	9788121285308	13th Part II	Thana	Ed.: James M. Campbell	1770	357
113	9788121285285	14th	Thana - Places of Interest	Ed.: James M. Campbell	3290	659
114	9788121285261	15th Part I	Kanara	Ed.: James M. Campbell	2340	348
115	9788121285247	15th Part II	Kanara	Ed.: James M. Campbell	1740	348
116	9788121285223	16th	Nasik	Ed.: James M. Campbell	3490	698
117	9788121285209	17th	Ahmadnagar	Ed.: James M. Campbell	3860	772
118	9788121285186	18th Part I	Poona	Ed.: James M. Campbell	2930	586
119	9788121285162	18th Part II	Poona	Ed.: James M. Campbell	2680	537
120	9788121285148	18th Part III	Poona	Ed.: James M. Campbell	2500	503
121	9788121285124	19th	Satara	Ed.: James M. Campbell	3450	692
122	9788121285100	20th	Sholapur	Ed.: James M. Campbell	2730	547
123	9788121285087	21st	Gazetteer of the Bomaby Presidency: Belgaum	Ed.: James M. Campbell	2570	514
124	9788121285063	22nd	Dharwar	Ed.: James M. Campbell	4200	841
125	9788121285049	23rd	Gazetteer of the Bombay Presidency:Bijapur	Ed.: James M. Campbell	3550	712
126	9788121285025	24th	Kolhapur	Ed.: James M. Campbell	2250	450

S. NO.	ISBN NO.	VOLUME	TITLE	AUTHOR	PRICE	PAGES
127	9788121285001	25th	Botany	Ed.: James M. Campbell	2040	408
128	9788121284981	26th, Part I	Materials Towards a Statistical Account of the Town and Island of Bombay - History	Ed.: James M. Campbell	2500	504
129	9788121284967	26th, Part II	Materials Towards a Statistical Account of the Town and Island of Bombay - Trade and Fortifications	Ed.: James M. Campbell	2690	538
130	9788121284943	26th, Part III	Materials Towards a Statistical Account of the Town And Island of Bombay - Administration	Ed.: James M. Campbell	2450	702
131	9788121284929	27th	General Index	Ed.:R. E. Enthoven	2190	428
			MADRAS DISTRICT GAZETTEERS			
132	9788121258814	1st	Anantapur	W. Francis	1140	227
133	9788121258555	2nd	Malabar	C. A Innes & F. B Evans	3010	602
134	9788121258791	3rd	Bellary	W. Francis	1890	377
135	9788121258777	4th	Statistical Appendix For Chingleput		280	56
136	9788121258753	5th	Coimbatore	K. N. Krishnaswami Ayyar	3420	628
137	9788121232814	6th	Madras District Gazetteers District Gazetteer Cuddapah	C. F. Brackenbury	1120	285
138	9788121258715	7th	Statistical Appendix For Ganjam		370	73
139	9788121256766	8th, Vol. 1st	Godavari District Gazetteer	F. R. Hemingway	650	320
140	9788121256803	8th, Vol. 2nd	Godavari District Gazetteer	F. R. Hemingway	160	83
141	9788121258678	9th	Statistical Appendix For Kistna		640	127
142	9788121258654	10th	Statistical Appendix For Kurnool		270	54
143	9788121258616	11th	Madura	W. Francis	1900	379
144	9788121258579	12th	Statistical Appendix For Madura		740	148
145	9788121258630	13th	The Nilgiris	W. Francis	2190	437
146	9788121234276	14th	Madras District Gazetteers Gazetteer Of The Nellore District Brought Upto 1938		1150	386
147	9788121258517	15th	North Arcot		590	118
148	9788121258494	16th, Vol. 1, Part I	Salem	F. J. Richards	1710	343
149	9788121258593	16th, Vol. 1, Part II	Salem	F. J. Richards	1800	360
150	9788121258456	17th	South Arcot	W. Francis	2400	480
151	9788121258470	18th	Statistical Appendix For South Canara		400	80
152	9788121258432	19th, Vol. 1st & 2nd	Tanjore: Main Volume and Statistical Appendix		2070	401
153	9788121258395	20th	Tinnevelly	H. R. Pate	2740	547
154	9788121258418	21st	Statistical Appendix For Tinnevelly		320	64
155	9788121258371	22nd, 1st & 2nd	Trichinopoly: Main Volume and Statistical Appendix	F. R. Hemingway	2440	487
156	9788121241953	23rd	Vizagapatam District Gazetteer	W. Francis	760	385
			PUNJAB DISTRICT GAZETTEERS			
157	9788121255943	1st	Ambala District 1883-84		620	124
158	9788121255967	2nd	Amritsar		1180	236
159	9788121255981	3rd	Delhi		1300	260
160	9788121256001	4th	Ferozepore		950	188
161	9788121256025	5th	Faridkot		350	70
162	9788121256049	6th	Gujranwala 1893-94		1270	254
163	9788121256063	7th	Gujrat	C. E. Luard	1140	228
164	9788121256087	8th	Gurdaspur 1891-92		1260	252
165	9788121256100	9th	Gurgaon 1883-4		1020	203
166	9788121256124	10th	Hazara	H. D. Watson	2290	458
167	9788121256148	11th	Hissar district and Lohar State		1840	367
168	9788121256162	12th	Hoshiarpur		1420	283
169	9788121256186	13th	Jhang		1070	213
170	9788121256209	14th	Jhelam		1010	202
171	9788121256223	15th	Jalandhar District 1883-84		540	108
172	9788121256247	16th, Vol. XIV-A	Jullundur District, with maps and Kapurthala		1990	398
173	9788121256261	17th, Pt. I	Kangra (Proper)		1450	290
174	9788121256285	17th, Pt. II	Kangra (Kulu, Lahual, Spiti)		1800	357
175	9788121256308	18th	Karnal		1930	386
176	9788121256322	19th	Kohat		1540	307
177	9788121256346	20th	The Lahore District 1883-84		1220	244
178	9788121256384	21st	Ludhiana and Maler Kotla		1680	335
179	9788121256407	22nd	Lyallpur		735	147
180	9788121256421	23rd	Mianwali		1170	234
181	9788121256445	24th	Montgomery	P. J. Fagan	1590	318
182	9788121258364	25th	Multan (1901-02)	E. D. Maclagan	2400	480
183	9788121258708	26th	The Rohtak District 1883-84		980	196
184	9788121258746	27th, Vol. III A	Dujana State 1904		500	16
185	9788121256483	28th	Shahpur District		1780	356
186	9788121256506	29th	Simla District		800	159

S. NO.	ISBN NO.	VOLUME	TITLE	AUTHOR	PRICE	PAGES
187	9788121256520	30th	The Chamba State		2040	408
188	9788121256544	31st	The Chenab Colony 1904		1550	310
189	9788121256568	32nd	Kalsia State		270	53
190	9788121256582	33rd	Suket and Mandi		770	154
191	9788121256605	34th	Phulkian States, Patiala Jind And Nabha 1904		2070	414
192	9788121256643	35th	Simla Hill States		2220	443
193	9788121256667	36th	Sirmur		920	183
			RAJPUTANA DISTRICT GAZETTEERS			
194	9789362088994	1st, Vol. I-A & B	Ajmer-merwara (Text and Statistics Tables)	C. C. Watson	1230	246
195	9789362080882	2nd. Vol. II-A & B	Mewar Residency (Text and Statistics Tables)	K.D. Erskine	1700	339
196	9789362088444	3rd, Vol. III-A & B	The Western Rajputana States Residency And The Bikaner Agency	K.D. Erskine	3590	718
			UNITED PROVINCES OF AGRA AND OUDH DISTRICT GAZETTEERS			
197	9789362087560	Vol. I	Agra	H. R. Nevill	2260	452
198	9789362082466	Vol. II	Aligarh	H. R. Nevill	1300	260
199	9789362089779	Vol. III	Allahabad	H. R. Nevill	2050	409
200	9789362081346	Vol. IV	Almora	H. G. Walton	1670	333
201	9789362085658	Vol. V	Azamgarh	D. L. Drake Brockman	1750	349
202	9789362080547	Vol. VI	Bahraich	H. R. Nevill	1410	281
203	9789362085214	Vol. VII	Ballia	H. R. Nevill	1750	350
204	9789362084668	Vol. VIII	Banda	D. L. Drake Brockman	1750	349
205	9789362086518	Vol. IX	Bara Banki	H. R. Nevill	1720	344
206	9789362084101	Vol. X	Bareilly	H. R. Nevill	1640	327
207	9789362086631	Vol. XI	Basti	H. R. Nevill	1610	321
208	9789362083814	Vol. XII	Benares	H. R. Nevill	2290	458
209	9789362086105	Vol. XIII	Bijnor	H. R. Nevill	1820	363
210	9789362081674	Vol. XIV	Budaun	H. R. Nevill	1890	378
211	9789362086891	Vol. XV	Bulandshahr	H. R. Nevill	2100	419
212	9789362081520	Vol. XVI	Cawnpore	H. R. Nevill	2210	442
213	9789362088031	Vol. XVII	Dehra Dun	H. G. Walton	1710	342
214	9789362088710	Vol. XVIII	Etah	E. R. Neave	1600	320
215	9789362082992	Vol. XIX	Etawah	D. L. Drake Brockman	1390	277
216	9789362082220	Vol. XX	Farrukhabad	E. R. Neave	1620	324
217	9789362083869	Vol. XXI	Fatehpur	H. R. Nevill	1890	377
218	9789362085962	Vol. XXII	Fyzabad	H. R. Nevill	1700	339
219	9789362087997	Vol. XXIII	Garhwal	H. G. Walton	1270	254
220	9789362089892	Vol. XXIV	Ghazipur	H. R. Nevill	1600	320
221	9789362085436	Vol. XXV	Gonda	H. R. Nevill	1650	330
222	9789362080271	Vol. XXVI	Gorakhpur	H. R. Nevill	1890	378
223	9789362086129	Vol. XXVII	Hamirpur	D. L. Drake Brockman	1390	277
224	9789362087638	Vol. XXVIII	Hardoi	H. R. Nevill	1680	336
225	9789362081636	Vol. XXIX	Jalaun	D. L. Drake Brockman	1180	236
226	9789362084309	Vol. XXX	Jaunpur	H. R. Nevill	1750	350
227	9789362084187	Vol. XXXI	Jhansi	D. L. Drake Brockman	1960	391
228	9789362089168	Vol. XXXII	Kheri	H. R. Nevill	1650	330
229	9789362086778	Vol. XXXIII	Lucknow	H. R. Nevill	1760	352
230	9789362088635	Vol. XXXIV	Mainpuri	H. R. Nevill	1740	348
231	9789362080424	Vol. XXXV	Meerut	H. R. Nevill	2170	434
232	9789362081087	Vol. XXXVI	Mirzapur	D. L. Drake Brockman	2430	486
233	9789362085443	Vol. XXXVII	Moradabad	H. R. Nevill	1900	380
234	9789362082763	Vol. XXXVIII	Muttra	D. L. Drake Brockman	2140	428
235	9789362089915	Vol. XXXIX	Muzaffarnagar	H. R. Nevill	2260	451
236	9789362086143	Vol. XL	Naini Tal	H. R. Nevill	1890	377
237	9789362086761	Vol. XLI	Partabgarh	H. R. Nevill	1560	312
238	9789362081124	Vol. XLII	Pilibhit	H. R. Nevill	1570	314
239	9789362084453	Vol. XLIII	Rai Bareli	H. R. Nevill	1610	322
240	9789362088284	Vol. XLIV	Rampur	H. R. Nevill	1170	234
241	9789362083654	Vol. XLV	Saharanpur	H. R. Nevill	2190	438
242	9789362083142	Vol. XLVI	Shahjahanpur	H. R. Nevill	1510	302
243	9789362083623	Vol. XLVII	Sitapur	H. R. Nevill	1590	317
244	9789362089939	Vol. XLVIII	Sultanpur	H. R. Nevill	1330	266
245	9789362080851	Vol. XLIX	Unnao	H. R. Nevill	1530	305

BENGAL DISTRICT GAZETTEERS.

BAKARGANJ.

BENGAL DISTRICT GAZETTEERS.

BAKARGANJ

BY

J. C. JACK,

INDIAN CIVIL SERVICE.

CALCUTTA :

BENGAL SECRETARIAT BOOK DEPÔT.

1918.

PLAN OF CONTENTS.

TABLE OF CONTENTS.

CHAPTER I.

Physical Aspects.

CHAPTER II.

History.

CHAPTER III.

The People.

CHAPTER IV.

Public Health.

CHAPTER V.

Agriculture.

CHAPTER VI.

Natural Calamities.

CHAPTER VII.

Rents, Wages and Prices.

CHAPTER VIII.

Occupations, Manufactures and Trade.

CHAPTER IX.

Means of Communication.

CHAPTER X.

Land Revenue Administration.

CHAPTER XI.

General Administration.

CHAPTER XII.

Local Self-Government.

CHAPTER XIII.

Education.

CHAPTER XIV.

Gazetteer.

GAZETTEER

OF THE

BAKARGANJ DISTRICT.

CHAPTER I.

PHYSICAL ASPECTS.

THE district of Bākarganj forms the central district in the northern seacoast of the Bay of Bengal and lies between 21° 54′ and 23° 2′ north latitude and between 89° 55′ and 91° 2′ east longitude. It contains an area of 4,891 square miles, but a large portion of this is covered by the waters of the Meghnā estuary and other rivers which form the district boundary. Excluding these rivers, the area is 3,840 square miles. GENERAL DESCRIPTION.

The district is bounded on the north by Faridpur district, on the east by the Meghnā and Sāhābāzpur rivers, on the west by the Baleswar river (called Madhumati in its northern reaches) and on the south by the Bay of Bengal. Boundaries.

The name of the district is derived from a certain Āgā Bākhar, a prominent person at the Moghul Court at Dacca in the first half of the eighteenth century. He was owner of the Buzrugumedpur pargana, which is the largest pargana in Bākarganj and in the centre of the district, and also *wādādār* of the pargana of Selimābād. His headquarters which included a flourishing market were fixed at a place which he named Bākarganj, and which afterwards became for a short time the headquarters of the district when it was first formed into a magisterial jurisdiction. Origin of name.

The present headquarters and principal civil station is Barisāl, which is situated in 21° N. and 90° E. Headquarters.

Bākarganj first became an independent district under the British administration in the year 1817, when it included part of what is now Khulnā and also most of the Mādāripur subdivision which is now in Faridpur. Subsequently the island of Previous boundaries.

Sāhābāzpur was transferred in 1822 to Noākhāli district, but was rejoined to Bākarganj in 1869. The Khulnā portion of Bākarganj was made over to Jessore in the year 1861, at which time the then main stream of the Madhumati was made the western boundary of the district. The subdivision of Mādāripur was made over to Faridpur in the year 1873, at which date Bākarganj obtained practically its modern boundaries. In 1912 a small transfer of land took place on the northern boundary with the district of Faridpur and on the eastern boundary with the district of Noākhāli.

GENERAL CONFIGURATION.

Bākarganj is an alluvial deposit, but the date of its formation is not known. It appears probable, however, that it consisted of a chain of islands separated by wide rivers in the thirteenth century. These have gradually consolidated into the modern district and the process is still going on in the large area which is covered by the waters of the Meghnā. This deposit has been the work of three rivers, the Padmā, the Brahmaputra and the Meghnā, but it seems that the Brahmaputra, which to this day carries far more silt than the other rivers, had the chief work in filling up this part of the delta. The island of Sāhābāzpur is generally higher than the level of ordinary high tide, and contains in the interior only a few depressions, none of which are permanently filled with water. The mainland, on the other hand, is generally below the level of high tide, and as a result during three months in the flood season is for the most part entirely under water. Even in the cold season large areas, especially in the west of the district, are marsh and elsewhere in almost every thana there are small depressions from which water is never wholly absent. The high tides and the flood are carried over this part of the district with great completeness by the small streams and distributaries which cover the country. On the other hand, in the cold season, when the water in the rivers is low and the tides at their lowest, a great deal of water is drained from the marsh by the streams which at other times are engaged in filling it. The soil of the district is, therefore, entirely alluvial. It appears to be impregnated with salt to a considerable extent in the Sāhābāzpur island and on the sea-face. There is no stone or gravel anywhere in the district. There are, however, large deposits of pure sand at the seacoast, where also there is a belt of forest of varying thickness.

Natural divisions.

The district consists of two sharply defined parts. On the east there is the island of Sābābāzpur, which is well raised and generally free from marsh and a network of streams. On the west is the great mainland block of a stiff clay soil, which disappears for three months each year under flood water and which is intersected in every direction not only by large rivers but by a multitude of large and small streams. Between Sāhābāzpur and the mainland at the mouth of the estuary of the Meghnā, there is a large number of scattered islands which are gradually being consolidated into a compact block of land which will, when completely consolidated, have the character of the present island of Sāhābāzpur.

The river system of Bākarganj is very important from the economic aspect, from the aspect of communications and from the aspect of administration. In the first place, there is the river Meghnā, which separates the district effectually from its neighbour on the east and which also throws out a channel, the Ilsā (or Tentuliā) river, which separates the island of Sāhābāzpur as effectually from the rest of the district. The islands which the Meghnā throws up at its mouth are separated from each other and the mainland by such wide channels as to become not easily inhabitable. In the second place, the Baleswar (or Madhumati) divides the district as completely from its neighbour on the west. Within the mainland block of the district there are seven large rivers which flow generally north and south, four, the Tarki river, the Ariāl Khān, the Safipur and the Noābhāngani rivers, in the north-east of the district; and three, the Biskhāli river, the Bighāi river and the Lohāliā river, in the south of the district. The northern four are really channels of the Padma river after its junction with the Brahmaputra river. The water of these combined rivers slips away westward by many watercourses in the district of Faridpur, which unite to form the Ariāl Khān river, which enters the district in two main channels, the western under the name of the Turki river and the eastern under the name of the Ariāl Khān river. The Noābhāngani is a later distributary of the combined rivers after their junction with the Meghnā, and appears to have been formed as a result of the historic floods on the Tistā in 1787 A. D. It flows almost due westward for some miles and then separates into two channels which flow southward, the eastern retaining the name Noābhāngani and the western being known as the Safipur river. The Ariāl Khān then sweeps eastward and rejoins the waters of the Ilsā river, taking with it all the waters of the Safipur, the Tārki and the Noābhāngani rivers. RIVER SYSTEM.

From the Ariāl Khān and from the Ilsā rivers a great deal of water escapes again westward by many petty rivers and streams, which unite to form the Lohāliā, the Bighāi and the Biskhāli rivers.

The Baleswar on the extreme west is also fed by some streams which bring water from the Biskhāli and from the Ariāl Khān through the Barisāl rivers. The northern distributary of the Madhumati is the Kāliganga river, which is also fed by water from the marshes of Swarupkāti, from which source the Baldiā river is formed. These two rivers join the Barisāl river and the Swarupkāti river to form the Kāchā river, which takes all their waters to the Baleswar river.

It may be mentioned that all these rivers are tidal, but fresh water comes down at all times of the year. In the southern rivers the water is salt in the cold weather, but only in the Baleswar and the Kāchā rivers in the flood season. All the rivers mentioned have a very great width. The Meghnā is eight miles wide where it enters the district, and although the main stream flows under Noākhāli yet the two Bākarganj channels, the Ilsā and the Sāhābāzpur, are three miles wide. The Baleswar has an average width of half a mile above the junction of the Kāchā and two miles below it. The Tārki, the Ariāl Khān, the Noābhāngāni and the Safipur rivers are nearly a mile wide and the Ariāl Khān after the junction of them all is over two miles wide. The Lohāliā, the Bighāi and the Biskhāli are each more than a mile wide.

Smaller streams.

The country between these great rivers is covered with a maze of smaller rivers and petty streams to an extraordinary extent. Most of the larger streams take their rise in the great rivers and most of the smaller streams join the larger streams together, but every depression is surrounded by numerous watercourses and every homestead is surrounded by a moat which is usually connected with one of the smaller streams, thus carrying on the work of distribution. As a result, in most of the mainlands of the district, it is impossible to walk in any direction for any distance without meeting an unfordable stream and it is impossible to walk far without meeting a large river.

Marshes and natural drainage.

Apart from the river system, the most distinctive physical feature of the district is the great marshes. These reach their greatest size in the north-east of the district and cover most of Gaurnadi and Swarupkāti thanas, but there is a large marsh in Bhāndāriā thana and apart from small depressions there are tracts of marsh also in Jhālakāti, Galāchipā and Patuākhāli thanas. The best description of the marsh country is that given by Mr. Pellew (Vol. XXXIX No. 78 of the "Calcutta

Review "), although it should be said that the channels through the higher banks of the rivers tend to shoal and thus to obstruct the deposit of silt in the *bils* during the flood season and the emptying of the water from the *bils* when the floods subside.

"Although in a district so essentially flat, a complete system of natural drainage would scarcely be looked for, we find that, in fact, the whole district, except where the great Meghnā and Ariāl Khān rivers have obliterated the old features of the country by recent deposits over its northern and eastern portions, may be divided into distinct drainage districts, each of them containing corresponding features. In undulating tracts of country the drainage ordinarily radiates from elevated centres towards the circumjacent coast-line. In alluvial formations, on the contrary, owing to the excess of deposit on the edges, the water flows inwards from an elevated surrounding and enclosing ridge to a central basin, from whence it is conducted to the exterior, along watercourses piercing through this surrounding ridge. And this order is followed, not merely in tidal districts like Bākarganj, but in all alluvial formations, however elevated, as, for example, in Silhet.

"Each of the drainage circles or districts of Bākarganj possesses its central basin or reservoir of swamp, towards which the surface slopes in every direction from the exterior. On the exterior edge of the area, where it abuts on the large tidal rivers (which everywhere divide one drainage circle from another), the land is well raised and covered with villages. The intermediate space is covered with rice cultivation, and the centre is a lake or *bil*, varying in size and depth with the season of the year. From points not very far from the centre of this *bil* or marsh, and quite submerged in the rains, numerous little watercourses proceed in every direction towards the edge. These can only be recognized by the fact that a current flows along them, and by the narrow submerged rims of deposited earth which enclose them on either side, and partially separate them from the *bil* proper. Beginning almost in nothing, many combined to form others, which, though still within the *bil*, and with banks concealed by its waters, present more defined features. At last, by the coalescence of many, a watercourse is formed, with banks which, though but a few feet wide, and sloping rapidly towards the *bil* water, rise in the cold weather above the swamp's surface. After further convergence of such channels, we find ourselves in a khal of moderate dimensions, with banks which are not submerged except in the height of the rains; but we are still many stages from the great rivers whose banks are permanently above the water, and which are some hundreds of yards in width. It is useless to particularise further. The numerous khals which originate in the depths of the central reservoir terminate in some two or three considerable channels, which open into the main watercourse. Between this latter and the *bil* there is no water communication, except through these two or three channels and their ramifications. Even if a short cut were artificially made direct into the *bil*, it would, in a few rainy seasons, by sucking in at the ebb tide the water from all directions, create for itself a branched system of terminations under water, which, in the dry weather, would be exposed to view. The whole system depends on the principle that inundating waters, if in a position to lay down deposits, do so chiefly upon their actual banks, and thus tend to shut themselves off from the tract of submerged country beyond. As the banks rise, the rush of water over them at ebb and flood is intensified, and at length bursts open channels of communication. These throw up enclosing banks in their turn, which process gives birth to new connecting channels piercing these new banks, and the process is repeated till the communicating channels become so small as scarcely to be noticed.

"It is obvious that in this manner the drainage of flat surfaces is performed in the most effectual manner. In undulating or mountainous countries, the drainage derives sufficient force from gravity to maintain the channels open, but in alluvial flats the slow passage of the water would scarcely suffice. If in a tidal district the drainage channels merely flowed from the interior of each patch of land towards the circumference, they would soon fill with sediment brought in by the tide, which would ebb and flow in them with but slight velocity; but where these channels are the only means of communication between two considerable bodies of water constantly differing from each other in level, an adequate rate of speed is maintained. In the rainy season, the drainage reservoirs are connected much more directly with the exterior than during the remainder of the year. The water from various causes stands at an average at least six feet higher than in the dry season, and completely submerges all the interior articulations of the system of relieving channels. Only the larger and more external have their banks above the water; the smaller feeders are supplied both from their extremities and over their own banks. The greater volume of water which then requires passage is thus amply provided for; whilst in the dry weather, when the drainage volume is weak, the water is unable on account of the fall in its level to leave the reservoir except through the extreme ends of very small channels. The banks of the different classes or grades of channels, each in turn, begin to fulfil their proper functions as the level decreases, and in this manner the water-way is always exactly proportioned to the volume to which it is required to give passage. In districts of alluvium raised above tidal influence, the rise and fall of the rivers during the rainy season produces similar effects. The water in the swamps being only connected with these by narrow channels piercing the banks of the rivers, is always, unless the river remains very long at exactly the same level, either above or below that level, and the channels are incessantly occupied in restoring the balance.

"The swamps, or drainage reservoirs, are themselves an interesting feature in the physical geography of Bākarganj. They vary greatly in size in accordance with the area of the tract they drain, and the amount of *filling up* which they have undergone. In the eastern portion of the district, the alluvium from the Meghna has completely obliterated the natural drainage organisation, which has become enveloped in one uniform mound sloping towards the west, and forming the right bank of this immense watercourse. In the west of the district, where the system of natural drainage prevails which we have endeavoured to describe, the swamps during the rainy season fill up the whole of each drainage tract, except its extreme margin, and the banks of the primary channels which penetrate that margin. In the dry weather they are reduced till they form only the nucleus or central portion from which the relieving channels take their rise * * * * * * * * From the *bil* on every side the country rises with considerable slope, the first firm ground being generally found in the watercourses. The drainage towards the *bil* is along successive terraces of rice fields, each a few inches lower than the next above it. The water is retained in the higher ground for cultivation by means of the little *hiras* or banks (here constructed of straw as well as of earth), common throughout Bengal. It may be repeated that all the surface drainage of the tract surrounding each *bil* flows towards it, and never into the penetrating channels, whose banks are invariably higher than the ground outside, and always slope away from the channel."

The bore. There are two interesting physical phenomena in Bākarganj: one is the bore and the other the Barisāl guns. There is a very strong bore at spring tide in the estuary of the Meghnā. This estuary forms a funnel and as the tide sweeps round both sides of the Bay of Bengal it meets at this funnel, which consists for the most part of submerged chars with deep waters between them. The bore is hardly perceptible in the deep water, but advances like a wall over the submerged chars. As the funnel contracts, the wall gets higher. There is a bore at all periods of the year, but it is only high, rapid and furious during the spring tides, when the mass reaches the height of 14 or 15 feet. There are really two bores which meet; the first in point of time is known as the Deulā bore, which comes up between Dakshin Sāhābāzpur and Hatiā and forces its way inland in both islands through all the watercourses and streams. The Chittagong bore passes up the channel between Sandwip and Noākhāli, turns westward under Noākhāli and then southward until it meets the Deulā bore which turns it back again.

The "Barisāl guns." The "Barisāl guns" are sounds resembling the discharge of cannon which occur at regular intervals of a minute or two apart in May and June at the beginning of the rains. These sounds are not confined to Bākarganj as they are heard in Faridpur and Jessore and I believe as far north as Jalpaiguri. They are supposed to be most frequent in a south wind and before rain and to be heard best in the evening, perhaps because at that time there are fewer competing noises. They were heard with extraordinary distinctness before the earthquake of 1896. They have never been satisfactorily explained, but they are now generally supposed to be an atmospheric phenomenon. It should be added that the sound always comes from the south.

GEOLOGY. The district is a typical part of the alluvial delta formed by the Ganges and the Brahmaputra and their feeders. The soil is either a sandy loam, where the rivers are large and have an easy access to the sea, or a stiff clay, where the land has been deserted by the great rivers after formation and has been covered for a considerable period by heavy forest. In the lower parts of the interior the soil contains a great deal of decayed vegetable matter. In the south of the district and especially in the Meghnā delta and the Sāhābāzpur island, the soil contains a considerable impregnation of salt. There is no stone or gravel to be found in any part of the district.

BOTANY. Timber trees.

The only forest in the district is situated in the south and produces many varieties of timber and an abundant supply of firewood. Thirty-three varieties are enumerated as follows :—(1) *gāb* (diospyros embryopteris) ; an extract from its fruit is applied as a covering for native boats as a preservative against decay and sea-worms ; (2) *haritaki* (terminalia chebula), the gall-nut tree ; the fruit and galls are much used by dyers who with a mixture of alum and galls obtain a yellow dye, and with ferruginous mud an excellent black ; (3) *sundri* (heritiera minor) ; a strong wood used for a variety of purposes ; large quantities are exported to the Calcutta market as firewood ; (4) *pasur* ; used for the manufacture of native furniture, and for posts ; (5) *keorā* (sonneratia apetala) ; used for platforms, making boxes, boats, etc.; (6) *kirpā* (lumnizera racemosa); used for making small boats, for posts, rafters, etc., of houses ; (7) *bairā* (zizyphus jujuba) ; (8) *karai* ; used for posts, etc.; (9) *dumsir* ; used for making posts, etc.; (10) *garān* or *gātiā* (ceriops roxburghianus) ; the timber is used for making posts and the bark for tanning ; (11) *sonāil* ; the timber is used for making posts and the bark for tanning purposes ; (12) *jin* ; firewood ; (13) *lohākhairā* ; firewood ; (14) *phulsi* ; firewood ; (15) *singra* ; firewood ; (16) *chhailā* ; firewood ; (17) *kankra* (bruguiera rheedii) ; firewood ; a hard and durable wood ; (18) *nāringā* ; used for making the handles of billhooks, axes, and spades or mattocks ; (19) *balai* ; firewood ; the inner bark also yields a strong fibre ; (20) *uriam* ;- used for making small boats, platforms, etc,; (21) *gāmbhār* or *gámur* ; used for native drums, picture frames, etc.; (22) *bāin* for posts and planks ; (23) *gomā*; used as firewood ; (24) *bāilā* ; firewood ; used for making handles ; (25) *māndār* ; firewood ; (26) *hizal* ; firewood ; (27) *kāfila* ; fencing posts. In addition to the above are the following small trees and shrubs :—(28) *archakā* (sonneratia acida) ; a good firewood ; (29) *bhorā* (rhizophora mucronata) ; a durable wood of a dark red colour ; (30) *gila* (salicornia indica) ; a shrub from which the natives obtain barilla for soap ; (31) *bodāli* ; used for the same purpose as the above ; (32) *hentāl* (phœnix paludosa) ; the young trees are used for making walking-sticks, the older trees as rafters for huts ; the leaves are used for thatching ; (33) *karanja* ; the wood is used as fuel, and for making charcoal ; the oil of the fruit is used for medicinal purposes. It is possible that some of the timber trees have been imported into the district. Other trees which occur occasionally in the district are the casuarina, simul or cotton-tree, pipal, banyan, box, babul and cassia florida. Most of these are found in Barisāl and other headquarters. They are probably all imported.

Fruit trees.

Of fruit trees 29 may be enumerated. It is impossible to say how many of them are really indigenous, but it would appear that most of them are imported and very few grow wild.

(1) Cocoanut (cocos nucifera); (2) betelnut (areca catechu); (3) date (of which the fruit does not ripen well, but the tree gives *tāri*); (4) *tāl* or common palm; (5) wild plum; (6) *coranja*; (7) papia; (8) mango; (9) *amra*; (10) bael; (11) pomegranate; (12) lichu; (13) *kāmrāngā*; (14) *gāb* (the juice is not eaten but used for pitching boats); (15) tamarind; (16) custard apple; (17) fig (not eaten); (18) pomelo; (19) lemon (of which there are several varieties); (20) orange; (21) citron; (22) pineapple; (23) plantain; (24) nail; (25) *pāilā*; (26) *jāmrul*; (27) jack; (28) *latkā*; (29) *chālitā*. There are apparently only two fibres in the district, jute or mesta and hemp, neither of which grow wild but are cultivated. Reeds (*hoglā*) grow in the marshes and on the river banks, while *nal* grass grows chiefly in the marshes. Both are used in the preparation of mats. Thatching grass (*chhan*) grows chiefly on the river banks.

Drugs.

The following is a list of drugs which are furnished by the district: (1) *bel*, anti-dysenteric; (2) *dhaturā*, narcotic and antispasmodic; (3) *supāri* (betel or areca nut), astringent; (4) *bāsak*, expectorant and styptic; (5) *kurchi*, anti-dysenteric; (6) *punarnabhā*, diuretic; (7) *gulanchā*, anti-periodic, tonic; (8) *lālchitā*, purgative, irritant (used for procuring abortion); (9) *nim*, tonic, anti-periodic; (10) *bhānti*, tonic, anthelmintic; (11) *lātā*, tonic, anti-periodic; (12) *haritaki*, laxative, aphrodisiac; (13) *bairā*, astringent; (14) *shatamuli*, alterative; (15) *amlaki*, astringent; (16) *bairkuli*, anti-periodic; (17) *shonāl*, laxative; (18) *brihati*, anti-periodic; (19) *bhumikusmánda*, alterative; (20) *pārul*, anti-periodic; (21) *gaināri*, anti-periodic; (22) *brahmajaistha*, expectorant; (23) *dārimba*, anthelmintic; (24) *teoriā*, purgative; (25) *ākānda*, laxative; (26) *āpāng*, anti-periodic; (27) *pitháni*, neurine tonic; (28) *dhaniā*, aromatic, carminative; (29) *chhālāni*, neurine tonic; (30) *bālā*, astringent; (31) *ghritakumāri*, laxative; (32) *muthā*, anthelmintic; (33) *tentul*, laxative; (34) *khetpānprā*, anti-periodic; (35) *dronaphul*, emetic; (36) *nishindā*, emetic, expectorant; (37) *saluphā*, neurine tonic; (38) *sathi*, anthelmintic; (39) *suāshambhu*, anti-periodic; (40) *gajapippali*, anti-periodic, anthelmintic; (41) *ādā*, carminative; (42) *joyān*, carminative, stomachic; (43) *palāsh*, anthelmintic.

FAUNA.

The district was formerly full of the larger mammalia, and tigers at the time of the Permanent Settlement were so common in Gaurnadi that a special reward had to be offered for their destruction. In the marshes, which were then much more extensive than they are now, large herds of wild buffaloes used to roam. In later times tigers have retreated into the forest in the south of the district from which they are gradually being trapped and shot out. They seem to have entirely left the Sāhābāzpur island, although forty years ago they were very numerous. Rhinoceros was at one time found in the Sundarbans and perhaps along the banks of the Baleswar river, but it has certainly not been seen in the district for many years. The buffalo is still numerous in the Sundarbans, in the islands of the Meghnā archipelago and in the Bhāndāriā *bil*. It has disappeared from the other marshes. Deer (chital or spotted) are found in the Sundarbans and in the Sāhābāzpur island and swamp deer in the Bhāndāriā *bil*. Barking deer is also found in the Sundarbans. Leopards are found everywhere, even in Barisāl town. Amongst other animals which are found everywhere are the jackal, wild hog, porcupine, otter, mongoose, rat, mouse, civet cat, wild cat, flying fox, common bat and porpoise. Wild hog and otter are specially common in the Sāhābāzpur island. The fruit-eating tree-cat exists in the south of the district and the scarlet bat is also found.

Game birds.

The game birds of the district are not numerous. Snipe are only found in a few places, duck do not come so far south in any numbers, geese are common in Sāhābāzpur, where also plover, especially golden plover, are very numerous. In the Sundarbans jungle fowl are to be obtained. A complete list of the game and water-birds in the district is as follows :—

(1) bittern, chestnut (rare) ; (2) coot, bald ; (3) coot, purple ; (4) crane, large white (rare) ; (5) crane, kulin (rare) ; (6) curlew, black ; (7) curlew, white ; (8) curlew, grey ; (9) dove, common ; (10) ring-dove ; (11) dove, bronze wing ; (12) dove, rufsus ; (13) duck—, pinheaded, pintail, white eye, golden eye, pochard-red head, pochard-red crest, gadwall, shoveller, spoonbill, brahmani or ruddy-sheldrake (*chakwa*), widgeon ; (24) teal—, grey, bluewinged "*gargany*," whistling, lesser whistling ; (28) goose—, barheaded, blackbarred, grey, cotton (cotton teal) ; (32) egret ; (33) cattle egret ; (34) paddy-bird, common (*bogla*) ; (35) paddy-bird,

black; (36) florican; (37) godwit; (38) grebe; (39) heron, blue; (40) heron, night; (41) ibis, black (black curlew ?); (42) ibis—white; (43) jabirn; (44) jacana, bronze; (45) jacana, pheasant; (46) lapwing, crested—"did-he-do-it"; (47-48) plover—, golden, grey; (49) ortolan ("*bagheri*"); (50) partridge, swamp (*kya*); (51) peafowl (very rare); (52) pelican; (53) pigeon, green (*harial*); (54) pigeon, bluerock; (55) quail, bush; (56) quail, black-breasted; (57) quail, button; (58) waterrail-dank; (59) redshank; (60) sandpiper; (61—63) snipe—, common, jack, painted; (64) junglefowl; (65) stork, adjutant (rare); (66) stork, great shell-breaker, (*shomokbhongo*); (67) stork, lesser shellbreaker (*shomokbhongo*); (68) stork, blacknecked (*ramsalik*); (69) stork, blacknecked beefsteak bird (*mānikjore*); (70) waterhen; (71) snakebird.

Other birds.

A complete list of the other birds in the district is as follows.—

(1—3) vulture—, common brown, raj, white; (4) fisheagle or osprey; (5) marsh harrier; (6) kestrel; (7) sparrow hawk; (8-9) kite—, common brown, whiteheaded red fish-kite; (10-12) owl—horned, small grey (athene), brown jungly (small); (13) raven; (14) crow; (15) crowpheasant or griff's pheasant; (16) jay; (17—19) mina, brown and white, black and white, "*pawai*"; (20) cuckoo; (21) nightjar; (22) kingcrow; (23) koil; (24) anvil bird; (25-26) golden oriole, large, small; (26—29) kingfisher—, large, black and white; medium sized, chestnut; white and blue; very small (very brilliant); (30) robin (*dyal*); (31) bulbul; (32) nunia; (33) fly-catcher, small green; (34—36) parrot, green, large and small; plumheaded; (37) akupaku; (38) magpie; (39) *sātbhāi*, seven sisters-ground thrush; (40) *minivet*; (41) jungle warblers (2 or 3 kinds); (42) woodpecker; (43) honey-bird; (44) tailor bird; (45) weaver bird; (46) sparrow; (47) reedsparrow; (48) lark, two kinds at least; (49) swallow; (50) martin; (51) swift; (52) tern; (53) seaswallow; (54) razorbill; (55) seagull; (56) riverkite (*gāngchil*).

Fish.

An incredible variety of fish is caught in the district, including salt-water fish in the southern rivers, fresh-water fish, tank fish, and swamp fish. The most common edible varieties of each kind are :—

(*i*) *of salt-water fish.*—Korāl or bhetki, (2) hilsā (ılsā), (3) bhol, (4) kharsul, (5) med, (6) tariā, (7) tapsi (all salt water fish also occur in fresh water).

(*ii*) *of fresh-water fish.*—Rui, (2) kātal, (3) āir, (4) pāngās, (5) dhāin, (6) boāl, (7) chital, (8) kāun-māgur, (9) gāngkai, (10) mircā, (11) ghaniā, (12) silan, (13) rithā, (14) chāpilā, (15) kājli, (16) nāndul, (17) bāchā, (18) poā, (19) bhātā, (20) tuldāndi, (21) pheshā, (22) golishā, (23) tengrā, (24) kāchki, (25) bāush, (26) ghāgrā, (27) sākos or sāplāpātā.

(*iii*) *of tank fish.*—Bāin, (2) bāliā, (3) phali, (4) pāptā, (5) bhedā, (6) bātāshi, (7) tātkini, (8) kākilā, (9) chelā, (10) dārkhinā, (11) malandi, (12) puti (all of the fresh water fish shown under II also occur in tanks. Rui, kātal, mircā, silan, boāl are commonly found in tanks).

(*iv*) *of swamp fish.*—Kai, (2) māgur, (3) singi, (4) khalisā, (5) saul, (6) gazār, (7) cheng.

Shark come up the rivers occasionally from the Bay of Bengal. One was caught in 1870-71 off the seacoast of the Sāhābāzpur island, which was about 48 feet long and was exhibited in Barisāl.

Reptiles and insects.

The most common reptiles are mentioned in the following list :—

(1) *magar* or man-eating crocodile ; (2) *ghariāl* or fish-eating crocodile ; (3) *guisāp* ; (4) *gecko* ; (5) common small house lizard ; (6) long-tailed lizard; (7) python (common) ; (8) ophiophagus elaps (in Sundarbans "hamadryad") ; (9) cobra (common) ; (10) *karāit*, blue, bangarus coeruleus (rare) ; (11) *karāit*, yellow, *rājsāp*, bungarus fasciatus (rare) ; (12) *dhaman*, ptyas mucosus ; (13) *haria*, grass snake (of sorts) ; (14) water-snake, black and yellow check pattern ; (15) water-snake, *dhorā* ; (16) grass snake, bright green, non-venomous, 3 feet long ; (17) blindworm.

In addition to these there are many varieties (probably all Indian) of salt-water snakes in the big rivers in the Sundarbans and no doubt there are many varieties of fresh-water and grass-snakes not mentioned in this list. Of crustacea the following may be mentioned :—

Chingri, prawn (grows to 2 feet long, but usually small); *chāmuā chingri*, a stinking un-eatable shrimp; crab, two varieties, the red which is found on the beach of the Sundarbans and the dark which is found on trees; the land crab and the scorpions. Of amphibia the frog, bull-frog and toad are found. Insects are very numerous and comprise many varieties of the following kinds:—

Butterflies, moths, gnats, black ants, large and small, red ants, white ants, mosquitos, crickets, cockroaches, centipedes, fleas, bugs, dragon flies, common flies, blue-bottles, bees, wasps, hornets, beetles, pamari, mowā and ledā.

CLIMATE. The climate of Bàkàrganj resembles in its chief features that of the great alluvial tract of Lower Bengal of which it forms the eastern margin. It is damp at all times of the year and has an equable temperature, due in part to its maritime situation and in part to its being beyond the reach of the dry westerly winds of the Indo-Gangetic plain. The cold season lasts from the middle of November to the end of February and is generally dry except for occasional rain at Christmas, but humidity is almost as high as in the rainy season and fogs occur. Sea breezes begin to blow in March and gathering strength with the advance of the hot weather result at intervals in nor'-westers, which are on the whole most frequent in May. The monsoon sets in about the middle of June and rain is fairly continuous until the middle of September. In some years heavy falls of rain occur in October owing to the influence of storm in the Bay.

Temperature and humidity. The highest temperature recorded at Barisāl is 101·8° and the lowest 42·4°. The mean temparature is 77°, while that of May, the warmest month, is only 83° and that of December and January, the coldest months, is only 65°. The diurnal range is as usual greatest in the dry season, when it reaches 23° in January and in the damp cloudy months it does not exceed 11°. At Barisāl even in the driest month the relative humidity exceeds 80 per cent. and during the rainy season it is above 85 per cent.

Rainfall. The mean rainfall in the year in the district as a whole is 85 inches distributed over 98 days, but it is greater on the coast than in the interior. In the wettest year on record, 1902, the rainfall amounted to 120·71 inches and in the driest, 1879, to only 55·63 inches. The average number of rainy days is 1 in November, December, and January; 2 in February and March; 4 in April; 9 in May; 17 in January; 20 in July and August; 14 in September and 6 in October.

Statistics of the rainfall at the various recording stations are given below for the cold weather November to February, the hot weather March to May and the rainy season June to October.

The figures are the average of the ten years 1892 to 1901 :—

STATIONS.		November to February.	March to May.	June to October.	Annual average.
Patuākhāli (coast)	...	3·59	12·59	78·24	94·42
Daulatkhān ,,	...	2·49	16·27	80·13	98·89
Bāuphal (central)	...	2·57	13·45	74·78	90·80
Bholā ,,	...	2·83	13·13	71·08	87·04
Pirozpur ,,	...	3·05	11·78	62·07	76·90
Barisāl ,,	...	2·94	13·51	62·30	78·75
Gaurnādi (north)	...	2·67	13·71	52·70	69·08
Mean of district	...	2·88	13·49	68·75	85·12

CHAPTER II.

HISTORY.

FORMATION AND EARLY HISTORY.

ACCORDING to the most probable theory Bākarganj was at one time an inland sea or lagoon behind the Sundarbans, which had already been raised as a chain of islands in approximately their present position by the action of the tides in compelling the great rivers to discharge their silt. This lagoon was slowly filled by the deposit of silt from the rivers which traversed it, as the Ganges raised the level of the lagoon working from west to east and the Meghnā and Brahmaputra filled up the eastern portion. Land was apparently first formed as a series of detached islands on the banks of the rivers, which were themselves ten or fifteen miles wide. The detached islands then consolidated into several compact land groups, which gradually gained so much upon the lagoon as to form a single mass. In the south of the district the country must have consisted largely of islands separated by salt lagoons until quite modern times, as salt was manufactured at many inland places in Buzrugumedpur (thana Bākarganj) and Selimābād until the beginning of the ninteenth century; in such places all the salt has long ago been washed out of the soil. In the east of the district the process of consolidation is still not complete as the island of Sāhābāzpur has not as yet been incorporated geographically into the district. If this account be accurate, the first mention of population might be expected in the north of the district or in the Sundarbans. A copper-plate grant of three villages to Brahmans by Kesab Sen under the date 1136 A.D. was found in the Idilpur pargana (thana Mehendiganj) in the north of the district. There is nothing to show that the villages were in Bākarganj, but it is not improbable, since other copper-plates as well as coins have been found in the contiguous parts of Faridpur. The inscription on the copper-plate indicates that that part of the country was then occupied by a degraded people, called the Chandabhandas (J. A. S. B., January 1838). There is a tradition that the Sundarbans were occupied and prosperous at an early date; but there is no evidence to support it, while the absence of trade at the head of the Bay of Bengal under the Hindu administration would make it antecedently improbable. If any part of Bākarganj was inhabited when the Hindus ruled Bengal, it was probably only the extreme north of the district as part of the Hindu kingdom lying mainly south of the Buriganga river which was ruled from Rāmpāl (in Dacca district). This kingdom maintained its independence for nearly a century after Bakhtyar Khiliji had conquered the rest of Bengal and only fell to the sons of the Emperor Balban at the end of the thirteenth century. In 1330 A. D., Muhammad Tughluk appears to have completely conquered Eastern Bengal and to have included the delta of the Meghnā in a province which was ruled by a Governor at Sonārgāon. It was probably at this period that the Hindus dispersed over Eastern Bengal and founded the kingdom of Bāklā in Bākarganj. The Chandradwip Raj family (Bakla-Chandradwip is the name used in their papers) counts 22 generations from its entrance into the district which, allowing for the shorter-lived generations of Bengal, would date that event about the time of the break-up of Hindu rule in Eastern Bengal. Hindu kings and kingdoms have rarely either annalists or serious historians, and Bāklā was no exception. Moreover, such papers as the raj may have kept were burnt by a mad king at the beginning of the eighteenth century. The Chandrawip Rāj family appears first to have settled in Mehendiganj and later in Kachuā (thana Bāuphal) and to have maintained—like others of the petty Hindu princes on the outskirts of Eastern Bengal—some sort of independence during the Afghan rule, particularly during those frequent periods when the Afghans were fighting for mastery amongst themselves. Blochmann writes that about 1450 A.D., the Meghnā delta formed part of the province of Muazzamabad under the name of Fathiabad and Bāklā was from 1487 to the middle of the sixteenth century certainly included in the dominions of the great Afghan house of Hussain and Sher Shah. The kingdom of Baklā appears at this time to have achieved considerable prosperity and to have been visited by the Arab traders, who had found their way into the Bay of Bengal. It already contained a considerable Muhammadan population and the oldest building in the district is a mosque built in 1465 A.D. at Masjidbāri in thana Patuākhāli. The first mention of incursions by the Arrakanese pirates occurs however in the fifteenth century, although they did not become formidable until the beginning of the seventeenth century.

1500—1638 Moghuls, Maghs and Portuguese.

From the sixteenth century there is more of fact and less of conjecture in the history of Bākarganj. In the middle of the century Akbar broke the power of the Afghans and brought Eastern Bengal under the rule of the Moghuls. Bāklā was included in Todar Mull's assessment (1582 A. D.) and is described by Abul Fazl. It was a *sirkar* containing four parganas, Ismailpur commonly called Bogla (Bāklā), Srīrāmpur, Shāhzādapur and Adelpur, and was assessed at Rs. 1,80,000. It furnished a force of 320 cavalry and 15,000 infantry. It was visited by several European travellers, assuming that "Bengala" is to be identified with it, by Varthema of Bologna in 1507, by Le Blanc of Marseilles in 1576, by Ralph Fitch in 1586, by Melchior De Fonseca in 1599-1600 and by Sebastian Manrique in 1628—1641. An excellent summary of their accounts of the district is given by Beveridge (pp. 28—39, 169—180 and 444-45). Bāklā was sufficiently important at this time for its Raja to be described as one of the twelve Bhuiyas of Bengal. But its downfall had already begun. It is not clear whether this downfall was due to the destruction wrought by a stormwave or to the incursions of the Arrakanese and Portuguese—probably both contributed. The stormwave is described by Abul Fazl as occurring in 1584 A. D. and as drowning the king with 200,000 of his subjects, "the whole *sirkar* was overwhelmed and laid waste"; but the fertile lands of the delta have a great power of recovery and the effects of this inundation seem to have disappeared when Fonseca visited the country 15 years later. It was otherwise with the ferocious invasions of the Maghs (Arrakanese). The King of Arrakan had risen into power in the fifteenth century, but only became formidable as an invader when he employed Portuguese to build and fight his ships. The first Portuguese to visit the country was John D' Silveyra in 1517 A. D., who arrived with four vessels from the Maldives to start a factory at "Bengala", but ultimately settled down at Chittagong, where he maintained himself by piracy in the estuary of the Meghnā and by assisting the local princes in their wars with one another. All the local princes, including the Raja of Bāklā, appear to have employed Portuguese, but their chief settlement was at Chittagong and their chief employer the King of Arrakan. With the aid of the Portuguese the Arrakanese overran all the islands in the delta, including Sandwip, which supplied salt to the whole of Bengal, and then made an expedition in force up the Meghnā in 1608 A. D., which was, however, defeated by Islam Khan. After this failure the most famous of these Portuguese mercenaries, Sebastian Gonzales Tibao, deserted the King of Arrakan and with the help of the Raja of Bāklā conquered Sandwip for himself in 1609 A. D. The Raja of Bāklā lent Gonzales some ships and 200 horses in return for a promise of half the revenue of the island; but Gonzales not only kept Sandwip for himself, but fell upon Sāhābāzpur and other territories belonging to the Raja and annexed them. Gonzales was only able to maintain his independence until 1615, when the Raja of Arrakan fitted out a great expedition, defeated Gonzales and annexed Sandwip. Then, as recounted by Du Jarric, "desiring to pursue his design of conquering all the kingdoms of Bengal, he suddenly threw himself upon that of Bāklā, of which he possessed himself without difficulty as the King of it was absent and still young." The Maghs (Arrakanese) on this occasion ravaged and despoiled the country which the Hindus evacuated. Manrique, who visited Sāhābāzpur between 1628 and 1641, describes it as entirely depopulated. The Raja of Bāklā eventually settled at Mādhabpāsā (in thana Barisāl), but the other leading Hindus dispersed over the district and began the reclamation of the west and centre.

1639—1770 Zenith and decline of the Mughal rule.

Although the capital of Bengal had been removed in 1608 to Dacca, the Mughal administration found itself quite unable to withstand the Arrakanese, who continually made ruthless and destructive raids until the time of Shuja Khān, the ill-fated brother of Aurungzeb, who became Governor in 1639 A. D. He defeated them in a two-days battle at Sujabad (in Nalchhiti thana, now diluviated) and protected Bākarganj with a ring of forts at Sujābād, Rupasia near Jhālakāti and Indrapasa near Rajapur. It is significant that these forts were placed in the centre of the district; the south appears to have been abandoned to the Maghs. Sultan Shuja's rule was vigorous and effective in other directions also and the public revenue was improved by a fresh assessment in 1658, the details of which are now lost. He was succeeded by Mir Jumla, the best of the Dacca Viceroys, and by Shaista Khan, who finally subdued the Maghs by taking Sandwip and Chittagong in 1666 A. D. During the vigorous rule of these three Viceroys Bākarganj passed definitely under the direct rule of the Mughals, the local Rajas of Bāklā subsiding into unimportance at Mādhabpāsā. Relieved from the dread of the Maghs, Bākarganj shared in the general prosperity of Eastern Bengal, which distinguished the last half of the seventeenth century. Reclamation and revenue increased apace. Cultivation extended rapidly in Buzrugumedpur in the centre of the district, while an attack was begun upon the forests of Selimābād in the west of the district, which were still, if local tradition is to be believed, separated by a wide river from the eastern parts. This prosperity was checked by the removal of the capital from Dacca to Murshidābād in 1707 and by the great increase in taxation associated with the name of Jaffar Khān and the assessment of 1721. Bākarganj as one of the districts at the extremity of the province was amongst the first to feel the effects of the weaker administration of the Naib Nazim. The zamindars fought amongst themselves and cultivation did not expand as might have been expected, while dacoity and robbery reached alarming proportions. Even the lands of the oldest families were not secure against the greed of Muhammadan adventurers; thus the Mazumdars of Chakhar got possession of Chandradwip for a time and Aga Bakhar seized Selimābād as well as Buzrugumedpur. Aga Bakhar, of whom some account is given by Beveridge (pages 43—47), was *de facto* ruler of Bākarganj from 1741 until his death in 1753. He obtained a footing in the district apparently by suppressing the rebellion of the Hindu zamindar of Buzrugumedpur, but was of an intriguing disposition and did not scruple on one occasion to obtain the assistance of 1,000 war-boats from the King of Arrakan in a quarrel with a Tippera Chief named Umed. After 1750 he was Governor of Chittagong, but lived at Dacca, where he assassinated the Naib Nazim in 1753 and was himself killed on the following day. His influence in the Bākarganj district was inherited by Raja Rajballabh, for some time Dewan of Naib Nazim. Nowaris Muhammad, who got possession of Selimābād until 1758, dispossessed Aga Bakhar's heirs of Buzrugumedpur in 1760 and obtained a share of Uttar Sāhābāzpur and other lands in the north of the district. In order to secure his influence in Bākarganj, he settled a company of Portuguese mercenaries in Sibpur (thana Bākarganj). Subsequently he became Deputy Governor of Dacca, but was ultimately drowned by Mir Kasem along with that son, Kissen Das, who was the occasion of the war between the Nawab and the British which ended in the battle of Plassey. In addition to these internal disturbances, Bākarganj was during the century still exposed to the ravages of the Maghs, and at the beginning of British administration the south of the district was described by Grant and shewn in Rennell's survey as depopulated by the Maghs. A large part of the revenues of Bākarganj were alienated throughout the century for the upkeep of the Nowara or fleet against the Maghs, all the zamindaris along the banks of the big river and especially Shaistanagar, Shahzadpur and Chandradwip containing Nowara lands, in some cases on a feudal tenure. Thus the Raja of Chandradwip held *hissajat* lands on an obligation of personal service against the Maghs as well as for the maintenance of 42 *khos* boats with 32 oarsmen each. These Nowara lands were resumed, mainly in the year 1767. The Hindu zamindars, however, employed Muhammadans or Portuguese to fight their battles, and it was during this century that the Muhammadans occupied the riverside lands in place of the Hindus who had retreated from Magh pollution into the interior. The Maghs were not the only external enemies who vexed the district during this disturbed period. In 1748 the Mahrattas penetrated into Bākarganj and occasioned alarm in Dacca. They were defeated near Ponabalia by Ram Bhadra Roy, but it is doubtful if the Mahrattas engaged were more than a handful of men who had strayed from the main body.

EARLY BRITISH REFERENCES.

After the British assumed the Government of Bengal, Bākarganj early attracted their attention chiefly on account of its position on the trade routes from Calcutta to Dacca, but also because of its great production of rice and because it was a centre for the manufacture of salt. The first reference to the district is contained in a letter of 1762, in which the disturbances created by European traders are complained of. The Nawab and the Governor in the same year had some correspondence about the oppression connected with the salt manufacture. This correspondence contains apparently the first reference to Barisāl : "The duties on the salt, which were paid at Burry-saul Chokey, belonging to the Shahbunder, amounted to near Rs. 30,000." In 1770 during the great famine rice was imported from Bākarganj to Murshidabad, arriving, as Mr. Becher observed in his account of the famine, at a most critical time. Apparently 33,913 maunds were purchased. At a previous date (1755) boats loaded with rice had been stopped by Raja Rajballabh at Bākarganj and had only been released by a company of military. During these early years the district was managed as part of the province of Dacca and no officials visited it. Probably the mart at Bākarganj itself was the only portion known to the authorities. The first Europeans to settle in the district were the Portuguese who had been established at Sibpur (thana Bākarganj) by Raja Rajballabh about the middle of the eighteenth century, but a Scotsman named William Robinson, who was shipwrecked off Saugor, settled at Madhupur near Nalchhiti in 1766, and lived for about 30 years, and his descendants are still in the district.

Creation of the Bakarganj District. It was soon found necessary to make separate arrangements for the administration of so large and distant a part of the province of Dacca. As early as 1781 a Civil Judge with magisterial powers was appointed with his seat at Baraikaran in thana Nalchhiti. He was joined at Baraikaran by a Commissioner in the Sundarbans, who was appointed in 1784 for "suppressing the depredations of dacoits." The headquarters of these officials were removed in 1792 to Bākarganj, which was made one of the stations of the Dacca Court of Circuit in 1793, and where the Commissioner in the Sundarbans first obtained magisterial powers by Regulation IX of 1793 and was then abolished by the Regulation VII of 1797. By this Regulation Dacca was divided into two zilas or districts, of which the southern was Bākarganj. The headquarters of the district were removed by Mr. Wintle in 1801 to Barisāl and the Judge accompanied the Magistrate in his transfer. This early creation of an independent district in Bākarganj was due entirely to the notoriety of the rivers as the haunt of desperate dacoits. The prevalence of river dacoity had been mentioned by the Jesuit missionaries in 1600 A. D., and had reached such proportions in the middle of the eighteenth century that even Europeans were not protected by their prestige from attack. The dacoits went about in large gangs which were well organised under prominent men such as Muhammad Hayat and Ainaddin Sirdar, who were transported in 1790 and whose property was confiscated. They did not shrink from wholesale murder to secure their booty, and they were so active in kidnapping that many boats full of children, both girls and boys, went from the rivers of the district to the great slave markets at Sandwip and Chittagong. The district which was constituted in 1797 included the Kachuā thana west of the Baleswar river as well as the islands of Sāhābāzpur and Hatiā, but not Gaurnadi, which with the eastern part of Mādāripur was only transferred to Bākarganj in 1806, nor the pargana of Idilpur which belonged to the jurisdiction of the city of Dacca until 1816. Owing to defective means of communication in the large rivers these boundaries were found unwieldy and the islands of Sāhābāzpur and Hatiā were transferred to Noākhāli in 1882, although they still remained under the jurisdiction of the Judge of Bākarganj. In 1861 the portion east of the Baleswar river was transferred to Jessore (now Khulnā), some villages in the north-west being at the same time transferred to Bākarganj in order to make the Madhamati (or Baleswar) river the district boundary on that side. In 1869 Dahshin Sāhābāzpur was retransferred to Bākarganj at the request of its inhabitants; but to prevent the district becoming unwieldy by this addition, the northern parts consisting of the modern thanas of Pālong, Mādāripur and Kotwālipārā was transferred to Faridpur in 1873 along with the subdivision of Mādāripur. The boundaries of the district are substantially the same to-day. All magisterial work was centred in Barisāl until 1854, when a subdivision was formed at Mādāripur In 1859 another subdivision was formed at Pirozpur. In 1869 the subdivision of Dakshin Sāhābāzpur, which was created in 1845 and is one of the oldest in Bengal, was transferred to Bākarganj along with the island. In 1871 another subdivision was created at Patuākhāli, but in 1873 the subdivision of Mādāripur was transferred to Faridpur. In the confusing administrative system of Bengal revenue and magisterial jurisdictions have never been completely identical, and at first they were entirely different. From 1786-87 there was a Collector of Buzrugumedpur, who was responsible for the collections in Chandradwip, Selimābād, Buzrugumedpur and the neighbouring parganas to the amount of about 8½ lakhs of rupees. This Collectorate was again amalgamated in March 1787 with Dacca. For 20 years after Bākarganj was formed into a separate magisterial jurisdiction, its revenue administration was conducted by the Collector of Dacca, who rarely visited the district. In 1814, however, the Registrar of the Zilla Court at Barisāl was appointed Assistant Collector to collect the revenue of Bākarganj, and finally in 1817 Bākarganj obtained a Collector of its own and henceforth its revenue business was transacted at Barisāl. The jurisdiction of the Collector was never and indeed is not now quite the same as the jurisdiction of the Magistrate, as the boundaries of the different estates under his control are not always, although mainly, conterminous with the boundaries of the district. The offices of Magistrate and Collector were not combined until 1862.

THE PERMANENT SETTLEMENT AND THE MANUFACTURE OF SALT.

The early history and the early correspondence in Bākarganj during British rule are concerned with the Permanent Settlement, the salt administration and the suppression of serious crime. The Permanent Settlement is dealt with else-where and needs no description here. Its immediate and ultimate effects upon administration were not the same. At first it freed the local officials from exclusive attention to revenue business and enabled them to give more attention to the general well-being of the inhabitants. Later, as conditions became more settled and administration of the modern type became possible, it contributed to keep the official in greater ignorance of the inhabitants and their needs than elsewhere. Bākarganj was a large centre of salt manufacture, until it was given up. Sāhābāzpur and Manpurā were so largely given over to it that they became partially depopulated, while Buzrugumedpur, Selimābād and the Sundarbans were also full of salt *tafals*. Wherever there was manufacture of salt, there was great lawlessness and extreme tension between the salt manufacturers and the inhabitants, resulting in frequent quarrels between the Magistrate of the district and the salt officers. The salt department had a great reputation for misconduct, and were alleged to use coercion of the most grievous kind in order to force advances upon the *molunghies*. The manufacture of salt certainly retarded the development of the district, and it was a good thing for the inhabitants when it was given up.

THE HISTORY OF CRIME.

As has been remarked, the separate magistracy was formed in order to "suppress the depredations of dacoits." In addition to dacoities by organised river-gangs and to kidnapping, there were numerous riots and affrays, in which many men were killed. The more powerful landlords retained bands of clubmen to support them in their quarrels. The suppression of serious crime absorbed all the energies of the Magistrate, and rioting flourished unchecked until the latter part of the nineteenth century. Crime was so prevalent that in 1801 over 300 men were arrested for dacoity and murder, chiefly in Dakshin Sāhābāzpur, while there were 750 prisoners in the jail on serious charges. In 1806 the Magistrate wrote that all the gangs had been broken up, although in the same year he reported that 152 persons had been implicated in murders and 1,747 in robberies. In 1808, although the President of the Court of Circuit expressed "his great satisfaction in the decrease of serious dacoities," there were still 23 murders, 6 dacoities with murder and 95 dacoities without murder. In 1809 a vigorous attempt to deal with dacoity was made by the appointment of a Superintendent of Police for the divisions of Calcutta, Murshidabad and Dacca, who set to work vigorously through an army of *goendas* (informers) and *guerendas* (persons employed to apprehend), so that by 1815 dacoities had been reduced to one with murder and nine without murder. At the same time the number of affrays, which appear to correspond to the serious riots of modern days, were 3 with murder and 105 without murder. It may be noted that in 1811 the hatred of the *goendās* bore fruit in the murder of five at one time by dacoit sirdars. The Magistrate in 1815 reported that the police were not only sharers of the booty, but sharers of the pay of the dacoit sirdars, who were employed by the landholders in their quarrels in the collection of rents; he complained also that much dacoity was concealed by the police. The police were, however, understaffed and there were at that time no village watchmen. On the other hand, a strong force of patrol boats was retained to deal with river dacoits, numbering in 1818, 14 boats with a crew of 182 oarsmen. In 1819 there were 15 murders, 1 dacoity with murder, 6 without murder and 176 house-breakings. Subsequently, serious crimes were considerably reduced owing to the able efforts of the Magistrate, Mr. Thomas Bruce, who was described as the "able and intelligent regenerator" of the district. It appears, however, that serious crime was still concealed, and only cases which were reported by the parties appear in the statistics. In 1850 there were 15 murders, 5 dacoities with murder and one affray with homicide, while some of the gangs such as that of Gagan Miān described by Mr. Beveridge (pages 234 to 238) were practically in a state of rebellion against the administration. In 1858 there were 32 cases of murder reported and in 1859 25. In 1861 the reform of the police was undertaken. The main features of the reform were the introduction of a new body of regular police under the stricter supervision of local officers, and the institution of village watchmen. The reform resulted at first in better reporting of crimes and afterwards in a great reduction. Thus, in 1871 dacoities had risen to 28 and in 1872 there were 26 murders and 189 riots of which 12 were accompanied by loss of life; whereas by 1887 murders were reduced to 13, dacoities to 2 and riots to 54. The passing of the Criminal Procedure Code in 1882 and of the Evidence Act about the same time affected conviction in serious cases to such an extent that the criminals obtained great immunity in a district which, by its innumerable streams and ditches and its isolated homesteads surrounded by screens of trees, made crime easy to conceal and difficult to detect. The results are seen immediately in the figures. Whereas in 1872 to 1882 the reduction in serious crime had been great and continuous, it began to increase in 1886 in a most alarming manner. Thus, in 1892 there were 41 murders, in 1893 57, in 1894 82 and in 1895 94. Murder by gunshot, which in a district full of ditches is extremely easy to effect, became so common that the district had to be disarmed in 1896. This measure had an immediate effect upon the figures, but murder still remained very frequent, and in the period from 1908 to 1914 there was an average of 40 murders a year. Throughout the whole of this period rioting has been very common, but as no distinction is kept in the figures between serious riots and trivial scuffles, the statistics are not of great value. Rioting about land and rent which had been very frequent has lately been much reduced as a result of the settlement operations. An examination of the figures during the century suggests the conclusion that the criminal code is too far in advance of the conditions in the district. It is certainly curious that crime should have showed a continuous and progressive decline until the introduction of the new criminal code and that thereafter serious crime should not only have increased portentously but have shown no signs, despite exceptional measures, of returning to the earlier standard.

CHIEF EVENTS, 1782—1860.

Apart from crime, the history of Bākarganj is more full of incident than other districts, but the chief events of historical importance are natural calamities. In 1787 a flood created great havoc in the north-east of the district, while in 1822 the great storm wave devastated the south-east and the islands. Both of these events are, however, described in Chapter VI. In 1792 occurred the attempted insurrection of one Bolaki Shah, a fakir, who collected an armed force and erected a fort at Subandia, which contained 7 cannons, 12 ginjals, several muskets and two men employed in making gunpowder. He was apparently apprehended by a Naib with a force of 88 sepoys. In 1794 a sea-going ship, the "Eliza", and in 1808 the brig "Moria" came up to Bākarganj mart, while it is recorded in 1794 that the Civil Surgeon, Mr. Harper, was in partnership as a boat-builder with Mr. Gill, whose family is still connected with the district, and that they employed a Frenchman named Antoin Piazi. At this time the Government stored rice at Bākarganj, where they maintained 52 *golas* or granaries. In 1812 there was an outbreak in the jail and 12 prisoners were shot before it was suppressed, the Magistrate, Mr. Battye, nearly losing his life.

Cholera epidemics were very common, occurring in 1817, 1818, 1822 and 1825. In the last year 25,050 persons are reported to have died between the 22nd of August and the 10th of September, during which short time 20 women performed "sati." During all this period the European community in Barisāl was very small, the officials rarely numbering more than three; and as early as 1827 it was reported that there had been for a long time a general objection to accept the post of Judge and Magistrate of Bākarganj. In 1845 there was a serious defalcation in the treasury, on account of which the Collector was degraded and the treasurer was sentenced to seven years' imprisonment. This Collector, who was originally in the Navy, had married a Bengali lady and used to celebrate the Charak Puja in front of his house. There were no disturbances in Bākarganj during the Mutiny, and as indigo had never obtained any footing in the district there were no such riots as occurred a little later in Nadia and Jessore.

The introduction of modern administration, 1860—1915.

After the Mutiny and the passing of the Company, modern administration began in the district. The chief steps by which it was introduced in Bākarganj were the Rent Law (Act X of 1859), which gave rights to some of the tenants and substituted regular courts for rioting in the decision of land disputes; the thak and revenue surveys of 1859—1865, which surveyed the limits of estates and reduced the causes of quarrel amongst landlords; the formation of subdivisions (1859—1871), which brought criminal and civil courts closer to the population; the formation of the District Board in 1887 and the introduction of steamer traffic into the district about the same time; the Bengal Tenancy Act of 1885 and the preparation of the record-of-rights in 1899—1908, which secured the position of the cultivator and pacified agrarian disputes by providing accurate information concerning every tenancy in the district. The other remarkable events which have occurred in the district in later years were the storm-wave of 1876, which swept the east of the district and the islands of most of their inhabitants and cattle, and of which an account is given in Chapter VI; and the agitation which arose out of the first Partition in 1905, the effects of which have not as yet entirely subsided.

CHAPTER III.

THE PEOPLE.

GROWTH OF THE POPULATION.

THE first official census of the population of Bākarganj was taken in 1872. The boundaries of the district were then very different from the present boundaries. There had previously been many estimates of the population, including the estimate of the Revenue Surveyor; but it is clear that such estimates can have been of no value, as although the Revenue Surveyor had not only seen the whole district but had enumerated all the houses in it, yet his estimate differed by 140 per cent. from the first census which was taken about ten years later. Calculations based upon the amount of land occupied at the time of the Permanent Settlement and the rate of increase which has been observed between the dates of different censuses would indicate that the total population in 1801 cannot have been more than a million, of which at least half was to be found in the Sadar subdivision. The population has considerably more than doubled in a century. At the first census it was at 1,887,586, although it would seem that this was certainly an over-estimate, as by 1881 it had only grown to 1,900,889, whereas the increase in the next decade was 13 per cent. In 1911 the total population was returned at 2,428,911, an increase of 5·98 per cent. in ten years. The rate of increase in the previous decade was 6·45 per cent., so that 6 per cent. may be taken as the normal rate of increase in recent times in the population in Bākarganj. In the last 30 years the population of the district has increased by 28 per cent. In the same period the increase in the Dakhin Sāhābāzpur subdivision has been 50 per cent., in the Patuākhāli subdivision 35 per cent., in the Pirojpur subdivision 23 per cent. and in the Sadar subdivision 20 per cent. During the last decade the increase in the Sadar subdivision has only been 4 per cent. and in the Pirojpur subdivision there has been actually a decrease, while in Patuākhāli the increase was 20 per cent. and in Sāhābāzpur 18 per cent.

Sadar subdivision.

Dealing with the subdivisions separately it will be found that the Sadar subdivision has twice the density of any other subdivision. In some of the thanas the population appears to have reached the limit which the land can support. Thus Jhālakāti thana, which has 1,213 people to the square mile, reports a decrease of 4 per cent. in the population since 1901, while Nalchiti and Bākarganj had insignificant additions to their population during the last ten years. In 1881 these two thanas had a population of 214,000 and thirty years later 226,000, so that the increase in thirty years is only 6 per cent., but even in 1881 the population was nearly 1,000 to the square mile. Barisāl thana is equally densely populated. It shows an increase of 20 per cent. in 30 years, which is no doubt chiefly due to the headquarters of the district being situated within it and becoming a centre of considerable trade. The only two thanas in this subdivision which have been progressive in population throughout the period are Gaurnadi and Mehendiganj. Gaurnadi has indeed added 43 per cent. to its population in 30 years and increased the number of persons per square mile from 703 to 1,031. Mehendiganj has a much smaller density of population than any other thana in the subdivision, but although the people are very prosperous and the land is fertile, the increase in population is not what might be expected. It is, however, very subject to diluvion.

Pirojpur subdivision.

In Pirozpur subdivision the only thana which showed any considerable increase of population in the last ten years was Matbāriā. In the other three thanas there has been a decrease which, in Pirozpur, amounted to 6 per cent. Pirozpur is a densely populated thana and even in 1881 contained 1,014 people to the square mile, which perhaps explains the fact that the increase in 30 years has only been 4 per cent. In Bhāndāriā, where the increase had formerly been considerable and there is a large marsh to reclaim, the decrease in the population is no doubt due to the fact that the Baleswar and the Kāchā rivers have become saline, a phenomenon which cannot have been without serious effect upon Pirozpur also. In Swarupkāti thana there has been in the last decade a small check in what was formerly a rapid increase in the population. As this thana has large *bils* which are in process of reclamation it is not clear why the population should have become stationary. The density per square mile had, however, become very high in the dry parts of the thana.

Patuākhāli subdivision.

In Patuākhāli subdivision, where the general density of population is much less, the growth has been, as might be expected, much greater in the southern than in the northern thana; thus in Patuākhāli and Bāuphal the population has been increased by 22 per cent. in 30 years and by 7 per cent. in the last

10 years, whereas in Amtali and Galāchipā the increase has been 56 per cent. in 30 years and 15 per cent. in the last 10 years.

Sāhābāzpur subdivision. In the Sāhābāzpur islands both the thanas have had a progressive population throughout the whole period, Bholā showing an increase of 35 per cent. in 30 years and 11 per cent. in the last 10 years and Barhānaddin of 70 per cent. and 26 per cent. Generally speaking the increase of population in the southern thanas is due to migration from the northern thanas. There is little immigration from other districts and the natural increase in population would therefore appear to be 6 per cent. throughout the district : in the more densely populated thanas it would appear that the struggle for existence resulted in emigration.

MIGRATION. Emigration outside the district is very small. Only 40,000 natives of Bākarganj were counted outside the district, most of whom were agricultural labourers, whose residence outside was very temporary. Of the emigrants only 14,000 were women, while the districts in which most of them were enumerated were Khulnā and Faridpur, in those parts which formerly belonged to Bākarganj. Apparently the total number of Bākarganj men who have really emigrated to other parts is only 6,000. Immigrants number 60,000, most of whom were temporary labourers, boatmen and traders from Dacca, Faridpur and Noākhāli. Here also most came from Khulnā and Faridpur.

SEX. Between the sexes there is really considerable equality, although the enumeration in the district showed 105 males to every 100 females. Of the natural population, the people born in the district, the excess of males was only 2½ per cent. Apart from Barisāl thana, where the male excess is due to the town, the excess is most noticeable in the following thanas :—15 per cent. in Galāchipā, 12 per cent. in Barhānaddin, 10 per cent. in Bholā, Matbāriā and Amtali, where it is due partly to the presence of foreign boatmen and agricultural labourers who have left their womenkind at home and partly to the number of colonists who have not as yet got ready their homesteads for the reception of their families in the land of promise. In Gaurnadi and Swarupkāti women are in a small majority, due chiefly no doubt to the absence of the bread-winners and school boys amongst the higher castes.

TOWNS AND VILLAGES. The population is almost wholly rural. The great majority of the people are engaged in agricultural pursuits and they have hitherto developed no tendency to flock into the towns. There are no new industries that have been developed and the growth of trade, except in the headquarter town, has been slow. Two per cent. of the inhabitants live in urban areas, the remainder congregating in 5,009 villages. The total population of the five towns is 48,618, and even in Barisāl, which is the only town of any importance, over one-half of the population is interested in agriculture. Jhālakāti is purely a trade centre, Nalchhiti a decayed mart, Pirojpur and Patuākhāli overgrown villages with a bazar and the courts and a sprinkling of traders and officials. During the last decade the population of Nalchhiti and Pirojpur has considerably decreased. On the other hand, the population of Barisāl has increased by nearly 20 per cent. and developed continuously since 1872. In the towns Hindus generally outnumber Muhammadans and males outnumber females; thus in Barisāl there are 15,488 males and only 6,985 females, while in Nalchhiti they are three times and in Jhālakāti four times as many males as females. In Jhālakāti, however, the proportion of females is growing rapidly.

RELIGION. Hindus and Muhammadans.

The great bulk of the inhabitants are Muhammadans, who number 1,693,905 and form 70 per cent. of the population. Practically all the remainder are Hindus, who number 719,557. The Mussalman is found everywhere, but is strongest in the south of the district and in Sāhābāzpur. The Hindu is found chiefly in the west of the district, but is only as numerous as the Muhammadan in two thanas, Swarupkāti and Gaurnadi. In Patuākhāli subdivision Hindus are only 12 per cent. of the population and in Sāhābāzpur only 14 per cent. During the decade 1901 to 1911 the increase of population amongst the Hindus was only ·8 per cent., whereas amongst Muhammadans it was 8 per cent., and generally speaking throughout the whole period during which censuses have been taken the Muhammadans have been gaining at the expense of the Hindus. Indeed it is probable that there were as many Hindus as Muhammadans in the district in 1800 A. D.

Christians.

The number of persons belonging to other religions is only 15,449, of whom 6,541 are Christians and 8,906 Buddhists. The Christians are chiefly protestants of the Baptist denomination, although there are about 1,000 members of the Church of England and 1,000 Roman Catholics. The Baptists came to the district as a result of the efforts of the Serampore Missionaries, Messrs. Carey, Marshman and Ward, and their converts are chiefly Chandāls of the Gaurnadi *bils*. They have increased very largely since 1872. Their converts joined them at first largely in a spirit of revolt against caste bondage and zamindari oppression, and much opposition was experienced at the hands of the landlords, which culminated in the kidnapping and confinement of several families of converts on the 1st of July 1855 in an outrage which as "the Bāropakhya case" became one of the *causes celébrés* of the Calcutta High Court. The best known of the early missionaries in Bākarganj were Mr. Page and Mr. Sale. The attention which has always been given to the education of children has been redoubled in the present century, when handsome new schools for boys and girls have been built in Barisāl in connection with the mission. The English Church Mission was founded by Mr. Barerio, but has been taken over by the Oxford Mission, which maintains excellent schools in Barisāl and an administrative centre in the *bils* at Jobārpār in Gaurnadi. The Roman Catholic Mission is connected with the Goā Church and is established at Sibpur in thana Bākarganj. It contains 841 adherents. There is another mission established by the Church of Rome at Barisāl. There was at one time some ill-feeling between the Goā and the Calcutta priests, but the disagreements were settled by a concordat between the Pope and the King of Portugal in 1870. The Sibpur Mission appears to be dwindling in numbers as in 1872 it counted over a thousand adherents.

Buddhists (Maghs). The Buddhists are Maghs, who came from Arrakan at the end of the eighteenth century, reclaimed the Rābnābād islands and then spread over the Sundarbans. They are very nomadic in their habits and appear to be incapable of settling quietly for very long in the land which they have cleared of forest. They are excellent wood-cutters. In recent times they have deserted many of their former settlements and tend to concentrate in villages which they hold direct from Government and to leave the land of private landlords. They object to an enhancement of rent and to close contact with Bengalis. They live in timber houses raised on piles, which contributed to save them during the cyclonic wave of 1876. Both the Christians and the Maghs have increased very rapidly during the last ten years, the rate of increase being about 20 per cent in each case. In addition there are a few Koches in Pirozpur subdivision who were settled by the zamindars to fight for them with bow and arrow, a few Tipperas in Idilpur and a small colony of Bunās near Barisāl, who were brought by the indigo-factors or as policemen about the middle of the nineteenth century.

MUHAMMADAN CASTES. The Muhammadans of the district must have been largely converts, but conversion has not been vigorous during the last 150 years. They still cleave to some extent to Hindu customs, observing the *navānna* and the *dussera* puja and talking of their castes, but the preaching and vogue of the Ferāzis and the followers of Keramatali have gradually made them more consistent followers of the Prophet. The census report divides the Muhammadans into the following castes:—Jolāhā (weavers), Nikāri (fishermen), Bediā (gipsies), Behārā (palanquin bearer), Dhāi (midwife, etc.), Sheikh, Pathan and Syed. The Behārā is now an ordinary cultivator and most of the fishermen cultivate some land. Bediās are really vagrants without any definite religious belief, who call themselves Hindu or Mussalman indiscriminately. They are few in number and live by juggling, hunting, begging or by theft. Jolāhās are established in considerable colonies in populous centres and still weave strenuously for a declining market. The Nikāris are found on the banks of the big rivers. One-third of the Jolāhās and Nāgarchis (musicians) live in Gaurnadi, the Behārās chiefly in the northern thanas and the Bediās chiefly in the southern thanas. There is also a wandering gipsy tribe—Bebājiās—who profess Muhammadanism, but do not intermingle with other Muhammadans. They live in boats, but have headmen at fixed headquarters, principally in the south of the district but also in Jhālakāti and similar marts, to whom all disputes are referred. They live by woodcutting, fishing and peddling and they are peaceful, industrious, orderly and honest. The great bulk of Muhammadans are Sheikhs, who with few exceptions till the soil. Pathans are reported chiefly in Barisāl and Bākarganj. They are often small traders and rarely engage in agriculture. It is probable that many Syeds and Pathans have no real claim to the classification.

Most of the Bākarganj Mussalmans are Sunnis like most other Musalmans in Eastern Bengal; but the Ferāzis, a puritan sect, are very numerous, specially in the southern parts of the district. The Ferāzi wraps his dhoti or waist-cloth round his body without closing his legs from his aversion to anything like the infidel trousers. The sect was founded in Faridpur by Hazi Shariātullā and increased greatly under his son Dudu Miā, who died in 1862. The first enthusiasm amongst the members of this sect appears now to have died away. They are to be found in strongest numbers in thanas Bhāndāriā and Matbāriā. Ferāzis

Another sect of Muhammadans follows the teaching of Maulvi Kerāmatāli, a learned law doctor and disciple of the Wahabi Syed Akhmad, who acquired notoriety by stirring up the tribes beyond the north-western frontier to a religious crusade against the British in the early part of the nineteenth century. After Syed Akhmad's departure for Mecca about Followers of Kerāmatāli.

1822, Kerāmatāli arrived in Bākarganj with the object of teaching the Muhammadan faith, and his followers increased rapidly and were later joined after the death of Dudu Miā by large numbers of the Ferāzis. This sect, which was founded as a protest against the abuses which had been allowed to creep into Muhammadan worship, now outnumbers the Ferāzis and is very strong in the Sāhābāzpur island.

HINDUS. Amongst the Hindus, castes are more numerous and are still to a large extent engaged in their functional occupations. It is impossible, however, to say with any accuracy how they are employed as the census report gives no information on the subject except in relation to the whole province. No doubt the provincial figures form a rough index to the district proportion, but it is certain that amongst the higher caste only Kayasthas engage in agricultural pursuits, and very few of them. The Nāpit is the rural doctor or the medicine man as well as the barber. The Sudra is often an agriculturist as are many other castes whose traditional occupations no longer provide a comfortable subsistence. The Sāhā, as elsewhere, has prospered and owns a great deal of land.

Principal castes. The numbers and distribution of all the principal castes are given in the statistical appendix. They are only five :—

Namasudras	...	...	322,988
Kayasthas	...	...	97,711
Brahmans	...	...	48,936
Nāpits ...	...	...	36,970
Kaibarttas ...	...	...	29,012

In 1901 Sudras numbered 35,727. Of the lesser castes the most important are the Baidyas, whose functional occupation is the practice of medicine, but who are increasingly turning to other professions. They have an influence in the district out of all proportion to their numbers and, apart from strong colonies in Barisāl and Nalchhiti, are almost confined to Gaurnadi and Jhālakāti. A rich caste is the Bārai, who grow *pān* (betel). They are confined chiefly to the north of the district, but have founded strong colonies in Bhāndāriā and Pirozpur. Of weavers there are two castes, Jugi, the more numerous, and Kāpali, who have now very generally turned to agriculture for livelihood. Jugis are found uniformly distributed throughout the country, but Kāpalis are confined to Gaurnadi and the Patuākhāli subdivisions. Kumārs, whose functional occupation is the making of earthen pottery and who are very faithful to it, are found chiefly in the northern thanas.

Other numerous castes which are uniformly distributed throughout the district are Dhobas (washermen), Sāhās (traders and wine-sellers), Kamars or Lohars, who are ironsmiths.

Namasudras.

The Namasudras are generally supposed to be Hinduised aborigines of the Dacca Division, who were driven into the marshes of the interior by successive waves of invasion. Considerably more than half of them inhabit the neighbourhood of the Gaurnadi and Swarupkāti *bils* to this day. They form 13½ per cent. of the total population and 45 per cent. of the Hindu population, but they have increased only by 1 per cent. in the last ten years, although in Gaurnadi, their chief stronghold, they have increased by 10 per cent. They are not enterprising colonists and form but a small proportion of the raiyats in the southern thanas, in which their numbers have actually diminished during the last ten years. As compared with the total population they are stronger in Pirojpur subdivision than elsewhere; as compared with other Hindus they are least numerous in Nalchiti and in Sāhābāzpur. In Swarupkāti and Bhāndāriā, two out of every three and in Matbāriā four out of every five Hindus are Namas. In Gaurnadi one-half of the Hindu population is Namasudra, and they are strong also in Mehendiganj and Jhālakāti. In occupation they are almost confined to agriculture, although a considerable proportion own a little land and earn their livelihood as agricultural labourers. A few are makers of roads and diggers of tanks. They are strong and vigorous especially in the marshes; but timid and peaceable. The girls marry early, and the many young widows are according to repute productive of much immorality in the caste.

Kayasthas.

Amongst the higher castes Kayasthas are most numerous and they show an apparent increase of over 20 per cent. in the last decade, but most of these were men of lower castes who took advantage of the opportunity offered by the census to claim an improvement in their status. The increase was almost entirely in the Sadar subdivision, every thana participating, Barisāl, Mendiganj and Bākarganj being most prominent. Kayasthas crowd all the professions, own many tenures and are numerous as naibs and muharrirs employed in the management of estates. It appears also that they are to a small extent engaged in cultivation. The high position and general prosperity of the Kayasthas are probably due to the fact that the Chandradwip Rajas are Kayasthas and indeed the leaders of the caste. There was formerly a famous caste,

Samaj, in Mehendiganj, and in Bānaripārā and Gābhā there are still *Kulin* Kayasthas, who rank very high throughout Eastern Bengal.

Brahmans.

Brahmans have somewhat decreased within the last decade. Outside the Sadar subdivision they are very few and within it they are most numerous in Gaurnadi, Barisāl and Jhālākāti. They are an insignificant element of the population in the south of the district. As elsewhere they crowd into the professions and other clerical employments. They are also large landed proprietors, while those who are uneducated still practise priesthood. Generally speaking the higher castes form about 6 per cent. of the total population and 20 per cent. of the Hindu population. In Nalchhiti they are as numerous as 40 per cent.: on the other hand in Patuākhāli and Dakhin Sāhābāzpur subdivisions they are only 2 per cent. of the total population and little more than 10 per cent. of the Hindu population. There was in ancient days a centre for pundits in Idilpur, which ranked even higher than Nabadwip.

Kaibarttas.

The Kaibarttas are partly fishermen and partly cultivators. The Mahisyas or Chāsi Kaibarttas number 13,517 and the Jalia Kaibarttas 15,695. The Kaibarttas are very numerous in thana Barāhānaddin, into which they have apparently immigrated from the district of Faridpur in recent times. Barāhānaddin Kaibarttas are chiefly Mahisyas. The Jalia Kaibarttas are uniformly distributed throughout the thanas of the district.

The Brahma Samaj.

The Brahma Samāj was established in Barisāl in 1861 and at first secured many adherents. Of late years it has declined in numbers and influence, although many of the most prominent men in the district of late years have belonged to the Samāj.

RELIGIOUS CEREMONIES.

The only peculiarity requiring special mention among the religious ceremonies of the Hindus of Bākarganj is the special reverence they pay to Manasā, the goddess of snakes, who is always represented among the family idols. It is not clear whether the extensive worship is due to the prevalence of deaths from snake-bite or is a relic of the old serpent-worship. A festival which is celebrated with unusual ceremony by Hindus of the respectable classes in the district is the *navānna* or the eating of the first rice grown in the year, for which a small area is sown with specially early rice. An auspicious day is selected in the month of Agrahayan (late November) and kinsmen often collect to celebrate the occasion with a full family gathering. Even the business of the Courts is often stayed for the *navānna* ceremony. Funeral cakes are offered on this occasion to the manes of the family ancestors, and Lakshmi, the goddess of food or riches, is worshipped with offerings of the new rice. The *kartta* or head of the family must see that the crows are appeased with balls of the rice mixed with sweets and plantains before he can spread his table with his guests. This is probably a relic of the old Hindu custom, which required every householder to feed birds and beasts before he could sit to dinner himself. If a crow does not consume the offering, the family look upon it as an ill-omen and live in great anxiety lest any danger should befall them during the year.

HINDU CASTE DISPUTES.

Caste disputes are very common amongst the higher castes in the district and arise out of very trivial causes, although it must be said that the falling away from orthodoxy has been so general that caste disputes must tend to lose all force. An example of such disputes may be quoted. In 1871 some school-boys on their way from Calcutta ate some pulse cooked by Muhammadan boatmen. One of the boys who had not partaken of the food related the matter. Social disputes and several criminal prosecutions followed and the Sadar sub-division was arrayed for a long time into two factions about the punishment of the boys.

RELIGIOUS FAIRS.

Of the twenty-one fairs in the district none are connected with a definitely religious observance, although those at Kālisuri, Kalaskāti and Lākhutiā which occur in October and November and last more than seven days have a religious origin. Kālisuri was the headquarters of a Muhammadan *pir* and contains his tomb (Saheb Arpin's Dargā). The *pir* was a preacher said to be sent by Timurlane. The Kalaskāti fair is held in connection with the Ganes Puja and the Lākhutiā fair in connection with the Rath Jatra. These fairs are not attended by more than five thousand persons.

LANGUAGE.

The language spoken in Bākarganj is Bengali and there are few words exclusively confined to the district. The pronunciation both among the upper and the lower classes is flat as compared with Western Bengal, but not so flat as in Chittagong. The Muhammadans use the dialect known as Musalmani-Bengali, which contains a large number of Persian and Arabic terms. Most of these words concern revenue, justice and administration; but some relate to the arts and sciences and domestic life.

LIFE IN BAKARGANJ.

The most characteristic feature of Bākarganj life is the absence of the gregarious instinct. The urban population shows no sign of growing and lives very largely in widely-separated homesteads. The big bazars and markets outside the towns do not attract a residential population, while there is no such thing as a village site in the whole of Bākarganj. Ordinarily each family lives on an ample plot of land which is surrounded by a deep moat and by a thick belt of trees and usually the homestead is not flanked by another homestead, but is further separated by paddy land from the nearest habitation. This isolation is almost universal with cultivators, both Hindu and Muhammadan, and accounts for the absence of all communal sentiment and co-operation. The *bhadralok* or respectable classes amongst the Hindus tend to congregate in villages such as Gāilā, Gābhā, Bānaripārā, Kalaskāti, Kirttipāsā and Basanda; but even in such villages the homesteads are usually separated by moat and garden from their neighbours.

CHARACTER OF THE PEOPLE.

This absence of the gregarious spirit and of communal sentiment is responsible very largely for the difficulty of administration. All executive action is made more difficult, when each family instead of each village or each community needs to be individually addressed. More especially is it difficult to introduce reforms or legislation which involve a change in the habits of life in the people. Apart from this, modern conditions can only be slowly introduced in a country where communications are so slow. Even in the elementary duty of coping with serious crime the administration has been much hampered by dilatory means of communication and by the isolation of the homestead. This has probably been responsible for the continued prevalence of dacoity, murder and rioting in Bākarganj, when other districts had become pacified and settled. The people of Bākarganj bear a bad reputation throughout Bengal for turbulence; but it does not appear that this reputation is deserved. They have been much oppressed by their landlords in the past, who have flagrantly broken the law, and yet the authorities were not able to give redress. They found that a resort to lynch law in the murder of *naibs* and *mriddhās* went unpunished and that no serious attempt was made to cope with rioting. It is only natural in these circumstances that rioting and murder should flourish and increase. It is true that murders of passion are also common; but it is difficult to draw any inferences from this fact, when at one time they had almost disappeared and when since they have again increased they have been committed with so large an impunity. There is no doubt much truth in the remarks of Mr. J. H. Reilly, in the "Police Report" quoted in Hunter's Gazetteer (page 230); but they are certainly not the whole truth, as murder almost disappeared after they were written. Mr. Reilly, who knew the district well, remarked :—

"It is difficult to explain why the crime of murder is so common in Bākarganj. On asking the people, the only answer they give is that 'the men of the *Bhati Des* (tidal country) are very passionate.' The people are quite right that the men in the southern portion of Bākarganj are prone to violent and sudden outbursts of passion. I attribute this disposition to freedom from all wholesome social restraints, and to the feeling of independence in having money at their command, which has a tendency to make these men domineering. In the older districts it is well known that the inhabitants congregate together for mutual protection against robbers, and live in communities. The country is divided into clusters of houses forming villages, with the cultivated land lying round each village. The men and women associate with each other, and are acquainted with each other's affairs. But in Bākarganj the features of the country are very different, and there are, strictly speaking, no villages. Each man builds his homestead on his own land, generally on the highest spot appertaining to his holding, without any reference to his neighbours. The consequence is, that the homesteads are far apart from each other, with dense plantations of cocoanut and betel-nut surrounding each homestead. Families, for this reason, have little communication with each other, and owing to the numerous khals or watercourses, and the swampy nature of the country, neighbourly visits are seldom exchanged between them. I believe this isolation of families has a great effect upon the character of the people. In the older districts owing to the social relationships subsisting between families, domestic disputes are settled either by neighbours or by a Panchayet of the villagers, and a man finds himself restrained in his temper and manners by the fact that the eyes of his neighbours are upon him ; if he beats his wife, it is known at once in the village, and forms the gossip of his friends. But in Bākarganj, owing to the isolation of families, the owner of the homestead is sole arbiter and ruler, independent of every social restraint. If a man of bad temper, he often develops into a despot or domestic tyrant. This will explain how a man of this lordly disposition, whose pride has been fostered by wifely homage, returning home after a hard day's ploughing, and finding his rice uncooked or cold, seizes a club or a knife, and either batters or hacks his wife to death. It is crimes of this class that are so common in the district—hasty and violent ebullitions of temper, leading to sudden murder. I believe the household habits of the people, caused by the secluded lives they lead, will account in a great measure for the social and domestic murders so prevalent in the district. The prevention of murder among such a race is not the work of the police officer; it is the work of the schoolmaster and teacher, who, by inculcating a purer religion and a higher standard of humanity, may civilise these savages, and soften their hearts and manners; until that is effected, murder will continue to be common in the district."

Whether this independence of public opinion and lack of restraint is responsible for the prevalence of murder or not, it is probably responsible for the extent to which abduction and kidnapping of eligible girls takes place amongst Muhammadans. A girl is regarded by her relatives as a gold mine and is often married at the same time to two or three different men. It is also responsible for the public manner in which widows are kept as concubines amongst the Namasudras. But the cultivator has an easy life and during most of the year has little or no work in the fields. It is in accordance with universal experience that in such conditions offences should come. Idleness has no doubt much of the crime in Bākarganj to answer for. It cannot, however, be held on mature consideration that the inhabitants of Bākarganj are as turbulent or as bad as they are painted. It cannot be denied, on the other hand, that there are wild elements in the population and that their crimes are of a peculiarly ferocious type. The murder of whole families, including children, is not uncommon, while the weapons most in favour are a large curved knife (dão) which inflicts frightful wounds or the fish-spear which pierces the body with its fifty prongs and cannot be extracted without tearing the flesh to pieces. The criminal annals of Bākarganj are very interesting and would repay a detailed account. They include stories of professional murderers, of long vendettas in which the threatened man slept for years in an iron cage and never left his house, of snakes trained to poison men in their sleep. They contain also many tales of old men and women slain by their own sons or kinsfolk, sometimes with their own consent, in order to accuse the enemy of a deed for which he may be hanged, while one thana (Rājāpur) has a sinister reputation for this form of crime with cases of fathers killing their own little children in their blind desire to ruin their enemies.

CHAPTER IV.

PUBLIC HEALTH.

A COMPARISON of vital statistics for any lengthy period is rendered impossible by the changes in the system of registering births and deaths which have taken place from time to time. In 1869 the duty of reporting deaths was imposed upon *chaukidars* and in 1867 the system was extended to births; but the returns were incomplete and the registration of births was discontinued except in the towns until 1892. The system now in vogue still depends upon the *chaukidar*. VITAL STATISTICS.

The statistics are perhaps accurate enough for comparison between different years. They show a very constant ratio of about 34½ deaths per mille from 1892. The three years 1906-08 were the most unhealthy, the unhealthiness of 1908 being due chiefly to fever and that of 1906 and 1907 to cholera. The ratio in 1908, the unhealthiest year of the three, was 38 deaths per thousand of the population. The birth-rate in the ten years 1893—1902 was 37 per mille and in 1903—1911 it had risen to 40 per mille, being as high as 45·36 in 1904. The death-rate has been much reduced of late years, being 24·58 in 1914. The district is not generally considered unhealthy, and although the drinking water is often bad the homesteads are far more sanitary in their arrangements than the ordinary crowded village site. The comparatively high death-rate is undoubtedly due to the dearth of qualified doctors.

According to the returns submitted year by year, by far the greatest mortality is due to fever, but the ignorant *chaukidar* responsible for the returns is far from being a medical expert. All deaths not due to cholera and other obvious forms of disease, especially when associated with a high temperature, are classed indiscriminately under the general head of fever. The ratio of deaths from fever in the decade 1893—1902 was 21·29 per mille, and in the decade 1901—1910 it was only slightly less and only in two years was it less than 20. In 1911, however, it was as low as 15·25. PRINCIPAL DISEASES. Fever.

In the view of the Civil Surgeon the district of Bākarganj cannot comparatively speaking be said to suffer severely from malarial fever. Cases of enlarged spleen, though common enough, are by no means so frequently met with as in some other parts of the province, nor are those cases of malarial cachexia, characterized by much enlarged spleen, grave anæmia, and oedema of the extremities, so frequently seen in the hospitals and dispensaries of the district as elsewhere. In its physical features the district would appear to offer unrivalled advantages for the propagation of mosquitoes and thereby for the incidence and spread of malaria. The level of the land is low, of the subsoil water high, the whole district is indeed a swamp, albeit a cultivated one. Villages consist of collections of scattered homesteads, each house, secluded in its grove of cocoanut and *supāri* palm trees with much riotous jungle, is built up on a high mud plinth, necessitating for its construction the excavation of a proportionately extensive tank. Each house, therefore, may be said to maintain its own mosquito-breeding establishment at its door. The houses themselves are, in the main, well built lofty structures with corrugated iron roofs, but internally are no cleaner, lighter nor better ventilated than the more old fashioned thatched huts which are the particular delight of the anopheles mosquito. It may be that the inhabitants of the district, being generally well fed and comfortably situated, are in a better position to resist the malarial influences, by which they are surrounded, or, as the Sanitary Commissioner for Bengal remarked in the annual report for 1904 : "The river districts of Bengal, viz., Khulna, Dacca, Bākarganj, Tippera and most of Faridpur, are the least malaricus; in these districts the rivers are open, tidal, and clean banked, and that is the reason." What immunity there is, however, is at best a comparative one, for the decade 1891—1900 the average death-rate per 1,000 of population was 21·18, since when it has only varied from 18·69 in 1901 as a minimum to 20·72 in 1903 as a maximum, the mean average total rate for the last five years from all causes being 34·25. The types of the disease met with in the district differ in no way from those seen in other parts of the country. No scientific classification, based on a large number of microscopical examinations of the blood of patients suffering from fever, has yet been carried out, without which it is impossible to speak with certainty; but clinically the usual varieties are recognized. Black-water fever apparently does not occur. The problem of prophylaxis is at the present time attracting much attention. Oiling of tanks and similar measures which are attended with practical disadvantages have been given up in favour of quinine prophylaxis; and indeed the very favourable results which have been obtained in jails give encouragement to the hope that the extension of the facilities for the purchase of quinine by the rural public will be attended by the happiest results.

Cholera

After fever the greatest mortality is caused by cholera, which appears frequently in an epidemic form. In the decade 1893—1902 the deaths from cholera numbered 3·06 per thousand, and in the decade 1901—1910 3·45 per thousand, rising as high as 5·61 in 1906 and 6·03 in 1907. In the early part of the nineteenth century cholera was much more virulent, thus in 1825 the deaths from this cause must have numbered more than 20 per thousand. In January and February when the water is low in the streams of Sāhābāzpur and Gaurnadi, cholera is always probable; but its great vogue in Bākarganj is due to the dependence of the district upon tanks for its drinking-water. Every homestead has a tank, which is used indiscriminately for all purposes besides drinking. As most of these tanks are connected with the rivers and regularly washed out by them, there is no particular danger in this; but in the months of February the water gets very low and very putrid. The Bākarganj peasant will not drink well water, and the only means of avoiding cholera is to build good tanks in every village and preserve them for drinking purposes—a course upon which the District Board has with some success embarked. It is unfortunate that the landlords by the high fees which they exact make it very difficult to increase the size of private tanks or to keep them clean by regular re-excavation.

Other causes of death.

Bowel complaints are very common in the district, but according to the statistics they are not a frequent cause of death, thus in 1893—1902 only ·21 and in 1901—1910 only ·16 deaths per mille were reported annually from this cause. It is probable, however, that better reporting would have increased these figures. Small-pox is very rare, only ·11 per mille in 1901—1910. The deaths from other causes average 9·52 per mille and from injuries ·55 per mille. A very large number of deaths from snake-bite are reported; but it is usually considered in the district that snake-bite is used in cases of sudden, unaccountable and suspicious death in order to avoid the unwelcome visit of the police. It is also currently reported that poisoning is more common than the figures indicate, especially by wives of their husbands.

SANITATION.

Outside the municipalities any attempt at sanitation in the modern sense is unknown. In 1870 orders were issued to clear jungle in the neighbourhood of villages; but little has been done in this respect and least in those more congested villages in which the *bhadralok* or respectable classes live, and in which therefore something might be expected. Such villages are usually full of the rankest undergrowth. In other villages, sanitation is difficult to introduce and perhaps not urgently necessary. As explained, there are no village sites, each homestead stands apart from its neighbours in an open and healthy manner, the moat and tank are in the south connected with tidal rivers and washed out daily. There is often a good deal of miscellaneous jungle in the garden, which might very well be cleaned; but it is not usually right at the walls. The houses, being made of mat walls and thatched roof, are cool and airy and they are usually very roomy. In regard to drinking water, there is more scope. The numerous tanks are often overgrown with weeds and in a filthy condition. The District Board has, however, done much in this direction by the provision of tanks (usually 120′ × 90′) for drinking water in places where drinking water is hard to obtain. These tanks are fenced in to avoid contamination. A more extensive campaign is however desirable, which should embrace the cleansing and re-excavation of all impure tanks and the enlargement of private tanks as far as possible to a sanitary size. The hostility or rather rapacity of the landlords would need to be conciliated. In the municipalities more has been done in the direction of sanitation, jungle is cut down, a system of conservancy is enforced and pure water is secured. As a result the death-rate is much lower than in the rural districts.

VACCINATION.

When vaccination was first introduced, there was a great deal of opposition; but by 1887 it was in vogue in the north and east of the district. In the south and west of the district it was introduced generally somewhat later, as the hostility of the Muhammadans was fanned by the Mullahs. A large staff of vaccinators is now maintained and the number of vaccinations rose from an annual average of 62,000 in 1893—1902 to an annual average of 119,000 in 1901—1910 and of 140,000 in 1908—1910. In the latter years the vaccination accomplished amounted to a protection of 6 per cent. of the entire population annually.

MEDICAL INSTITUTIONS.

The district contains four hospitals and 30 charitable dispensaries. There is, however, no medical school. The total number of qualified doctors is only 157, which is quite insufficient for the population. Most of these are crowded into the Sadar subdivision or rather four thanas. There is a large number of *kabirājes* or native practitioners, and homeopathic treatment is very powerful. Considering that the population is predominantly Muhammadan, there are remarkably few *hākims*; but the number of quacks in the southern thanas is very large. In Chāndsi there are some hereditary native doctors (the Namasudras) who have a great reputation as surgeons and who attract patients from all the neighbouring districts. They chiefly operate for piles, fistula, etc. The hospitals are all in the subdivisional headquarter towns. The buildings are good and there is accommodation for in-patients; but in the subdivisions at least the in-patients are chiefly the victims of violent crime. The hospital in Barisāl is an excellent building, built in 1911-12, and an attempt has been made by building suitable wards to inculcate the hospital habit among the general public. Both hospitals and dispensaries are chiefly resorted to in surgical cases, with the important exception of midwifery, in which Hindus and Muhammadans alike cling to ancient and somewhat barbarous customs with which a great deal of religious observance is mingled. In the provision of dispensaries the District Board has always maintained a progressive policy. In 1870 there were only two dispensaries in the district, at Barisāl (founded in 1847) and at Pirozpur (founded in 1865). In 1901 the number had grown to 41 with an average daily attendance of 40 in-door and 1,356 out-door patients. Some of the less numerously attended dispensaries were then shut down and in 1911 there were altogether 30 in existence with an average daily attendance of 51 in-door and 1,048 out-door patients. The total expenditure was Rs. 69,867, of which 10 per cent. was provided by the provincial Government, 65 per cent. by the District Board and Municipalities and the remainder by fees and subscriptions. Of the dispensaries 12 are in the Sadar, 6 in the Pirozpur, 7 in the Patuākhāli and 5 in the Sāhābāzpur subdivisions. It is unfortunate that the charitable purpose of the local authorities has been somewhat defeated by the class of doctor employed. Many charge for the medicines with which they are supplied gratuitously, some are very lazy and nearly all charge unauthorised fees, which are often so heavy as to discourage the resort to them of the poorer classes altogether. The District Board has somewhat neglected the south of the district in the provision of dispensaries, but it is difficult to obtain doctors who will consent to live there.

The following table shows the extent to which dispensaries were used in the different parts of the district in 1911 :—

	Sadar.	Pirozpur.	Patuâkhâli.	Sâhâbâzpur.	Total.
Total population	985,184	550,418	574,972	318,337	2,428,911
Number of dispensaries ...	10	7	8	5	30
Expenditure—					
Establishment ... Rs.	11,359	4,835	5,109	2,934	24,237
Medicine, diet, etc. ... Rs.	7,000	3,766	4,659	2,425	17,850
Diseases treated—					
Bowels	11,015	4,549	8,009	3,868	27,441
Fever	18,812	13,081	7,802	3,989	43,684
Cholera	278	95	139	89	601
Eyes, etc.	1,750	1,480	588	838	4,656
Injuries	1,563	681	960	1,029	4,233
Miscellaneous	65,420	41,799	54,485	43,753	196,457
Number of operation ...	2,289	1,216	1,122	696	4,323
Total number of patients ...	101,127	62,901	73,105	45,262	281,395
Average per 1,000 of the population.	104	115	129	145	493

CHAPTER V.

AGRICULTURE.

BĀKARGANJ is from its conformation entirely a rice district and, being a very recent alluvial deposit which is still so low that during the flood period it goes under water, it is only in small areas that the soil is suitable for other crops. Rainfall does not exercise so great an influence upon the fortune of the cultivators as in other parts of India. The rice crop needs rain at the right time, but rain is certain and delay although damaging is never completely ruinous to the whole crop. For the spring and autumn crops rain is more important, but they form too small a proportion of the district crop to produce a famine or even a scarcity in the case of their failure. The greatest danger the cultivator has to fear is cloudy weather before the winter rice is harvested when the pāmari insect commits great destruction. GENERAL CONDITIONS. RAINFALL.

In Bākarganj floods spread by the great rivers play a more important part than rain in the fortune of the crop. If floods are good the water should begin to accumulate in June, should rise gradually until September and should fall as gradually. Sudden rises when the autumn or winter rice is young are very disastrous, unless they are followed quickly by fall, when damage is confined to the country very close to the Meghnā. The floods are very rarely late, but sometimes subside too early with disastrous effect to winter rice in the higher lands. The Meghnā and the Ariāl Khān bring down a large quantity of silt in the flood season. On the western side of the district the country is not so well served, as the Baleswar (or Madhumati) loses most of the silt in the northern part of the district and therefore has little to spare for the southern part. The numberless watercourses distribute the silt almost universally and there are only a few parts of the district which are so unfortunately placed as not to be served by them. Floods.

The part which rainfall plays in the agricultural economy of the district is of course important. Rain is indeed needed at the end of March, to make ploughing easy, but after ploughing is over extreme heat without rain is required to kill Main.

weeds. Rain is again necessary in June for broadcast sowing and for the preparation of seed-beds. In October the flood subsides and rain is required to give vigour to the young paddy. In November, when the paddy is in flood, heavy rain will destroy the ear. Rain or rather cloudy weather in December, as has been said, is very destructive to the crop.

Salt-water inundations.

Inundations from the Bay during the passage of cyclones are not infrequent in the southern part of the district and do great damage. They usually occur in June before the breaking of the monsoon, or in October and November after the monsoon is over. Smaller inundations affect the coast for several miles inland and deposit a layer of salt, which not only destroys the crop of that season but reduces the fertility of the soil for some seasons afterwards. Incidental effects felt in that portion where the wave is at its height are the destruction of cattle and the impregnation of all tanks which supply drinking water with salt. At infrequent intervals storms and waves of great magnitude occur which are liable to cover the entire district or the greater portion of it with salt water and therefore affect the fertility of the whole, while in the southern parts such waves destroy the whole country and send temporarily a great deal of the land out of cultivation.

COMPARATIVE FERTILITY.

The fertility of the different thanas may be summarised thus:—

GAURNADI.—Soil moderate except in the riparian area and in the *bils*, where it is excellent for paddy, when the water is not too deep. In the higher lands, a light soil, only fit for *rabi* and autumn crops.

MEHENDIGANJ.—A good soil for all crops, and excellent for the areca nut. Some clay, but generally a sandy loam.

JHĀLAKĀTI.—Poor in the north-west, otherwise good, being fairly stiff clay.

BARISĀL.—A good clay soil generally, tending to poverty in the north.

BĀKARGĀNJ.—An excellent soil for paddy, as it is a stiff clay.

NALCHHITI.—A similar soil to Jhālakāti, but deteriorating in the interior from lack of alluvial deposit.

SWARUPKATI.—Poor in the north-east, but rich and valuable for garden crops in the south-east. The *bil* area gives excellent paddy crops where not water-logged.

PIROZPUR—Was an excellent clay soil both for paddy and orchards 15 years ago, now deteriorating owing to salt irruptions from the big rivers, which have recently become saline.

BHĀNDĀRIĀ.—Rich clay on the margin of the *bil*, deteriorating on the Baleswar side, but excellent on the Biskhāli bank and excellent for the areca palm in the north.

MATBĀRIĀ.—Excellent on the Biskhāli side, but sandy and saline on the Baleswar side and high in the centre.

BĀUPHAL.—A good soil for paddy throughout, and in the north an excellent soil for *rabi* crops.

PATUĀKHĀLI.—Exceedingly fertile, generally a very stiff clay.

GALĀCHIPĀ.—Exceedingly fertile on the mainland, but full of depressions in which the crop is precarious. A light but excellent soil in the islands.

AMTALI.—A heavy clay, exceedingly fertile throughout, but the banks of the innumerable tidal creeks require bunds to keep out the salt water.

BHOLĀ.—A light loam, fertile throughout, and excellent for the areca palm.

BARHĀNADDIN.—Fertile, except on the seaface, but very exposed on the south and east to irruptions of salt water.

The soil of the district although everywhere suitable for the growth of winter rice has naturally degrees of suitability. In the Sāhābāzpur island and the Meghnā estuary the soil is a sandy loam, and clay is only found in depressions. In Matbāriā and the western part of Āmtali the proportion of sand is large. In both cases, however, the soil gives good crops, although not so heavy as in the centre of the district. The best crops are obtained in the interior of the mainland and particularly in Bākarganj, Bāuphal and Patuākhāli thanas where the level is lower and the soil is stiff clay. Āmtali contains less clay, but the remains of decayed vegetable matter from the forests, which recently covered it, give the soil great fertility. In Galāchipā, Bhāndāriā, Swarupkāti, Jhālakāti and the western portion of Gaurnadi, the soil also contains a great deal of decayed vegetable matter, which has remained when the marshes dried up. The eastern portion of Gaurnadi and Mehendiganj possess a soil which is more like that of Sāhābāzpur island than that of the centre of the district. SOIL.

The statistics collected in the district survey of 1900 to 1905 give a total area of 1,553,376 acres under cultivation, but owing to the fact that the autumn crops were not upon the ground at the time the surveyors compiled their figures it is probable that the real area under cultivation amounts to nearly 1,600,000 acres. Of this area 172,751 acres were covered by fruit-bearing orchards. The cropped area of the district should AREA UNDER CULTIVATION.

be estimated at a gross total of 1,650,000 acres, and, deducting 250,000 acres as the area twice cropped in the same year, a net total of 1,400,000 acres. Out of this total, 1,313,000 acres or 95 per cent. are under winter *āman* rice together with 172,000 acres under autumn (*āus*) rice and 5,000 acres under *boro* rice. Compared with the rice crop, the other crops are insignificant, and a larger area is under fruit-bearing orchards and garden produce than under all these minor crops together.

Of the minor crops pulses cover 64,000 acres, sugarcane 12,000 acres, condiments and spices 27,000 acres, oil seeds 25,000 acres and jute 27,000 acres. Wheat and barley are not grown at all. In the south of the district the preponderance of rice is even greater than these figures show, as a very small proportion of the land is under any other crop, and even *āus* rice is less cultivated than in the north of the district. Pulses and jute are chiefly grown in the Sadar subdivision. *Masuri*, *til*, jute and sugarcane are almost confined to the three thanas, Barisāl, Mehendiganj and Gaurnadi, *mug* to Bāuphal, Galāchipā and Sāhābāzpur, *khesāri* to Gaurnadi, Mehendiganj and Sāhābāzpur. The small extent to which jute is grown as compared with the neighbouring districts of Faridpur and Dacca is somewhat remarkable. Moreover it is only cultivated in Barisāl, Mehendiganj and Gaurnadi thanas in the north of the district. It is not certain what the reason is for this absence of jute. In the south of the district salt water probably damages the fibre, but in the north of the district this cause does not operate, and it would seem that the profits of rice have been sufficiently high to discourage cultivators from embarking in speculation with another crop.

RICE. It is not necessary to describe the cultivation of different crops in Bākarganj in any detail as this has been exhaustively done in Chapter II of the Bākarganj Settlement Report recently published. It may be merely said here that *āman* rice is almost entirely transplanted and is sown in the nursery in May and transplanted in August and reaped in December and January. There is, however, an early variety grown in Sāhābāzpur known as *rājasāl*, which is harvested in October and November. *Aghāni* is also reaped in November and is grown in well-raised land in the mainland of the district, but it is not grown in any great quantity as it is chiefly used by Hindus during the *navānna* or the ceremony of new rice. Most of the winter rice is not reaped by the cultivator, but by hired labour, which comes very largely from Dacca, Faridpur and Noākhāli districts. In Sāhābāzpur and in the south of the district ploughing and other parts of the cultivation also are done by hired labour. The best rice is grown in Bākarganj thana and sold at Charāmuddin hat and in Bāuphal and North Patuākhāli. Bākarganj rice is famous in the markets of Calcutta and Bengal, where it is known as *bālām* rice, from the *bālām* country boats in which it is generally carried into Calcutta. The estimate of the outturn of *āman* rice made by the district settlement authorities gives the average yield of the district at 22½ maunds of paddy per acre, being rather less in the north of the district and rather more in the south. There are, however, no data upon which a really satisfactory estimate can be made, and it seems very probable that when such an estimate can be made the average figure will be very considerably increased. *Aus* rice is usually mixed with *āman* and occasionally followed by it. It is sown in April, transplanted in June and reaped in August, almost entirely by hired labour, as the cultivators are at that time engaged in transplanting *āman* rice. It is rarely sold by the cultivator as he keeps it for home consumption.

The minor crops cover so small an area that it is unnecessary to give any details about their cultivation. Sugarcane was formerly more grown, but it has given place very largely to jute, partly because it is a troublesome crop, which requires capital, and partly because the iron pans for the extraction of *gur* are difficult to obtain and keep in repair. Perhaps also the ravages of jackals and the extortion of the owners of the markets where it is sold have also contributed to this reduction in its cultivation. *Pān* is a very lucrative crop which covers however only 1,300 acres chiefly in Gaurnadi thana. It requires considerable expenditure, skill and trouble in the cultivation, but produces as much as 600 to 1,000 rupees per acre. A garden lasts on the average four years, but it may last as long as six. MINOR CROPS.

Rabi crops are grown as catch crops and little attention is paid to them except in Gaurnadi. The *masuri* of Bākarganj is famous for its flavour throughout lower Bengal and the chief markets are Turki, Mulādi and Sārikal. The best *masuri* is grown in Chāndpāsā (Barisāl thana) and the best *khesāri* in Bākarganj thana, while Kālāiyā in Fāufal thana grows *mug* of a very special quality.

Amongst vegetables, the potato is little grown and tobacco only for home consumption. Chillies and *kachu* are the most important vegetables, but a large variety is grown in the *dhāp* gardens of the Jhālakāti marshes. Thatching grass and reeds also grow well in the district and fetch a good price.

ORCHARDS. Next to the rice crop the agricultural wealth of Bākarganj lies in its orchards. Almost every part of the district appears to grow fruit-bearing trees of considerable variety and in great profusion. In extent orchards cover 15 per cent. of the net cultivated area in the Sadar and Pirojpur subdivisions and more than 20 per cent. in thanas Mehendiganj and Pirojpur, whereas in Patuākhāli subdivision they cover only 5 per cent. The most important of the fruit-bearing trees which are grown in the district are the areca-nut (*supāri*) of which there are perhaps 35,000,000 in the district, the cocoanut of which there are 2,500,000 and the date palm of which there are a million. The timber of the palmyra is valuable, but the fruit is not of much consequence. The district in the north does not grow bamboo of very good quality, but the quantity is considerable and the district contains 350,000 clumps. They are most common in the Sadar subdivision and least common in the Sāhābāzpur island. Most cultivators with a homestead of any size grow one or two mango and jack-fruit trees and some plantains. The mango does not do well as it is small and not very sweet, while worms or disease carry off a good deal of the fruit. The jack-fruit is a very popular fruit with the cultivators, although coarse and rather bitter in its flavour. The timber of the tree sells at a very good price. Plantains are very numerous and are no doubt one of the most lucrative of the petty sources of income to the cultivators.

BETEL-NUTS. The income obtained from the three principal trees grown in the district cannot be estimated at less than a crore of rupees each year of which more than three quarters is obtained from the betelnut. The areca-nut (*areca catechu*) grows in all soils of the district, but a high sandy soil rich in salt seems to be most suitable. The trees are grown on every homestead, but in addition there are many formal gardens. The biggest gardens are found in Mehendiganj thana and in the Sāhābāzpur island. The areca-nut is most common in the Sadar subdivision, in Pirojpur and in Bholā thanas. In Mehendiganj there are 5,000,000, Jhālakāti 3,500,000, in Pirozpur and Bholā 3,000,000, in Bākarganj, Patuākhāli and Farahānuddin over 2,000,000. In the cultivation of the betel-nut there is considerable variety in different parts of the district, but a garden is usually raised above the high-tide level and is planted with a mandar tree (*erythrina indica*), which grows quickly, sheds its leaves and makes the soil rich. Saplings are grown in a nursery from ripe nuts, slightly slit at the crown and transplanted in July of the following year, or even in the third year when they are planted in rows about 4½ feet apart. The mandar is only cut down when the trees have grown a sufficient height to require no protection against sun or wind. The trees begin to bear in the eighth year. They flower in February and March and the fruit is gathered from September to December. The trees bear well for forty years and then begin to decline. The nuts are gathered by professional pluckers and are sold by number to *bepāris*, who sell to the merchants through *āratdārs*. The *bepāris* are usually local Muhammadans, the *āratdārs* Hindus in Nalchhiti, but elsewhere Muhammadans. The wholesale dealers are usually Burmese merchants. The price is very variable, but may be said to average about eight rupees per hazar of 11,000 nuts. The nuts of Mehendiganj and Sāhābāzpur, which are bigger and heavier than those of other parts, sell at a higher price. From account made during the district survey it would seem that the average number of nuts per tree is 230. Nuts are sold in four different states known as maghāi, jangā, tātti and majā. Tātti nuts are husked and dried before sale; jangā nuts are half ripe nuts partially husked and sunned; maghāi nuts, which is the form in which the Magh merchants of Burma purchase, are thoroughly washed and sunned as well as husked and steeped. The principal markets of the betelnut trade are Nalchhiti, Pātarhāt (in Mehendiganj thana), Sukdeb and Amāni (in Bholā thana), Gāluā (in Jhālakāti thana), and Bhāndāriā. The total quantity exported is about 800,000 maunds, of which two-third goes by steamer to Calcutta and one-third by country boat to Chittāgong and inland places as well as to Calcutta. The betelnut is subject to a disease of a very virulent nature which broke out in Bakarganj in 1894 and destroyed many gardens in a single fortnight. No cure was discovered, but the disease rapidly exhausted itself.

Cocoanuts.

The cocoanut (*cocos nucifera*) is grown in all soils, but grows best on heavy soil with vegetable matter and some impregation of salt. The nuts of thanas Jhālakāti and Swārupkāti are generally reported to be the best and are exported in considerable quantity. Cocoanut gardens are not so common as betelnut, nor so large; and cocoanuts are usually grown as an avenue to the homestead. In a garden the soil is trenched to a depth of three feet and a width of six feet at intervals of sixteen feet. Saplings are grown from seednuts, which are planted in the month of July. The tree begins to bear from the eighth year, flowers in November and again in

April and the fruit matures in six months. Nuts ripen in every month, but the regular plucking season is from May to September. The amount of fruit given by a tree differs very greatly. It probably averages about thirty-two nuts. Local oil-pressers prepare oil everywhere, but the fibre is used for fuel and not for rope-making.

Date palms. There are no orchards of date-palms in this district, although the trees are numerous. They grow better on raised land. The date-palm is commoner and gives a better juice in the north of the district and especially in Gaurnadi. The tree is tapped in November. The juice is sold as juice and not as molasses or tāri.

Increase in the cultivated area. A century ago the land area of the district was not only much smaller, but a greater proportion was uncultivated; thus in the island of Sāhābāzpur only a small part of the land then in existence was occupied, the greater part being under forest and grass, while in the mainland of the district a forest known as the Sundarbans not only covered about 650 square miles of the south, but little blocks of jungle and waste were scattered throughout the rest of the area to such an extent that the Collector at that time complained of the depredations caused even in Gaurnadi by tigers and other wild beasts. In the north-west of the district a huge area was covered by impenetrable morass, and there were smaller marshes in Bhāndāriā and Galāchipā thanas. So far as can be calculated, the land area of Bākarganj was about 3,000 square miles in 1770 A.D., of which not more than 1,675 square miles or 56 per cent. can have been occupied. In 1905 the land area had become 3,490 square miles, of which 3,230 or 92½ per cent. was occupied. The expansion of cultivation which these figures indicate has been enormous. Since the Revenue Survey that expansion seems to have amounted to 432 square miles or at the rate of 10 square miles a year. There is little waste land now left in the district.

Uncultivated area. In the occupied area 90 per cent. is under cultivation or culturable fallow, so that here little more can be brought under cultivation. The unoccupied waste measures 260 square miles, but a great part of this consists of char land or of marsh which is not at present fit for cultivation. The forest in the south of the district which may amount to a 100 square miles is now very rapidly being cut down. The unculivated area is 30 per cent. of the total land area in the district. Of this 1½ per cent. is new fallow, 4½ per cent. old fallow, 1 per cent. reeds and 1 per cent. thatching grass, while

18 per cent. is returned as unculturable, which included 6½ per cent. homestead, tanks and roads, 2 per cent. char, 1 per cent. marsh and 4½ per cent. forest. In Patuākhāli subdivision char is 3 per cent. and forest 18½ per cent., while in Sāhābāzpur char and forest are 7 per cent. and old fallow 10 per cent.

IMPROVEMENTS.

So far there appears to be no indication of any general improvement in the method of cultivation. The implements in use to-day are the same as have been used for generations past, and no attempt is being made by any landlord to institute model farms which will experiment with new crops, new methods or new implements. Manure is practically not used at all, and indeed owing to the annual deposit of silt by flood water, it is only in small parts of the district that manure would be of any value. The soil is so generous that it is doubtful if more careful cultivation would give any increase in yield commensurate with the trouble and expenditure. Fodder crops will no doubt be more grown in the off season, when the cultivator takes more pride in his cattle; otherwise it is not clear that there is any great scope at present for agricultural improvements.

AGRICULTURAL LOANS.

There is, however, great scope for improvement in the facilities extended to the cultivator for borrowing for agricultural purposes. Under the Land Improvement and Agriculturists' Loans Acts loans are granted to cultivators chiefly in Government estates. Under the former Act loans have been granted for the construction of homesteads in chars and other waste lands, for embanking streams and for reclaiming forest in the Sundarbans and elsewhere. The average amount granted was only Rs. 776 per annum in the ten years 1893—1902, but Rs. 4,904 per annum in the ten years 1903—1912. In 1913 it was Rs. 9,859 and in 1914 Rs. 5,126. The increase has been chiefly due to the insistence upon the construction of homesteads and clearance of jungles by colonists in Government estates. Agricultural loans have been granted more widely for the purchase of seeds and plough cattle, especially in times of distress. Thus in 1893—1895, when there was local scarcity, Rs. 17,000 was advanced and fully recovered, while in 1906 the loans amounted to Rs. 2,10,040, of which Rs. 1,80,000 was in Gaurnadi. These loans were recovered with more difficulty, as they had been injudiciously distributed. In 1910, Rs. 3,802 was advanced for the purchase of cattle to replace those lost by rinderpest in the epidemic which attacked the cattle in the south of the district. Altogether Rs. 36,158 was advanced in the years 1893—1902 and

Rs. 3,87,229 in the ten years 1903—1912. In 1913 the amount advanced was Rs. 19,983 and in 1914 Rs. 21,874.

CO-OPERATIVE CREDIT.

Co-operative credit was introduced into the district in 1910 with one bank at Barisāl under the designation of Barisāl Islamia Co-operative Urban Bank. The members of the urban bank in 1914 were 25 and the total working capital was Rs. 3,380. Besides this urban bank there is a co-operative central bank in Barisāl founded in 1913. The total number of the members of the central bank in 1914 was 112 and the total working capital was Rs. 79,766. Rural societies in 1914 amounted to 54 with 1,707 members and a capital of Rs. 1,04,161, mostly advanced by the Barisāl Co-operative Central Bank and partly by individual financiers, Dacca Central Bank and Barisāl Urban Bank. A very small portion was subscribed by the members. The progress made has not been as great as is desirable, chiefly perhaps owing to the aversion of Muhammadans, who form the bulk of the cultivators, to money-lending in any form. It is also due to want of education and of co-operative spirit. The Bākarganj district is so unwieldy a charge that co-operative credit has probably suffered in comparison with other districts from an absence of interest on the part of the district officials.

CATTLE.

A careful cattle census has lately been taken in the province, but the statistics and report have not as yet been published. It is known, however, that the cattle enumerated in the district were nearly 1,400,000, or more than one to every two inhabitants and four to every agricultural family. The Bākarganj cultivator is certainly extremely well off in cattle, especially in Sāhābāzpur and the south of the district. In the absence of the figures and report of this census, it is impossible to comment in more detail. The cattle include about 50,000 buffaloes, as enumerated in the settlement operations, which are divided between the Sāhābāzpur and Patuākhāli subdivisions. There is no special breed of cattle indigenous to the district, and although the District Board, Local Boards, Court of Wards and jail in Barisāl keep bulls from Sitamarhi, Bihar and Nagpur, their services are utilised to a very small extent. The cattle are generally of very poor quality and are fed on straw and what they can find on the *āils* of the fields. Oilcake is rarely given to them, and fodder crops are not grown at all. They are stalled generally in poor huts, which are so insufficiently raised that the cattle have often to stand in liquid mud or water. The appearance of the cattle is still more diminished by the rotting of their horns, apparently due to the swampy nature of the country. The breed of cattle is said to have fallen off, since the practice of dedicating bulls and turning them loose has been given up owing, it is said, to the High Court ruling that as such bulls were *nullius proprietas* no offence is committed in killing them. The Hindu is fearful of being accessory to their slaughter and so dedicates no more. In the south of the district and the Meghnā islands, large tracts of grass are kept for grazing (*bāthān*), in which the fee is one rupee a head, and as a consequence the cattle are stronger and better-looking. The buffaloes especially are grazed in such pastures. The Maghs use buffaloes exclusively for ploughing; but the Muhammadans keep them largely for their milk and for draught. Draught cattle and buffaloes are only found in the Sāhābāzpur island. There is little other live-stock in the district, although fowls and ducks are kept by every Muhammadan and goats by many. In the settlement operations there were, however, only 16 goats to every thousand of the population. There are practically no sheep, and ponies are only kept by Muhammadans for racing of which they are very fond. It may be added that a cow sells for Rs. 30 and a bullock for Rs. 50 as compared with about Rs. 20 in 1870. The value of a pair of buffaloes is Rs. 200 as compared with Rs. 135 in 1870.

PLOUGHS. CARTS AND BOATS.

Ploughs are twice as numerous as in Bihar, numbering 43 per hundred agricultural families. In the stiff soil of Patuākhāli every family needs and retains a plough. They are iron-tipped, but light, and otherwise the same as the ploughs of a century ago. Agricultural produce is moved entirely by boat, except in the Sāhābāzpur island. In Sāhābāzpur there are 3 carts to every 200 agricultural families and 3 boats to every hundred agricultural families. In the district generally there are 15 boats amongst every hundred families, but rather more in Gaurnadi, Jhālakāti and Patuākhāli thanas and as many as 33 in Swarupkāti thana with its large area under marsh.

CATTLE DISEASE AND VETERINARY ARRANGEMENTS.

Cattle disease has several times broken out virulently in the district. Thus in 1865 forty thousand were reported to have died and in 1910 the mortality was almost as severe. It may be added that the frequent stormwaves, although local in their destruction, often drown all the cattle of the locality. After the great waves of 1822 and 1876, the mortality amongst the cattle was terrible, being estimated at 98,834 head in 1882 and about 80 per cent. in 1876. A veterinary establishment was introduced into the district by the District Board in 1902.

Veterinary Assistants are retained and are expected to go out and treat cattle reported to be diseased. Altogether 3,617 cases were treated in 1914; but the service is not as yet properly appreciated by the cultivators.

CHAPTER VI.

NATURAL CALAMITIES.

STORM-WAVES.

Bakarganj is not subject to famine. Even in the worst years it probably grows enough rice to feed itself, though scarcity in some localities has occasionally prevailed. To compensate for this comparative immunity, the district has been liable to destructive inundations from the Bay of Bengal, which have been very frequent, although local, in the Meghnā delta, and have occasionally been on a tremendous scale. Since 1890, there have been four smaller storm-waves, the last of which occurred in 1910 and was felt most severely in the island of Mānpurā and in Kālameghā (thana Matbāria). Altogether about 100 lives were lost. A large number of cattle were drowned and much of the standing crop was destroyed. The cause of such storm-waves is somewhat obscure. They occur at the tail-end of cyclones in the Bay of Bengal; but only strike Bākarganj when the cyclone takes a north-easterly direction and travels inland. It is supposed that the force of the wind holds up the ebb-tide, and when the tide changes carries in the flood-tide as a wall of water several feet higher than its usual level. The funnel-shaped Meghnā estuary with its expanse of shallows gives to the ordinary spring-tide the proportions of a bore, and with a fierce gale behind it, it is not surprising that the bore attains great height and fury. All storm-waves are therefore felt with greater intensity in the Meghnā estuary and sweep over the islands dotted about there with terrific force. The greater storm-waves occur at very infrequent intervals—only three being recorded in history, viz.:—in 1584, in 1822 and in 1876, but they engulf every living thing in the country over which they pass. It has been suggested that the peculiar violence of such inundations is due to the fact that a cyclone has passed over the coast just at the time when the tide was turning and has driven the flood tide in with the maximum force of wind of which a cyclone is capable.

Storm-wave of 1584.

We have only a brief reference by Abul Fazl to the storm-wave of 1584. It struck the mouth of the Meghnā estuary where land formations were at that date much less extensive than they are now and swept up the Bākarganj bank to Kachuā (thana Bāuphal), then a flourishing and populous port. The account of this inundation in the *Ain-i-Akbari* (Gladwin's translation) is as follows :—"Sarkar Bākla is upon the banks of the sea ; the fort is situated among trees. On the first day of the moon the water begins to rise, and continues increasing till the 14th, from which time to the end of the month it decreases gradually every day. In the twenty-ninth year of the present reign, one afternoon at three o'clock, there was a terrible inundation, which deluged the whole *sarkār*. The Raja was at an entertainment, from which he embarked in a boat ; his son with many people climbed to the top of a Hindoo temple and the merchants betook themselves to the highlands. It blew a hurricane with thunder and lightning for five hours, during which time the sea was greatly agitated. The houses and boats were swallowed up, nothing remaining but the Hindoo temple on the height. Near 200,000 living creatures perished in the calamity."

Storm-wave of 1822

Far more accurate and detailed accounts have come down to us of the later storm-waves. The first of these was in 1822 : we have the following description in Beveridge [p. 329 ; *et seq.*].

"The great event in the history of the district in this country was the inundation of the 6th June 1822, which is still well remembered by the people as the banya or flood of 1229 B.S. It was this inundation which swept over the island of Hattia, in the Noakhali district, and destroyed nearly every inhabitant. Mr. Cardew was Collector of Bakarganj at the time, and on 9th June 1822 he reported as follows : 'It is my painful duty to report, for the information of the Board, the dreadful state to which this district has been reduced by a most violent hurricane and inundation, which has extended its ravages through the whole district. This office was many feet under water, and I am sorry to say that a great part of the records have been swept away, including the whole of the kanungo's papers, the Bhulua papers, and the greatest part of the stamps. In fact, the mischief has been so great that as yet I am unable to state what has actually taken place. On the 6th I held a sale for arrears of revenue which I was unable to complete.' Mr. Cardew adds that as the whole of the amlahs' property had been destroyed, he had advanced them two months' pay as *hāwālāt*. A rubakari or vernacular proceeding was drawn up about the affair. It recorded that 'on the 6th June a sale of estates was fixed, and some mahals were disposed of. In the evening of that day it began to blow violently, and soon after the waters rose to a dreadful height, so that to escape with life became difficult. The destruction was terrible, etc.'

'On the 9th June the hurricane became less violent, and the river subsided. A little after this time the serishtadar, etc., came into the Presence and stated what had happened in their offices. It was then impossible to hold cutchery; but the acting Collector proceeded with the above named officers to the office, when he found that about four feet of water had risen in the cutchery, and that many bags of papers had been carried out of the office, while others were scattered about wet and covered with mud, and that some almirahs had been driven from their places.' A rubakari, drawn up on the 18th July 1822, gave lengthy details of the papers which had been lost. Unfortunately, neither of the above rubakaris has been preserved, and I have only seen a condensed abstract of the first of them. 39,940 persons—namely, 20,125 males and 19,815 females—are said to have lost their lives in the inundation. In Khalisakhali thana alone 22,422 lives are said to have been lost and 10,984 in Baufal; and according to my notes the deaths in these thanas are not included in the total of 39,940. Also 98,834 cattle are said to have been lost, and Rs. 13,26,691-11-8 of property are said to have been destroyed: but Mr. Collector Phillips very reasonably objects to a list which professes to give even annas and gandas. A letter dated 9th July 1822 gives translations of the reports of the darogahs. The Baufal darogah's report was as follows: 'At midday on the 6th June 1822 a storm commenced, and increased by degrees. After nine o'clock at night it was so violent that men, cattle, and property were washed away. Many persons were drowned, and some having got on choppers (roofs of houses), were driven from one village to another. Others ascended large trees and remained there all night. Next morning it decreased, but the storm continued for seven or eight days. Sir, having made inquiries in this thana, I have ascertained that there are sixty-three villages: in those situated in the eastern part, on the other side of the large river, many men, cattle, and property were destroyed. In the western side of the thana the inundation was less. It is difficult to find out the names in a short time, but by enquiries it has come to my knowledge that in the villages within this thana 4,932 men and 6,052 women—in all, 10,984 persons—and 9,700 bullocks were drowned; besides which, the property of the population has been destroyed to an amount that is impossible to guess.'

The notice that the storm began at Baufal at midday is interesting, as it shows how long the storm took to travel from Baufal to Barisal, where the storm commenced in the evening. Baufal is south-south-east of Barisal, and from the fact that it and Khalisakhali thana and the islands in the Meghna suffered most, it appears that the storm came from the south-east. 'I am happy to say that the effects of the late inundation have not been so severly felt by the district in general, as I had at first supposed. To the west and north-west there was very little water. The thanas of Tagra (now Pirozpur), Kachua (now in Jessore), Baroikaran, and Burirhat have suffered only from the violence of the wind. The chief brunt of the inundation appears to have fallen on the thanas Chandia (Dakhin Shahabazpur), Khalisakhali, Baufal, Bakainagar (in which Barisal was situated), and Mendiganj (21st June 1822). The Collector also adds that he had great pleasure in being able to inform the Government that rice, which was a few days ago selling in the bazar at the enormous rate of ten seers of sixty sicca weight per rupee, has been reduced to very nearly its former price, and that this has been occasioned by the meritorious and active exertions of Mr. Dawes, the active Magistrate of the city of Dacca, in inducing the merchants of the district to forward supplies. Government took notice of the catastrophe, and sent in rice through the great house of Palmer & Co. A committee was also formed in Calcutta, which despatched a Major Stewart to distribute relief. Rice was also received from Jessore, from the assistant to the Salt Agent. On 9th July the Collector reports that constant supplies of grain arrive from Dacca and elsewhere, and that the station and the neighbourhood continue healthy. On 11th August he reports that rice and other necessaries are procurable in Barisal and the neighbourhood at lower rates than those stated in the invoice from Messrs. Palmer & Co. No details appear to have been ever given of the loss of life in Manpura and the other islands, but the Collector writes that most of the inhabitants of Manpura and the other islands had been swept into eternity. With regard to the jail, the Magistrate writes on 25th June 1822 that he had great difficulty in procuring food for the prisoners until the arrival of the very opportune supplies from Dacca and Narainganj and that he had been obliged to feed the prisoners upon damaged rice. However, no evil effects had followed, and the jail had never been healthier, there being only one man in the hospital.'

* * * * *

'I have just seen a letter from the acting Magistrate of Barisal, about 120 miles to the eastward of this station, detailing the effects of the late storm, which commenced there on the afternoon of the 7th. I scarcely ever perused a more melancholy account. Barisal is situated on the banks of the Meghna, which river, from the fury of the winds, broke over its boundaries in every direction, and inundated the whole country to an alarming depth. The river rose so rapidly that on the 8th, at night, they had upwards of five feet of water in their houses, and the current was so strong that the doors and windows were burst open, and a regular rush of water set in through the houses. This gentleman says he contrived to get two palanquins to the top of his house, and retreated thither with his wife and children as a last resort. The registrar and doctor's houses were carried away, or at least fell in from the violence of the storm. Nearly the whole property of the residents of the station was destroyed. Had this been the extent of the damage, however, it would have been of little consequence, comparatively speaking; but, alas! the sufferings of the native inhabitants are not to be described. No fewer than one lakh of lives are said to have been lost on this occasion, together with the whole of the cattle and grain of every description, both in store and what was on the ground. The dead bodies were floating in every direction, and carried with the current through the houses. The writer states that no rice was to be procured even for the prisoners, and that he felt he would be obliged to release them from jail, otherwise they must starve. From what information he could obtain, he believed that the district could not supply food for ten days' consumption to the inhabitants who had escaped this dreadful visitation. I should think the writer meant to include in the lakh the lives of the cattle lost, although I should certainly infer from the letter that 100,000 human being perished. I have not heard whether the storm reached beyond this district to the northward and westward.'

A meeting for the relief of the distress in Bakarganj was held in the Calcutta Town Hall on the 19th of June, and another on the 22nd idem. A subscription was opened, and eventually upwards of Rs. 18,000 were collected. (According to the latest reports of the committee, Rs. 18,433 sicca.) Major Stewart volunteered his services, and was sent to Bakarganj to distribute relief. The 'Calcutta Monthly Journal', speaking of his having finished the good work upon which he had entered with such philanthropic alacrity, says that the zeal and judgment displayed by him in its performance reflected on him the highest honour.

In the 'Calcutta Journal' for 1822 (page 192) the following curious incident is mentioned: 'One of our correspondents mentions that at Ratandi he saw a child, who being only a few weeks old, his curiosity was excited to know how it had been preserved during the tempest and inundation. In reply to his inquiries, he was told that it was born in a tree when the whole surface of the country was covered with water; and its mother was then questioned and corroborated this tale. The surprise of the inquirer was still further increased, however, when he came to learn that so far from this being a singular event, there were from thirty to forty females, some of whom having reached the period of natural delivery, but many more having the birth accelerated by terror and alarm, who gave birth to their infants in this dreadful situation, and yet so providentially is the wind tempered to the shorn lamb, that most of these individuals with their offspring lived, presenting a picture of misery and distress unprecedented, we believe, even in the imagination of the painter or the poet, and certainly without a parallel, as far as we remember, either in fable or in history.

'The servant of a gentleman in Calcutta, whose family live at Hattia, says that out of four brothers and their families only one of the brothers was found after the storm and inundation, and he was blown across the river to the northward upon the top of a chopper (roof).'

The following appears in Sandeman's 'Selections' dated Thursday, June 20, 1822: 'On Sunday last we received an account of the awful calamity with which the civil station of Burrisol has been afflicted. It is brief, but the facts are of the most melancholy description, and require not detail to awaken feelings of the liveliest pity and commiseration. The sufferings of thousands—men, women, and children—during the terrible night of the storm must have been truly dreadful.

'The storm commenced on the evening of the 6th, and before midnight the body of water had overtopped the Bund, which runs along the margin of the river, and was approaching the gentlemen's houses rapidly. Mr. Cardew, the Registrar, had just sufficient time to send a palanquin with some food in it to the top of the house for his wife. Immediately after, his dining-room was three feet deep in water, the current carrying everything before it with irresistible violence. In another house there was five feet water in the dining-room, and dead bodies, washed from the native huts, floating about the room, in which only a few hours before dinner had been served. One thousand lives were lost in the bazar alone, and the loss throughout the district is not to be calculated. A famine was apprehended as inevitable. No provisions were procurable for the prisoners, in consequence of which they were released on the second day.'"

It was probably the inundation which induced Government to build new cutcheries at Barisāl.

The next storm-wave of such magnitude occurred in 1876, but in the interval inundations occurred in 1825, 1832, 1855, 1867, 1869 and 1870, which caused considerable local destruction. The eastern part of the district and especially the Meghnā islands including Sāhābāzpur suffered severely in 1867 and 1869, although the storm of 1867 was chiefly vented upon other districts. In 1869 the station road in Barisāl was carried away, much damage was done to other roads and in the villages, many cattle were drowned and the *āus* crop was injured. It was followed in the Sāhābāzpur island less than a month later by an inundation which destroyed all the fresh water, and then by an epidemic which is said to have carried off one-tenth of the population. Storm-waves—1820 to 1876.

The storm-wave of 1876 again wreaked most of its destruction on Sāhābāzpur. The following brief description of it is to be found in the Report on the Census of Bengal, 1881, Vol. I, page 46 :— Storm-wave of 1876.

"It was full moon on the evening of that 31st October, and there was an abnormally high tide, which flooded all the low lands along the coast at the head of the Bay. From 10 P.M. of the same night to 3 A.M. next day a violent north wind blew, which brought down the waters of the Meghnā in usual volume. After a short interval of calm the wind changed round, and blowing furiously from the south and west, impelled the storm-wave with unusual force into the converging waters of the estuary. The storm-wave, like the ordinary tidal-wave, was retarded on the shallows at the entrance of the river. It accumulated there, and finally overpowered the mass of fresh water brought down by the Meghnā which had been unable to find an exit seawards during the last six or seven hours. It then rushed forward as a salt-water bore up the Sundip Channel and as a fresh-water bore up the other channels, till the vast mass of water gradually advancing northwards flooded the whole area of the islands to a depth varying from 10 to 45 feet. Fortunately the inundation did not last long, and subsided even more quickly than it rose, for, beginning at about 11 P.M., the water continued to rise until about 4 A.M., when it began to subside, and the greater portion of the flood water had flowed off before 8 A.M. on the 1st November."

The Civil Surgeon has left the following succinct account which gives a view from closer perspective of the local signs and effects of the catastrophe :—

"The sky had been cloudy for some days previous to the 31st October. On the evening of the 31st the wind blew from the south. Towards evening it moved to north-east and became violent at 9 A.M., increasing to a hurricane during the night. It continued till 5 A.M. of 1st November. During its continuance it veered to north and finally to west of north. On the morning of 1st November the direction of the wind was from due west. Much damage was done to the station and to the boats in the river ; 90 per cent. of the kutcha houses in the bazar were blown down ; large trees were uprooted and blown down ; the north and south walls of the Racquet court were also blown down. This building did not suffer in the cyclone of 1867. Slight rain accompanied, but there was no thunder and lightning. An aneroid barometer stood on the evening of the 31st at 30·200. From this it steadily fell till 4 A.M. of the 1st November, when it stood at 29·230. On the 30th ·01 inches of rain had fallen, on the 31st ·36 and on 1st November 3·04 inches. No change occurred in the relative humidity.

The whole district was affected as far west as Perozpur. The eastern thanas suffered most. There, in addition to the strong hurricane, a succession of the storm-waves broke over Dakhin Sahabazpur, Munpura, Bara and Chota Baisdia, and other smaller islands in the estuary of the Meghnā and Ganges. The same storm-waves also swept over the river-side portions of Bakarganj, Bowphul, and Galachipa thanas to a distance of from six to eight miles inland. Certain portions of Mendiganj and Barisal thanas were also slightly affected. On the east side of Dakhin Sahabazpur the height of the water was 24 feet. The least height was at Darial in Bakarganj thana, where it was only kneedeep.

The moon was full on the 31st October. There was a high tide, and the phenomenon known as the bore occurred. These causes combined with a high wind blowing from east to north banked up the water in the estuary and threw it over the land. Pressure from the south area of the cyclone also increased the water in the estuary to a great extent.

From 30 to 40 per cent. of the people and an immense number of cattle were drowned. The bodies were left exposed to be got rid of by decomposition. The tanks were in many instances polluted by dead bodies and in all cases they were filled by the *débris* left by the waters. The stench from the bodies, but more especially the deterioration of the drinking water, produced a severe outbreak of cholera in the middle of December. It is estimated that 100,000 people were drowned, and I am of opinion that from 3 to 4 per cent. of the remaining people died from cholera afterwards. Much sickness from bowel complaints followed the decrease of cholera in the second week of January. The people suffered much privation from their homes having been destroyed, want of clothes, having to live on new rice, in addition to great depression of mind due to the calamities caused by the cyclone. When the cholera was at its worst all who could leave went away to neighbouring places that had not been visited by the storm-wave."

The Lieutenant-Governor visited the stricken area immediately after the disaster and the following extracts are taken from his picturesque minutes :— .

"There was a severe cyclone in the Bay of Bengal on the night of 31st October 1876. But it was not the wind which proved so destructive, though that was terrible enough; it was the storm-wave, sweeping along to a height from 10 to 20 feet, according to different localities; in some places, where it met with any resistance, mounting even higher than that.

In the evening the weather was somewhat windy and hazy, and had been unusually hot, but the people retired to rest apprehending nothing. Before 11 o'clock the wind suddenly freshened, and about midnight there arose a cry of 'the water is on us,' and a great wave several feet high burst over the country. It was followed by another wave, and again by a third, all three waves rushing rapidly onwards, the air and wind being chilly cold. The people were thus caught up before they had time even to climb on to their roofs, and were lifted to the surface of the surging flood, together with the beams and thatches of their cottages. But the homesteads are surrounded by trees—palms, bamboos and a large thorny species. The people were then borne by the water on to the tops and branches of these trees. Those who were thus stopped were saved, those who were not, must have been swept away and were lost.

The bodies of the lost were carried to considerable distances, where they could not be identified. The corpses began to putrify before the water cleared off the ground, so they were left unburied in numbers all over the country. Weather-tossed sea-men in the Bay of Bengal saw many corpses floated out from land with the waves. Corpses were flung on to the sea-shore at Chittagong, and living persons were borne thither across an arm of the sea, clinging to the roofs, or beams of their own houses, as if upon rafts.

Most of the local native officials were drowned—Deputy Magistrates, Police Inspectors, Native Civil Judges, notaries and others. There were few resident landlords and few land-agents on the spot. The villagers mostly consisted of cultivators with various kinds and degrees of tenures, and of sub-proprietors—a substantial yeomanry in fact—and they were the richest peasantry in all Bengal.

The loss of cattle, cows and bullocks was utterly disastrous. Some part of the large herds of buffaloes was saved, these animals being excellent swimmers.

When the storm burst there was an abundant rice crop ripening for the harvest—the well-known deltaic rice crop which is much beyond the needs of local consumption, and affords quantities (measured by thousands of tons annually) for exportation to distant districts. A part was lost, that in which the plant had not advanced beyond the stage of flowering, and a part was saved, that in which the grain had formed or begun to form. That which is saved is now amply sufficient for the population now on the land.

Since the first few hours of inevitable destruction, not a life, so far as we can learn, had been lost from any preventible cause, nor has anyone been in extreme danger. Those who perished in that fatal instant of time passed suddenly beyond aid; but those who then escaped are still sustained, or are sustaining themselves, sufficiently well. The disaster, big though it be, has yet happened in the midst of plenty and of rural wealth. All round the fated and wasted area there are excellent crops and abundant stores. The local authorities acted with the utmost energy in giving temporary succour to the most distressed, in re-establishing social order, which had been suddenly broken up by the universality of the disaster, and in restoring public confidence. Those who have lost their agricultural wealth have still some left, and doubtless possess considerable credit. Soon, therefore, will boats come pouring in by the numerous channels and creeks, from districts teeming with water-carriage; soon will fresh cattle be swum or ferried across the rivers from the overstocked districts of Eastern Bengal; soon will the grain bazars be re-opened, and the rustic marts be filled with the surplus produce of neighbouring tracts.

Fortunately cholera, although it has been sporadic all over Backergunge, did not break out in this district with overwhelming severity.

* * * * * *

It may be asked whether any protective means against such calamities in future can be devised—any embankments or the like. This question will be duly considered; but at present I know not how to devise such safeguard, nor have I seen anyone who can suggest anything. The area to be protected would be too great to be encompassed with protective works. If embankments became breached in such a storm, they would afterwards do more harm than good, for they would prevent or retard the running-off and the subsidence of the waters. Perhaps the people might build perches for themselves on platforms and the like; but the trees which invariably surround the homesteads serve this purpose admirably, and it is to them that the survivors mainly own their escape. Another means of protection would be construction of a large mound some 30 feet high in the midst of each village, to which the people might fly on emergency. But this could hardly be managed unless the scattered hamlets should be much more concentrated into villages than at present; and it would involve a considerable change in the mode of habitation—a change in which the people would probably not acquiesce. They will, I fear, be found unwilling to undertake troublesome and expensive precautions, seeing that these disasters, though not unfrequent somewhere or other in a less severe form, do not visit the same locality in such intensity save at long intervals of time. Without specifying the exact date when the last event of such gravity befell the delta of the Megna—one case of this kind happened in 1822—most people say that there has been nothing like the recent cataclysm since the middle of the last century."

A special officer was deputed to inquire and report and the utmost was done for the relief of the sufferers. The damage done to property must have been gigantic. In human lives alone the storm-wave of 1876 exacted a heavy toll.

"The first estimate of the deaths by drowning was for the Backergunge district 105,000 persons. Fortunately this estimate was found to be too high, and careful investigation reduced the number of deaths from this cause to 73,914. In the cholera epidemic which followed the subsidence of the inundation the number of reported deaths was 41,537, giving a total of 115,451 deaths from both causes; and bearing in mind the many deaths which in such seasons are not reported, it is reasonable to assume that the mortality reached 120,000." (Census Report, 1881, p. 46.)

PROTECTIVE MEASURES.

In the event no protective measures have ever been taken, although a belt of forest has been retained on the seacoast so as to break the first fury of the cyclonic waves. Another disastrous wave will probably be necessary before comprehensive measures are taken to guard against the danger. There is no doubt that high plinths give the most effective protection; the Maghs, who build their houses of timber upon piles six or eight feet high, fared far better in 1876 than the Bengalis, although they inhabited the tract on the sea-face which suffered the extreme fury of the wave.

THE RIVER FLOOD OF 1787.

Floods on the Meghnā, when the rise of the water is very rapid, often make great havoc of the crops and villages on the banks. Immense destruction was done by one such flood in 1787 A.D., but there has been no repetition of devastation on this scale. The flood of 1787 A.D. was the famous flood on the Tistā, which appears to have been responsible for the change of course in the Brahmaputra and for the opening of the Noābhāngani. It did more damage in the northern districts than in Bākarganj, but was felt severely in the north of the district, and as it occurred when the winter rice was in ear, it was followed by a famine which caused great loss of life. The Collector of Dacca, who was then making investigations to conclude the Permanent Settlement, wrote to the Board of Revenue on 6th April 1790 of the effects of this flood as follows:—"This district (*i.e.*, Dacca, Jalalpur, which included part of Faridpur and Dacca, as well as Bākarganj) has been visited by the most dreadful calamity ever remembered by the oldest inhabitant of the district, which deprived it of upward of 60,000 of its inhabitants, who either miserably perished or were reduced to the painful necessity of forsaking their habitations in search of a precarious subsistence. Mr. Day visited some of the parganas when the famine raged with the greatest violence, and had ocular proofs of the extreme misery to which the wretched inhabitants were reduced. He saw the parganas inundated, whole crops destroyed and cultivation totally neglected. He had the mortification of beholding hundreds of the poor wretched inhabitants daily dying without the means of affording them the smallest relief." Idilpur, Srirāmpur and Maizardi were the parganas most affected in Bākarganj. Of Idilpur the Collector wrote that he has been told from respectable authority that the northern part of this *zamindāri* lost three-fourths of its inhabitants in the dreadful calamity.

FAMINE SCARCITY OF 1893 AND 1906.

As already explained the district is dependent upon the winter-rice crop and the orchards. It was calculated in the settlement report that in a normal year only 30 per cent. of the crop is required for the subsistence of its inhabitants. A general failure of the rice crop has never occurred. The crop depends more upon floods than upon rainfall, and a general failure of the floods is practically impossible. Famine is almost inconceivable in the district. Partial failures in certain localities occasionally occur, but their effects are much mitigated by the produce of the fruit-bearing trees, which begins to be available for sale when distress is becoming acute and which is unfailing, being dependent neither upon rainfall nor flood. The most serious of the partial failures of the winter-rice in modern times occurred in 1893 and 1906. The thanas which felt the scarcity in 1893 were Gaurnadi and Swarupkāti. The scarcity was due to heavy floods in the *bil* area.

The thanas which were most severely affected in 1906 were Gaurnadi, Bhāndāriā and Rājāpur. In the *bil* thanas the failure of the winter-rice was due to high floods. In Rājāpur and the south of the district cloudy weather at Christmas brought out the *pāmari* insect, which swept whole fields bare, just when the rice was in ear. The *pāmari* insect did not attack every field in a village, but the cultivators whose fields were selected were reduced to great distress. On both occasions relief measures were undertaken. In 1893 relief was confined to loans, of which Rs. 17,000 was distributed. In 1906 beggars, old men and women and widows with young children were severly affected by the absence of the usual village charity. Rupees 15,450 was spent in gratuitous relief and Rs. 2,10,040 in loans. There is no doubt, however, that much was not needed and was improperly given.

CHAPTER VII.

RENTS, WAGES AND PRICES.

PRODUCE RENTS.

RENTS in Bākarganj are paid either in cash or in kind, but cash rents are of much greater importance as they are paid for 95 per cent. of the occupied area. As a rule produce rents are most in favour with middlemen of the Hindu higher caste in the north of the district, and especially in the three ṭhanas of Gaurandi, Swarupkāti and Jhālakāti in which most of them reside. On the edge of the *bils*, where the produce very largely depends upon the amount and the rate of the rise and fall of the flood water and the crop is precarious, they may have some justification, but in other parts of the district they have no justification at all. The area held at a produce rent appears to be rapidly increasing. The more common form is known as *bargā* in which a proportion of the crop, usually one-half, but occasionally one-third, is paid as rent. The value of the produce at present prices is three times at least greater than the prevailing cash rent in the same area. The landlord in Bākarganj very rarely supplies the seed and never the plough or cattle, so that the *bargādār* has all the burden and expenditure of cultivation. In the *dhānkarāri* system, which is a modern development, the rent does not vary with the season, but a specific amount of produce, whatever the crop may be, is to be given. The amount is usually very large, little less than half of the anticipated produce in a normal year.

CASH RENTS.

The average rates of cash rent per acre paid by the several classes of tenants who cultivate the soil in Bākarganj are as follows :—

		Rs.	A.	P.
Cultivating tenureholders	...	3	8	5
Raiyats generally	...	4	8	10
Raiyats at fixed rates	...	3	1	11
Non-occupancy raiyats	...	3	12	8
Under-raiyats ...	...	7	3	9

Rents however vary in different parts of the district very considerably from the general rates ; thus in the Sāhābāzpur subdivision they are very much less and in the Patuākhāli subdivision very much greater. The lowest rents are found in thanas Gaurnadi, Swarupkāti, Barhānaddin and Bholā; the highest in thanas Patuākhāli, Amtāli and Bākarganj. Generally speaking, the tenants in the Sāhābāzpur islands are the best off, the land being fertile, the rents low and *ābwāb* not severe, while very little land is held on produce rent. In the Sadar and Pirozpur thanas generally rents do not exceed the district average and are not high compared with the produce of the land, but a good deal of land is held at excessive produce rent, while *ābwāb* are more severe than in Sāhābāzpur. On the other hand, in some other thanas and especially in Jhālakāti, Bākarganj, Bhāndāriā and Matbāriā, a great deal of land is held by tenureholders with secure rights and paying a moderate rent. The tenants in the Patuākhāli subdivision pay higher rents than elsewhere and very much higher *ābwāb;* on the other hand their land is undoubtedly the most fertile in the district.

There can be no question that rents have increased very much during the course of a century, and it is probable that they have doubled; on the other hand there has been a great extension of cultivation while prices have risen very largely. The price of rice, the stable crop of the district, has been rising throughout the century and its rise during the last 15 years alone has been sufficient to offset the probable increase of rent during the last century. There can be no question that in many parts of the district very heavy enhancements of rent have been made in the last 60 years and many which were illegal during the 30 years which have elapsed since the passing of the Bengal Tenancy Act; on the other hand the rents which were enhanced were often very low owing to the need of attracting colonists to the forest, *chars* and other waste lands. There is, therefore, considerable justification for the increase in rent. ENHANCEMENTS.

The total rental paid by occupiers of all classes for the land of the district has been estimated at Rs. 90,00,000 and the total gross produce has been valued at Rs. 9,75,00,000, the rent amounting therefore to less than 10 per cent. of the gross produce. It appears to be 12 per cent. of the net produce. It is however impossible to exclude from consideration the large amounts in the shape of *ābwāb* which landlords extort from their tenants in Bākarganj. *Abwāb* are illegal fees, fines and levies which are collected by landlords at a proportionate rate on the rents or a proportionate sum on the tenancy. It has been estimated that in Bākarganj as a whole they amount to one quarter of the rent, so that the total proportion of the STATISTICS OF RENT.

net produce taken by the landlord should be estimated at about 15 per cent.

WAGES: Non-agricultural.

Statistics of the wages paid for certain selected classes of labour and the rates current during the two decades, 1893 to 1912, will be found in the Statistical Appendix, and it will be sufficient to observe that they show a very large increase during the last few years. This is ultimately due to the general rise in prices and especially in the price of rice. Cooly labour is very scarce and was very scarce in 1870. Smiths, bricklayers, carpenters and weavers are paid so much by the job that daily wages are rather a precarious guide. In 1760 weavers apparently got Re. 1-8 per month and common carpenters twelve annas: by 1800 their wages were doubled, weavers and blacksmiths getting Rs. 3, boatmen Rs. 2-8 and carpenters Re. 1-8. Some idea of the low scale of wages and prices at this time may be gathered from the fact that prisoners in the jail did their own marketing and were allowed Re. 1-6 a month for the purpose, of which 15 annas was spent in rice. Wages rose steadily throughout the century, but were apparently fairly stationary between 1870 and 1890, day-labourers (*gharāmi*), agricultural labourers as well as smiths, masons and carpenters getting very much the same. Thus a cooly who got 3 annas a day in 1850, could only be had for 6 annas a day in 1870, but wanted no more in 1890, while an agricultural labourer wanted eight to twelve annas a day in 1870. A cooly now expects 8 annas a day and a boy who got 3 annas in 1890 wants 5 annas. Common masons, carpenters and smiths got 8 annas a day in 1890, but now expect 12 annas and a smith as much as 14 annas; superior masons and carpenters who got 10 to 12 annas a day now get a rupee and superior smiths who formerly got 12 annas now expect Re. 1-4. These are Barisāl rates and are probably slightly higher at all periods than rates in the district generally.

Agricultural.

A great deal of agricultural labour is hired in Bākarganj. For the smaller crops this labour is obtained locally, but in the harvesting of the *āus* and *āman* rice crops the labour is hired from all the surrounding districts especially from those in the north. In the south of the district practically the whole of the *āman* crop is harvested by foreign labour, while in Sāhābāzpur Noakhali (*badla*) labourers are employed for all the processes of cultivation except sowing. Wages in harvesting are one-sixth to one-eighth of the crop and for other processes about Rs. 8 per month together with food and clothing. A day-labourer gets 12 annas a day, but in the height of the season a rupee. Even in 1870 he got 8 to 12 annas a day.

PRICES. It is a commonplace that prices have been rising ever since the beginning of British rule. In very early days owing to lack of communications and the isolation of markets, the prices of rice were often purely local and differed in an extraordinary manner from year to year and from thana to thana. As might be expected the price of rice was at that time extremely low in a granary like Bākarganj. The Collector reported in 1797 that it was considered cheap in Idilpur, when paddy was selling at three maunds a rupee; but it seems doubtful if there were many years in which it was as cheap as this. In 1861 paddy sold at one maund and common rice at 26 seers for the rupee, while in 1875 common rice sold at 21 seers per rupee. In 1866, on account of the Orissa famine, the price rose as high as 8½ seers per rupee. After 1875 its price has risen as follows :—

			Seers per rupee.
In the 10 years ending	1884	...	19
Ditto	1894	...	14
Ditto	1904	...	13
Ditto	1914	...	8½

The price of salt, the other chief necessity of life, has been affected by the variations in the duty as well as by the laws of supply. In 1760 it was one rupee per maund and in 1767 the East India Company wrote that they would rather reduce the duty than see salt selling at Rs. 140 per hundred maunds: yet in 1800 it was selling at Rs. 4 per maund and in 1824 at Rs. 5 per maund for small quantities. The price was very much the same in 1875. It is now Rs. 2-4 per maund. The only other of which early prices are obtainable are bamboos which sold in 1807 at Rs. 3 per hundred and in 1820 at Rs. 4 per hundred, iron which sold at Rs. 6 per maund and lime which sold about 6 annas per maund. In 1874 freight by country boat to Calcutta averaged about 4 annas a maund and in 1914 it amounted to 3½ annas a maund by country boat and 3¼ annas by steamer. The prices of many articles in common use are given in Mr. Sutherland's report on Bākarganj in the "Statistics of the Dacca Division." They are Barisāl prices and they compare with modern prices as follows.—

Commodity.		Price in 1867.			Price in 1914.		
		RS.	A.	P.	RS.	A.	
Betelnut	...	6	6	10	12	0	per maund.
Garlic	...	2	12	2	5	0	ditto.

Commodity.		Price in 1867. Rs. A. P.	Price in 1914. Rs. A.	
Oil (cocoanut)	...	17 12 8	22 0	per maund.
„ (linseed)	...	15 14 8	30 0	ditto.
„ (mustard)	...	10 5 9	18 0	ditto.
Ghee	...	35 14 9	90 0	ditto.
Gur (sugarcane)	...	3 12 7	8 8	ditto.
„ (date palm)	...	4 10 5	6 0	ditto.
„ (imported)	...	......	4 0	ditto.
Sugar	...	6 0 0	9 4	ditto.
Salt panga	...	4 9 1	2 4	ditto.
„ rock	...	6 3 4	4 0	ditto.
Cotton	...	26 8 10	32 0	ditto.
Jute	...	3 0 0	4 0	ditto.
Sugarcanes	...	30 sticks per rupee.	32 sticks per rupee.	
Bamboos	...	6 per rupee	3 per rupee.	
Cocoanuts	...	one anna per pair.	1¼ anna per pair.	
Eggs	...	4 for an anna.	4 for 1¼ anna.	
Fowls (chickens)	...	8 per rupee	3 per rupee.	
Milk	...	18 seers per rupee.	11 seers per rupee.	

MATERIAL CONDITION OF THE PEOPLE. Agricultural classes.

Special enquiries regarding the material condition of the agricultural classes were made during the last settlement operations, and the result went to show that the average family was in a condition of considerable comfort. The danger of famine does not exist, and apart from tidal waves the most the Bākarganj cultivator has to fear is local scarcity. There is practically no class of landless labourer. It was reported by the settlement authorities that out of 360,000 agricultural families representing a population of 1,800,000, one-fifth were in affluent circumstances, three-fifths in comfortable circumstances and one-fifth in struggling circumstances. Amongst the last fifth will be included outcastes and gypsies. Even labourers with insufficient land for their own subsistence had always sufficient to eat, and widows with young families were the only cases of real hardship. It was calculated by the settlement authorities that the amount of land required for the subsistence of a family in Bākarganj was 3 acres, whereas the amount of land actually held by the average family was 4 acres or, as defined in the settlement report, the average holding contained ·6 of an acre more under rice than was sufficient for the family subsistence besides half an acre in addition of garden or miscellaneous crops, while in another half acre a second crop was taken. It is estimated that the average income of an agricultural family is Rs. 233 in the Sāhābāzpur subdivision, Rs. 224 in the Patuākhāli subdivision, Rs. 183 in the Sadar subdivision, and Rs. 131 in the Pirozpur subdivision. The poorest thana is Bhāndāriā, while Pirozpur is little better off, but here the comparative poverty is due to the fact that the large river dominating these thanas has recently become saline and thereby reduced the fertility of the soil. The amount paid in taxation is only 2 per cent. of the gross produce and 3 per cent. of the nett produce, of which one half is taken by Government, one-quarter by the District Board and one-quarter by the village to pay the chaukidars.

The amount of borrowing by cultivators for short periods is very considerable and the terms are onerous, but permanent indebtedness is not a great feature. It was reported by the settlement authorities as covering in usufructuary mortgages and otherwise only ·67 per cent. of the land held by raiyats and was more than 1 per cent. in only three thanas, the worst cases being Pirozpur and Bhāndāriā.

The material condition of the agricultural population of Bākarganj may be summarised as one of very general comfort. There is no thana in which any large proportion of the population is underfed. Homesteads are usually large and well built and the land covered by the homestead of the average family is one-fifth of an acre. The agricultural population is also well off in the matter of cattle. It is true that the district is very largely dependent upon the winter rice crop so that the agricultural population is somewhat restricted in its expenditure to one particular season of the year, but for purposes of food sufficient *āus* is usually grown when the *āman* supply is running short, while most of the money required to finance the ploughing and sowing for the *āman* crop is obtained from the sale of the timely fruit of the betelnut.

Non-agricultural classes.

Of the Bākarganj population 22½ per cent. is non-agricultural, but of these no small part is as landlord or landlord's agent depending upon the land. The industrial population is insignificant and the district contains less than the usual number employed in trade or domestic services. The only disquieting feature in the material condition of the people is to be found in the indigent circumstances of some proportion of the higher caste Hindus, who form somewhat too numerous a proportion of the total population in the Sadar subdivision and are therefore unable to obtain a subsistence by their traditional employments. They have as yet displayed no versatility or adaptability. The rapid increase in the price of rice has contributed to make their position precarious. Most of them are congregated in a small tract of country on the borders of Gaurnadi, Swarupkāti, Jhālakāti and Barisāl thanas, and also in Nalchhiti. The non-agricultural population which was only 16 per cent. of the total population fifty years previously, is still very small in the southern thanas and the Sāhābāzpur island, and is usually in even more comfortable circumstances in those parts than the agricultural population. Most of the non-agriculturists are to be found in the Sadar subdivision, especially in thanas Gaurnadi, Barisāl Nalchhiti and Jhālakāti, and in thanas Pirozpur and Swarupkāti of the Pirozpur subdivision. The traders and professional men are well off ; but weavers, fishermen and boatmen are generally not in such comfortable circumstances as the agriculturists.

CHAPTER VIII.

OCCUPATIONS, MANUFACTURES AND TRADE.

OCCUPATIONS.

BĀKARGANJ is essentially an agricultural district, 82·2 per cent. of the population being dependent upon agriculture for livelihood, including 18,605 rent receivers and 491,102 rent payers, while the agricultural labourers aggregate 38,131. Of the persons engaged in occupations other than agriculture, more than a ninth are found in the five municipalities and 378,258 in the rural areas who are not dependent solely on agriculture. Of the latter nearly 4·03 per cent. follow agricultural pursuits to a certain extent. Only 5·4 per cent. of the population is supported by industries, 5·1 per cent. by commerce and 6·8 by the various professions. Of the industrial population 40 per cent. are actual workers and 60 per cent. dependents. Among them 16,707 are fishermen, 22,604 weavers, 6,365 potters, 4,610 basket and mat makers, 6,593 boat builders, 963 tanners, 2,705 gold, silver and iron smiths, 15,396 food-stuff sellers, besides numerous tailors, masons, ceramics, etc., numbering 57,445 in all. Of the professional classes 39 per cent. are actual workers including 5,704 priests, 2,733 teachers, 3,978 medical practitioners, 1,085 lawyers, and 3,626 public administrators. Among those engaged in other occupations 14,859 are beggars, 5,481 domestic servants, 30,905 general labourers.

INDUSTRY: Fishery.

The statistics of occupation show clearly that Bākarganj is in no sense a manufacturing district. The only industry of any importance other than agriculture is fishing, which supports 16,707 people, chiefly on the banks of the Meghnā and the Ariāl Khān. Fish are exported dried to Chittagong and *bil* fish are to some extent exported to Calcutta, but generally speaking the fish are caught for purely local consumption.

MANUFACTURES.

There are only four factories in the district, and one of these is purely a repairing workshop maintained by the steamer company at Barisāl. The only manufactured article which is exported from the district is oil, for which there are two mills at Jhālakāti, employing 123 persons, of whom 86 are skilled workmen, and 2 are women and 2 are children under 14 years of age. The fourth factory is for *surki* and brick-making and is located at Barisāl, where it gives employment to 143 men and 13 women. The workshop of the Steamer Company employs 152 men, of whom 107 are returned as skilled workmen. Manufactures for the local market are still considerable, although declining. The number of weavers in the district in 1911 was 9,690, of potters 2,585 and of mat-makers 2,615, the number of people supported by weaving being 12,914, by pottery 3,780 and by mat-making 1,995. The weavers of Uzirpur and Bānaripārā make *dhotis* of the Dacca pattern which are still bought, and the weavers at Mādhabpāsā weave mosquito nets which command a large sale among the middle classes. The Maghs also make a coarse cloth for their own use; but machine-made cloth is gradually driving the weavers from their looms and the *swadeshi* agitation gave but a temporary check to the movement. *Chhālās* or gunny bags are made at Patihar and neighbourhood in thana Gaurnadi by the Kapali caste. Imported European enamelled ware and pottery is beginning to oust the products of local potter also. Earthenware products are, however, made largely in the north of the district and particularly near Nalchhiti. Uzirpur and its neighbourhood has a local reputation for making of *dāos* and sacrificial knives and other iron implements. Brick-making is only vigorous near Barisāl. Perhaps the most flourishing industries are boat-making and mat-weaving. Most of the large boats in the district are foreign made, but good *khos* boats are made at Debaikhāli and Syāmpur in the Mehendiganj thana, and good pansways (*pānshi*) boats at Ghanteswar near Agarpur, where nets are also manufactured, at Barsākāti in Pirozpur thana and at Sohāgdal in Swarupkāti thana. At the two last-named places very large cargo-boats are made. *Dingi* boats are made all over the district and especially at Jhālakāti, while the Maghs also hollow canoes out of *Keora* wood. There are no large yards, as boat-making gives occupation to but a few families at a time, though in many places. In shape and arrangement the boats built show no advance at all. Indeed the industry is in a primitive and unprogressive condition, although in a district so full of rivers and of boats there is great scope for a modern industry. No attempt has been made in the district to utilise motor haulage for country boats of any kind. Boat-building gives employment to 1,760 people and support to 4,833. The *bils* and *chars* produce a large quantity of reeds from which coarse mats are made in many places and exported outside the district. The *bil* reed is the *nal* (*arendo tepalis*) and the *char* reed the *hoglā* or large bulrush (*typha elephantinum*). A superior kind of mat known as *sitalpati* is made out of a reed called the *paritā* (*phrynium dichotornium*), which grows somewhat like a shrub in damp ground near homesteads chiefly in Bākarganj thana, where Rangasri and Helencha are the centres of the manufacture. The workmen are called *paitiyas*. Thatching is done by a special class of workmen, who use *chhon* grass, but sometimes reeds. The Maghs and the poorer classes use the *golpatta* or wild cocoanut for thatching. It also yields an excellent toddy. Cocoanut oil is made in a small way in many places, but in a large way at Amani (Bholā) and Nalchhiti. Salt is no longer manufactured, although at one time it must have supported a large part of the population. Woodcutting is a decaying industry owing to the rapid contraction of the Sundarbans, of which some part has provisionally been preserved for firewood. The chief centre of the trade is Jhālakāti, but there are also markets at Galāchipa, Amtali, Nalchhiti and Barisāl. The woodcutters are called *bāulis* and live in ordinary boats, while they carry the wood in strong open boats called *bāulia* boats. Their number is considerable and many combine woodcutting with agriculture. The woodcutters go to the Sundarbans in January and remain until April or May. They cut little good timber, but chiefly firewood. They load the firewood into the *bāulia* but lash *sundari* logs alongside as they do not float.

The inhabitants of the district have little inclination for trade. The exports have always far exceeded the imports in value, and it is significant that the export trade in rice and betelnuts is in the hands of foreign merchants. The district exports rice and betelnuts on a large scale, but also timber, mats, *pān* and fish to a small extent. The principal imports are salt, kerosine oil, European piece-goods, cotton twists, coal, sugar, molasses, corrugated iron, oil, tobacco and flour. Rice is exported chiefly to Calcutta, 24-Parganas, Dacca and Mymensingh and paddy to Calcutta. Betelnut (*supāri*) goes chiefly to Calcutta and Chittagong and betel leaves (*pān*) to Dacca; timber, mats and fish to Calcutta. The imports are almost entirely from Calcutta. The trade of the district is chiefly carried on by country boat and steamer, the country boats still moving a large proportion of the rice crop. Apart from rice the trade with Calcutta and Dacca is chiefly carried by steamer. The only sea-borne trade is between Barisāl and TRADE.

Chittagong. It is small but growing, and chiefly consists of betelnut and dried fish.

TRADING CENTRES.

The chief centres of general trade are naturally on the main route to Calcutta. Jhālakāti, which is situated where many rivers meet, is the largest centre of inland trade in Eastern Bengal after Goālanda, Chandpur and Narayanganj. Barisāl has lately become an important centre of the steamer companies and its trade is increasing greatly especially with Chittagong. Nalchhiti and Sahebganj (Bākarganj) are declining and no southern marts have achieved a great general trade. The chief markets for the export of rice are Bagā, Bāuphal, Nyamati, Bhāndāriā, Kaukhali, Kālāiā, Chaulakati, Charamaddin and Bhuria in the mainland and Bhola and Amani in the Sāhābāzpur island. The chief markets in the export of betelnut are Nalchhiti, Patar Hat, Galua, Kāliganj, Bhāndāriā, Bholā, Sukdeb and Amani. Jalabari has a special trade in cocoanuts, Amtali in timber, Matibhanga in reeds and fish Tarki in betel leaves (*pān*).

FAIRS.

There are altogether 21 fairs in the district, all called after the villages in which they are held. Some of the fairs have been held for more than a hundred years. In most of the fairs amusement occupies as large a place as trade, and the traders and shopkeepers generally are beginning to desert them. The principal fairs are those at Kālisuri, Kalaskāti and Lākhutiā which are held in October and November and last for more than seven days. The attendance is probably not more than 5,000. The most important of the other fairs are held at Jhālakāti, Aliganj, Lata, Sarikal, Rājār Hat and Chandkhali. The average attendance is not more than 2,500. The fairs in any case are only contributory to the fixed and established markets.

WEIGHTS AND MEASURES.

There is no uniform system of weights and measures in the district, only the cloth-sellers' yard being everywhere the same. The unit of land measure is different in different parganas; in many a *kāni* measuring 20 by 24 *nals* is in use, but the length of the *nal* differs in each pargana, being as small as 11′ 3″ and as large as 17′ 3″. The most common systems are the Chandradwip *kāni*, in which the *nal* is 150 inches and the large or *shāhi kāni* (also in use in Noākhāli) in which the *nal* is 300 inches. In several parganas, of which the chief is perhaps Arangpur, the unit of land measure is a local *bighā*, varying in size according to the length of the *kātha* used in each case. Another measure of length is the *hāt*, which usually measures 18 inches. For weighing both solids and liquids, the maund is used ; but in addition to the standard maund of 80 tolas to the seer, there are the following local measures in use in different markets :—The Bākarganj maund of 96 tolas chiefly in the south of the district, the *kanchi* maund of 60 tolas to the seer mostly amongst the villagers, the Alamganj maund of 82 tolas to the seer used in weighing rice and paddy, the *kāni* of 67 tolas 10 annas to the seer used in measuring liquids in Bāuphal and Kālāiā, and the *kāni* of 64 tolas to the seer used in measuring oil and other liquids.

CHAPTER IX.

MEANS OF COMMUNICATION.

RIVERS. IN a district so completely intersected by rivers alternative means of communication must be a very late development. A glance at the map of Bākarganj shows that the river system of the district provides extremely convenient waterways north and south for both goods and passenger traffic. In the mainland of the district rivers which are large enough and deep enough to take boats of considerable size flow north and south in all parts, and there are usually sufficient streams to enable any villager to move himself or his goods to the big river or the nearest market. On the other hand rivers flowing east and west are few and have a strong tendency to shoal. There are in fact no avenues of communication which are open to boats of a large draught except the somewhat circuitous route from the Ariāl Khān through Barisāl, Jhālakāti, Rajapur, Kaukhāli, Matibhanga and then westward *viâ* Matibhanga to Khulna or *viâ* Tushkhāli to Calcutta. Formerly the district was not so lacking in deep streams, khāls or dons in local parlance running east and west. There was the Amua don from the Biskhali to the Baleswar and the Biskhāli khal connecting the Biskhāli in the west with the Bākarganj river in the east of the district. In the south there were several streams which permitted cross communications between the large rivers, of which the most important were the Bhāndāriā don, the Khag don and the Kukuā river. All of these have now silted up in the middle, while the northern route in the portion between Rajapur and Kaukhāli is only kept open with great difficulty.

STEAMER ROUTES. Steamers first began to use the rivers of Bākarganj shortly before 1880, but the steamer service has only begun to assist traffic within Bākarganj since the new route *viâ* Khulna and Barisāl was opened in 1884. Subsequently Barisāl has become an important steamer centre, not only for lines serving the interior of Bākarganj, but also as a station on the main route from other Eastern Bengal districts to Calcutta and as a terminus for branch lines from Chittagong, Noākhāli and Madaripur. The feeder services for the interior of the district are increasing rapidly. The north of the district is connected with Barisāl by a line using the Turki river; the east of the district by the Dacca steamers using the Safipur and the Noābhāngani rivers and by the Noākhāli and Chittagong rivers which call at several places in the Sāhābāzpur island; the west of the district by the two main routes to Calcutta, one of which goes north from Hularhat by the Kaliganj river and the other south through Tushkhāli by the Kāchā river. Other services use the Khairabad river to Pātuākhāli and Galachipa and the Bishkhāli river to Phuljuri. Altogether the district is very thoroughly covered by steamer communications, enabling goods and passengers to be transported to other parts of the province and to other parts of the district without any great difficulty. The extreme south of the district and the south of the Sāhābāzpur island are the only parts which can make any complaint. In order to reach the steamer routes or to travel east and west some miles have usually to be covered by travellers or goods from most villages. This is done by boat, and streams are sufficiently numerous except in Sāhābāzpur to enable the small boat to move about the district very efficiently. As, however, all the rivers in the district are tidal, great delays are inevitable in boat traffic, while, owing to the shallowness of even the widest streams which flow east and west, boats of large burden cannot be moved at most seasons of the year. Generally speaking, the need of the district in respect of the transport of goods lies in the improvement of communications east and west. It does not appear that this can be done by rivers except at great expense in deepening the channels.

Formerly there were no roads in the district, except a few miles in Barisāl, a short road from Bākarganj to Sibpur and Sabhi Khān's "jangals" in the north chiefly in Gaurnadi, which were high and wide, but were frequently breached and gradually falling into disuse and decay. Even after the formation of the Road Committee in 1870 the defect was very slowly repaired, and in 1873 there were only 29 miles of road in the neighbourhood of Barisāl. Of late years wide, raised, but unmetalled roads have been built by the District Board with great frequency, and there are now 387 miles of road in the district, of which 12 are metalled. These roads are not used by cart traffic in the mainland, partly because river traffic for the transport of goods is very convenient and partly because the roads are frequently broken by unbridgeable rivers. In the Sāhābāzpur island, however, these ROADS conditions do not exist to the same extent. In the interior of the island the streams are small and can be easily bridged, while even for small boats they provide means of transport only in the rainy season. In the island 121 miles of road have been provided, which are properly bridged and in constant use by carts. The roads radiate from Bholā, the subdivisional headquarters, two going south, one east and one west and two traversing the island from east to west. In the mainland the roads radiate from Barisāl connecting it with Patuākhāli (54 miles), Pirozpur and Saillarganj (29 miles), Bhurghata (22 miles) and Jhālākāti (12 miles). As these roads run north and south and are flanked by rivers on which steamers run, they are really of use only for foot passengers. There is, however, a useful road from Barisāl to Banaripārā (16 miles), while a road in Gaurnadi from Bātājor to Amboula through the marshes has been of the greatest assistance in opening up for cultivation of the tract through which it runs. It may be expected that in the course of time more roads running east and west will be provided as well as more roads to open up waste lands such as the Swarupkāti and Bhāndāriā *bils* and the Sundarbans tract. Apart from the main roads, there are a few embanked footpaths connecting village and village, or the villages with steamer stations and the main roads. Many more such are required. Except in the Sāhābāzpur island it is extremely difficult for a foot passenger in Bākarganj to make even a small journey rapidly in the absence of any bridges upon the numerous small streams which are to be found in every square mile of the district.

RAIL-WAYS. There are no railways in Bākarganj, although a railway has recently been proposed connecting Barisāl with Khulna. In the rest of the district it is doubtful if the immense cost necessary for bridging the rivers will ever enable a railway to become a profitable undertaking.

FERRIES. Ferries over the larger rivers are a somewhat important link in the chain of communications in the district. There are three Government ferries over the Biskhāli, Tentulia and Srimantapur rivers, which are settled at a revenue of Rs. 280. There are also 24 District Board ferries, eleven of which are in the Sadar subdivision, ten in Sāhābāzpur and three in Pirozpur. They brought in an income of Rs. 8,333 a year (average 1912—14). The most important is the Dapdapia ferry between Nalchhiti and Barisāl. Altogether there are 2 ferries connecting the mainland with the Sāhābāzpur island and 4 ferries connecting the Sāhābāzpur island with Hatia. Between Manpurā and

Sāhābāzpur there is a ferry twice a day. The ferry over the Barisāl river is under the Barisāl Municipality. The annual income of the municipality from this ferry is Rs. 2,275 (average of three years from 1912 to 1914).

CHAPTER X.

LAND REVENUE ADMINISTRATION.

GENERAL REVENUE HISTORY.

THE first historical assessment of land revenue in Bākarganj is that made in 1582 by Todar Mal, the great Finance Minister of Akbār. It does not appear, however, that this assessment was made in Eastern Bengal with the same careful investigation into the produce of the land and the assets of the villages as it is known to have been made in Bihar and elsewhere. The result of this assessment, so far as can now be ascertained, was the imposition of a khālsā revenue of Rs. 1,76,351 in addition to a jāigir revenue of an amount which is not known. Subsequently there was a great expansion in the revenue of this part of the country, especially during the administration of Shāistā Khān and previously of Sultan Sujā, who appears to have given considerable attention to Bākarganj and to have lived in it for some period. The revenue of Bākarganj at the assessment of 1728 is shown by Grant as Rs. 1,93,512 with jaigir additions, which were very large, and in the year 1765 as Rs. 7,25,850.

EARLY BRITISH ADMINISTRATION.

The early British revenue administration introduced in this part of Bengal a system of farming in great estates, but as a result of an enquiry made in 1769 the direct control of the revenue administration was entrusted to European officers in 1770, and Bākarganj was placed under the control of the Provincial Council at Dacca. Quinquennial settlements effected in 1772 failed to give any satisfaction, and subsequently annual settlements were made with farmers and zamindars, leading up to the decennial settlement of 1789, which was afterwards made permanent. During the whole course of this period the revenue business of Bākarganj was managed or rather mismanaged by the European Collectors of Dacca, by whom the extensive enquiries which preceded the decennial settlement were made and by whom the separation of tāluks was effected. During the early period previous to the decennial settlement, the revenue history of Bākarganj is largely bound up with the usurpations of the well-known Rājā Rājballabh Roy of Rājānagar, who was Dewan of Nowazis and later Deputy Governor of Dacca, and after his death to the intrigues of his sons. So far as can now be ascertained, the land revenue of Bākarganj as fixed by the decennial settlement, which was afterwards made permanent, was Rs. 8,23,665 upon an area which has been calculated at 2,422 square miles, as the Sundarbans were not included in it and a great deal of land has been formed by alluvium subsequent to it. This revenue amounts to a rate of 8½ annas per acre. The basis of this decennial assessment cannot have been very accurate, as exhaustive investigations were only made in a few estates, and even in those estates the rent actually paid by talukdars was taken as the assets for the purpose of assessment. From partition papers of the same period which exist in the case of the large parganas of Chandradwip, Selimābād, Buzrugumedpur and Dakhin Sāhābāzpur, it would appear that a very considerable profit was left to the zamindars; thus in Buzrugumedpur the rental of the tāluks was Rs. 2,46,000 and there were private lands belonging to the zamindars, yet the revenue fixed was Rs. 1,91,000. The rent of the tāluks, if it had been paid for 12 years, was apparently accepted without further enquiry. In many cases it was extremely small and can have borne no proportion to the assets of the land. A rough calculation, which has been made, would show that the value of the produce in the area then under cultivation at the prices then prevalent must have been eight times the revenue fixed, and the rental value of the land which was settled in perpetuity cannot have been less and may have been considerably more than double the revenue fixed. In accordance with the terms of regulation governing the decennial settlement, the engagement was made, as far as possible, with the real proprietors of the estates. It is clear, however, that in cases like that of Rājā Rājballabh the usurpations of the new class of zamindars were secured to them. Another feature of the decennial settlement was the separation of the tāluks which were historically independent of the zamindari within which they had previously been included. A large number of tāluks were granted independence in Bākarganj, but they were situated almost entirely in the north of the district and were very often not strictly entitled to independence at all, as being grants made by the zamindar himself.

SUBSEQUENT RESUMPTIONS.

The principal features in the subsequent revenue history of Bākarganj are the resumption and the reclamation of the Sundarbans, the resumption of alluvial accretions, the Revenue Survey and the Settlement operations of 1900-08. The Sundarbans were definitely resumed by comprehensive proceedings in 1831-33, which were undertaken in accordance with Regulation III of 1828. The total area then resumed were 610 square miles. The resumption of alluvial accretions, on the other hand, which was authorised originally by Regulation II of 1819, has been continuous throughout the whole period. Act IX of 1847 prevented indiscriminate resumption of accretions to private estates; and two regular surveys have been made in accordance with this provision, the first in 1881 by Babu Parbati Charan Ray, Deputy Collector, the second in 1912 following on the settlement operations. Islands on the other hand by virtue of Act IV of 1868 are resumable at any time. The total area resumed before 1847 was 293 square miles and after 1847, 217 square miles. In addition to the Sundarbuns and alluvium there have also been petty resumption of invalid lakhiraj including the Nowara jaigirs, which altogether amounted to 4½ square miles.

Owing to diluvion a large number of estates which were permanently settled at the time of the Permanent Settlement have been sold for arrears of revenue and purchased by Government in default of other bidders. Most of these estates were not very large, and it has always been difficult to discover their land. Altogether they number 395 and cover an area at present of 26 square miles. The zamindari of Buzrugumedpur was purchased very shortly after the Permanent Settlement owing to quarrels amongst the proprietors or to too heavy an assessment. It covers an area of 381 square miles.

REVENUE OF THE DISTRICT.

As a result of these proceedings the area which was permanently settled at the time of the Permanent Settlement and has not been sold now amounts to 1,980 square miles, and in the remainder of the district or 1,568 square miles other experiments have been tried in the assessment of revenue. It is unnecessary to detail these experiments at any great length as they are exhaustively reviewed in Part II and in Part III, Chapter II of the Bākarganj Settlement Report. Briefly the methods employed in early days involved engagement with a talukdar or farmer until the estate was fully brought under cultivation, when it was often permanently settled. In later days the policy in force has been to make settlement with the cultivators. The reclamation of the large forest in the Sundarbans was originally attempted through capitalists, but this was unsuccessful, and since 1909 a colonisation office has been formed which secures cultivators and supervises the reclamation by them of the forest. Until 1909 the revenue administration of the Sundarbans was under the control of a special Commissioner located at Alipur, but in that year it was transferred to the Collector of the district. The revenue of the district, which was Rs. 8,23,665 at the time of the Permanent Settlement, had, by the year 1910, amounted to Rs. 20,12,383 distributed as follows :—

	Rs.
Permanently settled at the time of the permanent settlement	5,82,593
Permanently settled subsequently ...	4,03,829
Temporarily settled	10,25,961

This is the real revenue of the district and not the revenue of the estates borne upon the revenue roll of Bākarganj. The district settlement operations accounted for Rs. 3,23,087 of this total. Owing to the number of temporarily-settled estates and to the great variety in the periods for which they have been settled the revenue demand of the district varies from year to year although it is always increasing.

THE REVENUE ROLL.

The first revenue roll was prepared in 1819 after the separation from Dacca and included 4,491 estates, of which 2,425 have been subsequently transferred to other districts. To this number 584 have been added by resumption and only 90 by partition. In 1910 there were 6,559 numbers on the roll, but owing to diluvion and transfers the real number was much less, thus :—

Permanently settled at the time of the Permanent Settlement	2,187
Permanently settled subsequently ...	797
Temporarily-settled private estates ...	207
Government estates	383
Revenue redeemed	15
Fisheries and ferries	9
Transferred to other districts, removed, amalgamated or diluviated	2,964

There are also 67 revenue-free estates covering 23,234 acres or 1 per cent. district area.

INCIDENCE OF REVENUE.

The incidence of revenue amounts to 14 annas per acre and is apparently greater than in any other district of Bengal. The general figure is, however, very misleading, as the incidence in the permanently-settled area is very much smaller than in the temporarily-settled area. The great bulk of the permanently-settled area is to be found in the north of the mainland part of the district. The south of the mainland contains the Sundarbans, while the pargana of Buzrugumedpur lies in the centre of the district with permanently-settled land to the east and west of it. In the Sāhābāzpur island the area permanently settled at the time of the Permanent Settlement is only 35 per cent. of the total area, although a large part of the remainder has been permanently settled subsequently. The incidence of revenue in the area permanently settled at the time of the Permanent Settlement is 8½ annas per acre, in Buzrugumedpur Re. 1-4 per acre and in the Sundarbans Re. 1-6 per acre. In the Sāhābāzpur island the incidence of revenue on the area permanently settled at the time of the permanent settlement is annas 8-6 per acre, on the area subsequently permanently settled Re. 1-9 per acre, and on the temporarily-settled area, including waste, Re. 1-14 per acre. The Government demand is very light as is apparent from the fact that the average rate of rent in the district is Rs. 4-8-10 per acre, and the total rental value of the district has been calculated at 90 lakhs of rupees or 4½ times the Government revenue. The total gross value of the produce is more than 9 crores of rupees, of which the Government revenue represents only about 2 per cent. In the permanently-settled area the Government revenue appears to be 32 per cent. of the estates, 12 per cent. of their rental value and not more than 1½ per cent. of the total value of the gross produce.

SURVEYS AND SETTLEMENTS.

The district was first surveyed in the course of the great revenue survey of Bengal in the years 1859-65. This survey provided a geographical map on a professional basis on the scale 4" to the mile, which is a very accurate representation of the country at the present day. It also provided in the *thak* map rough plots of each village on the scale 16" to the mile, which delineated the boundaries of estates within the village as measured by rod and compass. The chief value of the revenue survey in Bākarganj was the aid which it gave to the administration of the district. The chief value of the *thak* map was the prevention of constant disputes about boundaries between rival landlords and between landlords and their own lessees. The survey of the Meghnā diārā including the Āriāl Khān river was made in 1882 under Act IX of 1847 with the purpose of readjusting the revenue in accordance with the changes made in the riparian tracts by the movements of these rivers. The Dakhin Sāhābāzpur estate was surveyed in 1889 and a record-of-rights was prepared in order to pacify the disputes which had made the estate a serious administrative difficulty. A survey and a record-of-rights have been made in considerable number of other smaller estates usually for the purpose of the revision of the revenue, but sometimes for the purpose of adjusting disputes. With the exception of these areas, a survey and a record-of-rights were made of the entire district in 1900—1908. The specific object for which these measures were undertaken was to remove or to pacify the unrest and lawlessness which were so rife in the district, but they were also a part of the general policy which aimed at providing the whole province with a detailed record of the lands, rights and rents of every tenant as ascertained after accurate survey and investigation. These great operations were mainly undertaken in the interest of cultivating tenants, but they have supplied landlords with an accurate account of their estates which few of them formerly possessed and they are in various ways of great assistance to the administration.

LANDLORDS.

The result of the operation has been to show that the area occupied by landlords and tenants (not including unleased land at the disposal of Government) is 3,270 square miles, of which 1 per cent. is reserved by the owners, 3 per cent. covered by rivers, streams and roads, 5 per cent. granted free of rent and 91 per cent. leased to rent-paying tenants, 79 per cent. to tenure-holders and 12 per cent. to raiyats. The area actually occupied by tenure-holders is 606,548 acres, the balance being leased to raiyats who altogether hold 1,389,431 acres. Altogether 5,594 proprietary interests were recorded, which shows that on the whole there has been no very minute subdivision of proprietary rights. The area held by private proprietors in their own occupation is 28,255 acres, of which only 5,000 acres are cultivated, the remainder is chiefly waste in the forest and the marshes. Proprietors in Bākarganj are in very rare cases cultivators of their land. A very large number are absentees, and those who reside within the estate are almost all of the professional classes. The proprietors, however, hold a good deal of land as tenure-holders within their own estates or within the estates of other proprietors and it is chiefly from these tenures that they increase their income. Of the lands which they have leased a very small portion generally speaking has been leased to raiyats whose rents have been enhanced or can be in future enhanced. The great majority has been leased long ago to tenure-holders at a rent fixed in perpetuity. Thus as proprietors their income is not capable of any very extensive increase. As a body the proprietors in Bākarganj do not show any great capacity in the management of their estate. They are not very prosperous, but they display great ingenuity in divising means of retention of their ancestral property, however reduced their circumstances may be.

TENURE-HOLDERS.

Seventy-six per cent. of all the lands held by private proprietors has been leased to tenure-holders and the area held by tenure-holders who are tenants-in-chief amounts to 1,678,253, of which 606,548 acres are in their direct possession ; of this area 103,810 is held by rent-free tenants. Subinfeudation is the characteristic feature of the system of land tenure in Bākarganj. Not only are the tenures extremely numerous, but the degrees of subinfeudation are very great ; thus in many estates there are eight grades of intermediate tenures between the proprietors and the actual cultivators of the soil and the number very often extends to twelve grades and sometimes to twenty. The total number of tenures in the district is 356,830, to which may be added 107,178 shares which are entirely separate as regards management. There are 170 tenures in every square mile of the area which has been leased by proprietors to tenure-holders. Less than a thousand of these tenures are for temporary periods and very few of the remainder are held at a rent liable to enhancement. The permanent tenure-holders have by custom and very often by registered contract unfettered control over the land and tenures of their tenants on the single condition that they pay rent at the stated period. Of the total number of tenures 25,949 are rent-free grants and the remainder are rent-paying, of which 2,000 pay rent in kind. Each one of these tenures has by customs of the district a title (*mudāfat*) which consists of a revenue term such as *tāluk*, *jimba*, *hawala*, *miras* combined with the name of the original grantee or in some case the name of a purchaser or of a selected relative. Altogether 162 revenue terms are actually employed in the description of these tenures, of which a list is given in Appendix V of the Settlement Report. A considerable number of the tenures are very old, preceding in date the Permanent Settlement, but the vast bulk are of more modern creation. There seems to be no doubt that the physical conformation of Bākarganj was responsible for this subinfeudation. Dense forests had to be cut down which were divided by large rivers and numerous streams into a multitude of petty blocks which were difficult to manage or to supervise. The system of subinfeudation enabled the division to be made in a gradually diminishing scale to grade after grade of middlemen until at last the areas were sufficiently small for the reclamation of the forest to be arranged. No doubt also the system of subinfeudation was in origin largely the result of the coincidence that a numerous body of men whose capital was ordinarily small in amount lived in the district of Dacca from the headquarters of which the revenue arrangements of Bākarganj were controlled at the time that the British revenue system first came into force. The hawala which is the most characteristic of the Bākarganj tenures and with its derivatives, such as nimhawala, osat-hawala, osat-nimhawala, numbers 206,822, is very largely a small lease for the reclamation of forest granted to a man who was prepared to make his home in the grant and personally to supervise the reclamation. Generally speaking, the system of subinfeudation consists of three main classes : tāluks, which are grants from the zamindar or his lessees and are intended to create the interest of a landlord ; hawalas, which are leases given by the talukdars and their sub-lessees to substantial men for the reclamation of forests ; and karshas, which have been granted on payment to prosperous cultivators for land in their previous occupation. The last class is apparently an unique feature in land tenure, but promotion in status of the cultivators by the grant to them of the right of tenure-holders has been very common in Bākarganj. It may be due to the desire of the cultivator to achieve the superior status, which he found in the hawaldars who had taken the original lease of the land for cultivation, but it seems to have obtained a great vogue very largely as the result of a desire to plant slow-growing trees which no one would do with rights as insecure as those possessed by the raiyats, and of the opportunity which the great waves of 1822 and 1876 gave to the cultivators to improve their status. An excrescence of modern growth upon the system of subinfeudation is the assignment under the name of ijara, malguzar, etc., which has apparently been created chiefly to regularise the position of a manager amongst several co-sharers or to avoid the necessity of an outright sale. During recent years separate management by co-sharers amongst the tenure-holders has become very common and has been recognised by landlords, thus creating aliquot tenures with the right to grant sub-leases of the tenure-holders' aliquot and undivided interest in the tenure. The interests in land in Bākarganj village are thus a very complicated matter. There are usually several estates in each village. In each estate the proprietors have subdivided for the purpose of collecting rent from their tenants. In some of the subdivisions assignments have been granted permanently. Under the proprietors and their assignees, if any, come the tenants-in-chief. Under them tenure-holders of the second grade whose tenures are similar and who are more numerous. Under them a still more numerous body of tenure-holders of the third grade, and so on for the 8, 12 or even 20 grades of intermediate tenures which may exist in the village. Under the tenure-holders come the raiyats who cultivate the land, although a large part, indeed very nearly one acre out of every three, is cultivated by the inferior grades of tenure-holders. It should be noted that the rights of all tenure-holders are very generally the same. Their leases rarely contain special conditions. Of the total number of tenure-holders rather more than one-third cultivate all or almost all of the lands in their tenures which in the average measure only two acres. The rent for which such tenures are liable amounts in the average to Rs. 3-8-5 per acre, which is substantially less than the rate paid by the raiyats. Pure middlemen hold 45 per cent., and tenure-holders, who partly sublet and partly reserve, hold 20 per cent., of the total number of tenures. Subinfeudation is heaviest in the older part of the district and particularly in the parganas of Selimābād and Chandradwip, although it is not by any means absent in the recently reclaimed forest. There are very few tenures in the Sāhābāzpur island, in which although subinfeudation exists it has never obtained the grip or the ubiquity of the mainland. Tenure-holders in Sāhābāzpur are very frequently absentees, but in the rest of the district they are often residents within their tenures or within the village. Owing to the laws of inheritance most tenures are held by a large number of co-sharers amongst whom several may have sold their aliquot share to an outsider.

Rent-free tenants. Rent-free tenures are not an important feature in the Bākarganj system. Proprietors have granted about 6 per cent. of their estates free of rent, but few of the grants are large. Indeed the largest only measures 187 acres. The total number of these grants, free of rent, whether made by proprietor or by tenure-holder, is 26,000. The average area is, therefore, only 4 acres. Grants made by the proprietors alone measure in the average 10 acres, almost all grants to Brahmans. They have been conferred in the Hindu parts of the district and particularly in the parganas of Chandrawip and Shaistanagar. On the other hand they are almost non-existent in the island of Sāhābāzpur.

Raiyats. The total number of raiyati holdings is 565,531, of which only 2,150 are held by raiyats at fixed rates and only 15,569 by non-occupancy raiyats. The fields of these holdings are rarely in a compact block, being usually scattered throughout the village. Raiyats hold altogether 1,389,431 acres at an average rent of Rs. 4-8-10 an acre. The total area held by raiyats is equal to 63 per cent. of the land area in the district and to 72 per cent. of the cultivated area. The average size of an holding is 2·51 acre, although it is generally less than 2 acres in the north of the district and more than 4 acres in Barahanaddin, Amtali and Galachipa. The rights concerning trees are an important condition in Bākarganj. They appear to belong to the raiyat absolutely in all parts of the district.

RAIYATS AT A RENT IN KIND.

Of the total area held by raiyats 60,556 acres in 41,066 holdings are held at a produce rent, *i.e.*, 5 per cent. of the total raiyati area. They are chiefly found in Pirozpur and Sadar subdivisions. They are of two kinds:—*barga*, the most numerous, in which a fixed proportion of the crop is paid as rent and *dhankarari*, in which a specific amount of produce is paid as rent. The raiyats of *barga* holdings are locally regarded as tenants-at-will, and during the settlement proceedings an attempt was made to commute produce rents into cash rents in Gaurnadi, which created great opposition and considerable ill-feeling between the landlords and their tenants and ultimately did not achieve any great success.

UNDER-RAIYATS.

Under-raiyats hold 81,784 acres or 6 per cent. of the area held by raiyats; and their holdings, which number 76,120, average little more than an acre in size. The lease in most of these cases is permanent, very few temporary leases being found in the district. The rent varies very considerably, but is usually more than 50 per cent. greater than the rent of the raiyat-landlord. Only 2,336 acres are held by 2,545 under-raiyats of the second degree and 53 acres by 94 under-raiyats of the third or lower degrees.

SUMMARY DESCRIPTION OF LAND TENURE IN THE DISTRICT.

The following quotations from the settlement reports will serve best to explain the unique features of the Bākarganj system of tenancy:—

"The district of Bakarganj is notorious as the home of the most tortuous and intricate system of land-tenure in the world. To give a lucid description of that system is no easy task. Tables of statistics can no doubt be provided, but they are meaningless without the key of understanding; and understanding is to be acquired only by a patient investigation of the effect and growth of many diverse influences which have combined to produce so complicated a result. In the preparation of the record-of-rights it was found that the system was too complicated for the people who lived under it. Those who owned land very often did not know what land it was they owned, and those who cultivated very often did not know the title or estate of their landlords. The settlement camps were indeed regarded somewhat as lost property offices. Landlords came to find their lands and tenants came to find their landlords. Few were the days without their humorous surprise, when some tenure-holder found that he had spent a lifetime paying rent for nothing, as all the lands of his village had been brought into the account and his tenure had no place amongst them, or when some landlords who had believed that the land of a tenant lay in one village discovered that all the while it had been in another village far away.

To explain the case by comparison, it may be said that while in an average Bihar village of 100 acres, 84 acres will be occupied by raiyats and 13 acres by proprietors and rent-free holders, leaving only 3 acres to be held by intermediate tenure-holders, in a Bākarganj village of the same size 64 acres will be occupied by raiyats, 9 acres by the proprietor and 27 acres by intermediate tenure-holders. Of the 64 acres occupied by raiyats only 15 will be held directly of the proprietor and 49 will be held of intermediate tenure-holders. As an illustration of the multitude of these tenures, it may be added that in one zamindari alone Selimābād with an area which is but a tenth part of the area of Darbhanga district, there were found ten times as many intermediate tenures as in the whole of the Darbhanga district.

It is not, however, only the mere multitude of intermediate interests which makes Bākarganj land tenure peculiar, but the extent which in layer after layer they divide the cultivator from the proprietor. In every piece of land at the top is the proprietor paying revenue to Government and at the bottom is the cultivator who tills the soil ; but in Bākarganj between the two there are normally eight, often twelve and occasionally twenty grades of intermediate holders, each holding a separate and definite sublease of the land from the next higher in the scale. From the point of view of the cultivator his landlords form a ladder, of which each rung is occupied by a tenure-holder and the topmost by the proprietor. Viewing the village or estate as a whole, however, the interests in land spread out like a fan, the holders in each grade dividing their tenancies amongst a more numerous body of sub-lessees until the cultivators who are the ultimate sub-lessees form the most numerous body of all.

It may be convenient to summarise the foregoing description of the land system of Bākarganj in a picture of an ordinary village. Such a village will form part of several estates paying revenue to Government, but the land of these estates will be jumbled in a hotch-potch of small parcels throughout the village. The proprietors of these estates will have no connection with the cultivators of the land, but will have sublet to talukdars at a peppercorn rent the whole of their interest in the village with the exception of a few petty rent-free grants made to Brahmans. In every hundred acres of the land sixty-four acres will be occupied and cultivated by raiyats upon whom the Bengal Tenancy Act has conferred a right of occupancy, but in each field and in each holding the raiyat will not be a single person, but several members of the same family who jointly cultivate but divide the produce of the harvest into portions representing their inherited or acquired share in the holding. The fields belonging to a family will rarely be contiguous and will never be grouped within a ring-fence round the family homestead. In a large number of fields and holdings several families will have a share under different titles, but here again division will usually be recognized at the harvest and not during the process of cultivation. The field will be ploughed, sown, weeded and cut as a whole by the joint efforts of the co-sharers and specific portions will not be marked off as the claim of each co-sharer. The cultivators will ordinarily pay rent to some petty tenure-holder, but often a portion of the rent to each of several petty tenure-holders. The tenure-holder will rarely be a single individual, but usually a group of relatives. Between the cultivators and the talukdars there will be a vast sea of middlemen's tenures, all held under identical conditions and terms but all taking some small portion of the rent as their profit. The owners of the various tenures will be usually not a single person but a group of partners, originally members of the same family but often including purchasers. Most of the tenure-holders will be resident in different parts of the country and not in the village, many will be money-lenders and many will own several tenures in several estates. The tenure-holders will come personally or by agent to the village to collect their rents in February, but will otherwise take no interest in the village and have no part or lot in its affairs. Some of the tenure-holders will not trouble to take even the rent due to them, as the amount is nominal, and their interest will remain merely a paper entry in the village books. On the other hand a considerable proportion of the tenure-holders will be prosperous cultivators who live in the village and still cultivate twenty-seven out of every hundred of its acres. Such men will in many cases be middlemen in respect of some portion of their lands and cultivators of the rest. Most of the cultivators and many of the tenure-holders will be unable to explain the title of their landlord or the chain of tenures which connect him with the proprietors of their estate. No one in the village will be capable of pointing out the land of the different estates, still less of the different tenures in the village. No one, whether proprietor, tenure-holder or raiyat, will be capable of detailing with reasonable accuracy the tenures of the whole village, and very few of the more intelligent tenure-holders will be able to give accurate information about the tenures of any single estate ; even those few will be incapable of pointing out the land included in the tenures of which their other information is reasonably accurate."

CHAPTER XI.

GENERAL ADMINISTRATION.

ADMINISTRATIVE CHARGES AND STAFF.

THE administration of the district is in charge of the District Officer under the Commissioner of the Dacca Division. The District Officer is as District Magistrate in charge of the criminal administration and as District Collector in charge of the revenue administration. The extent of the Collector's revenue jurisdiction differs somewhat from the extent of the district, as his powers under some of the revenue Regulations and Acts are limited to the estates borne on the revenue roll of the district, which in some cases include land situated in other districts, and do not extend to the few estates with land in the district which are borne on the revenue roll of other districts. For general administrative purposes the district is divided into four subdivisions with headquarters at Barisāl (Sadar), Pirozpur, Patuākhāli and Bholā. The headquarters subdivision is under the direct supervision of the Collector, although there is a proposal to appoint a Subdivisional Officer; each of the other three subdivisions is in charge of a Subdivisional Officer exercising the powers of a Deputy Collector in revenue matters. The Subdivisional Officers are occasionally members of the Indian Civil Service, but usually members of the Provincial Civil Service. The Collector is assisted at the district headquarters by an Additional District Magistrate and a staff of Deputy Magistrates and Collectors consisting generally of 9 officers. They are employed upon both magisterial and executive work. There are in addition a special Deputy Collector in charge of Government estates and the temporarily-settled area and a special officer in charge of excise. There are usually 3 Sub-Deputy Collectors at the headquarters of the district employed chiefly on miscellaneous executive work, especially on the revenue side. Occasionally, a Joint Magistrate and usually an Assistant Collector are posted to the district. The Subdivisional Officers are each assisted by a Sub-Deputy Collector and in Pirozpur and Patuākhāli by a Deputy Magistrate for magisterial work. Little of the work connected with land revenue is transacted in the subdivisions.

REVENUE. The revenue of the district under the main heads was Rs. 27,25,118 in 1892-93, Rs. 31,15,110 in 1900-01, and Rs. 37,03,531 in 1910-11. This does not include the *chaukidāri* tax, which amounted to Rs. 4,55,937 in 1910-11. Of the revenue in 1910-11, Rs. 19,86,936 were derived from land-revenue, the other main heads being Stamps (Rs. 9,94,000), Cesses (Rs. 4,36,000), Excise (Rs. 1,68,000), and Income-tax (Rs. 90,000).

LAND REVENUE. Owing to the large area in the district under temporary settlement, land-revenue is capable of more expansion than in other districts of Bengal. The temporarily-settled area consists largely of waste fit for cultivation and colonization, while the periods for which more developed estates have been settled terminate at different dates. The land-revenue accordingly increases from year to year. The increase which was obtained in the recent settlement operations was Rs. 3,23,087. The land-revenue demand was Rs. 16,41,000 in 1892, Rs. 16,83,000 in 1900, and Rs. 19,32,000 in 1910.

STAMPS. As in other Eastern Bengal districts the revenue derived from stamps is not only very large, but rapidly increasing. It was Rs. 6,38,000 in 1892, Rs. 7,66,000 in 1901, and Rs. 9,94,000 in 1910. During the settlement operations, however, the receipts from stamps were abnormally large and the normal revenue may be taken at 9 lakhs of rupees. It appears to increase by 2 per cent. a year. The demand and the increase relate mainly to judicial stamps, which accounted for Rs. 8,51,000 in 1910, non-judicial stamps accounting only for Rs. 1,43,000.

The stamp revenue is an index to the litigiousness of the inhabitants. It amounts to 7½ annas per head of the population as compared with less than two annas in Darbhanga.

CESSES. The road and public works cesses are as usual levied at the maximum rate of one anna in the rupee. The demand in 1910-11 was Rs. 4,72,607, practically the same as in 1896-97. A fresh revaluation on the record-of-rights was concluded in 1912, but owing to errors in method it was cancelled and a new revaluation is now in progress. The rental of the district as estimated by the Settlement Officer is ninety lakhs of rupees.

EXCISE. The revenue from excise has been practically stationary since 1900. It averages to slightly more than an anna per head, which is less than half the average in Darbhanga. This is due chiefly to the fact that two-thirds of the population are Muhammadans. The excise revenue is as usual derived from imported liquors (Rs. 9,000), country spirits (Rs. 35,000), opium (Rs. 58,000), and hemp drugs (Rs. 65,000). The receipts from country spirits represent an expenditure of only Rs. 144 for every 10,000 of the population as compared with Rs. 1,910 in the Patna Division. Of the total sum Rs. 15,000 is obtained from the duty and Rs. 20,000 from distillery and license fees. *Tāri* and *pāchwāi* are not drunk at all and imported liquors are popular only with Europeans and the upper class Hindus. The revenue from country spirits is the same now as in 1892. The consumption of opium and hemp drugs is much more considerable. In the case of opium the revenue has risen from Rs. 35,000 in 1892 to Rs. 57,000 in 1910 or over 60 per cent., while in the case of hemp drugs the increase has been from Rs. 46,000 to Rs. 65,000 or over 40 per cent. The increase in both cases has been equally shared by the duty and license fees. The figures are given in the Statistical Appendices. Opium is largely consumed by the dissolute and was probably introduced by the Burmese merchants who came over for the betel trade. There is a certain amount of smuggling in the district. Of hemp drugs, only *Gānjā* is of any importance. *Gānjā* is the dried flowering top of the cultivated female hemp plant (*cannabis sativa*) and the resinous exudation thereon. The plant is not grown in the district. *Gānjā* is chiefly popular with low-caste Hindus.

INCOME-TAX.

The figures in the Statistical Appendix show that in 1910 11 the realizations were Rs. 89,769 from 1,454 assessees chiefly from Part IV, trade, especially money-lending and the renting of houses. Practically the same amount was realised in 1902-03 from 3,070 assessees, when the minimum income assessed was raised from Rs. 500 to Rs. 1,000. In the eight years since the minimum income was raised, the number of assessees has increased by 36 per cent. and the yield of the tax by 27 per cent.

REGISTRATION

There are 26 offices for the registration of documents under Act III of 1877. At Barisāl the special Sub-Registrar deals as usual with the documents presented there and assists the District officer, who is ex-officio Registrar, in supervising the proceedings of the other Sub-Registrars in the district. The number of documents registered in the district in 1914 was 111,931 as compared with 78,634 in 1894, the increase amounting to 42·3 per cent.

CIVIL JUSTICE.

The judicial staff entertained for the administration of civil justice consists of the District Judge, 2 Sub-Judges and 17 Munsiffs. Of the Sub-Judges all and of the Munsiffs 8 are located at Barisāl, 3 Munsiffs being located at Pirozpur, 4 at Patuākhāli and 2 at Bholā. Statistics of civil litigation will be found amongst the Statistical Appendices. It will be observed that the average number of suits in the district in the ten years 1893—1902 was rather over 30,000, whereas the average number in the nine years ending 1901 was 42,000, an increase of 40 per cent. This increase was chiefly due to the greater number of rent-suits filed as a result of the settlement operations, which enabled landlords to bring such suits without excessive expense. In 1911 the number of suits disposed of was 37,606 by Munsiffs by ordinary procedure and 7,586 by Small Cause Court procedure, 160 by Subordinate Judges by ordinary procedure and 754 by Small Cause Court procedure and 7 by the District Judge. The average value of a suit in the Munsiffs' Courts is less than Rs. 70. The number of civil appeals disposed of each year varies very greatly, and in the case of District Judges was much increased during the settlement operations. In 1911 Subordinate Judges decided 397 and District Judges 573 appeals.

CRIMINAL JUSTICE. Criminal justice is administered by the District and Sessions Judge, an Additional Sessions Judge, the District Magistrate, an Additional District Magistrate, several Deputy Magistrates and Sub-Deputy Magistrates at the headquarters and at each of the subdivisions. Altogether there are 14 Magistrates in the district with first class powers and 7 with inferior powers. There are in addition benches of Honorary Magistrates in Barisāl (9 members), Patuākhāli (4 members), Pirozpur (3 members) and Bholā (2 members). In all there are 18 Honorary Magistrates, of whom 4 are authorised to sit singly.

CRIME. The statistics will show that Bākarganj is a very criminal district and that serious crime is very frequent. Crimes of violence including murder are extremely frequent and offences against the public tranquillity very common. Rioting concerning land has been largely reduced since the record-of-rights was prepared, and the number of persons bound over to keep the peace has been diminished to an exceptional extent; but murder is as common as ever, rioting although checked is still very frequent and lawlessness still remains very considerable; theft and burglary are much more frequent than the statistics show, as many cases, especially those which occur on the rivers, are never reported, while still more never end in a prosecution. A historical sketch of serious crime in the district has been given elsewhere, in which the great and unchecked increase in modern times has been described.

POLICE. For police purposes the district is divided into 27 investigating centres, viz., Bārisal, Nalchhiti, Jhālakāti, Rājapur, Bākarganj, Gaurnadi, Muladi, Mehendiganj and

Badartuni (nine in all) in the Sadar subdivision; Pirozpur, Kaukhāli, Swarupkāti, Nazirpur, Bhāndāriā, Mathāriā and Bāmnā (seven in all) in the Pirozpur subdivision; Patuākhāli, Mirzaganj, Betāgi, Bāuphal, Galāchipā, Āmtali and Bargunā (seven in all) in the Patuākhāli subdivision; Bholā, Daulatkhan, Barhānaddin and Tazumnaddin (four in all) in the Sāhābāzpur subdivision. The machinery employed for the protection of person and property consists of the regular or district police, including the town police, and of the rural force of village watch, which is paid out of the *chaukidāri* fund. The former consisted in 1911 of one Superintendent and one Additional and one Assistant Superintendent, 2 Deputy Superintendents, 7 Inspectors, 76 Sub-Inspectors, 79 Head Constables and 627 Constables or a total of 794 as compared with 632 in 1902; and the latter of 521 dafadars and 5,465 chaukidārs as compared with 512 dafadars and 5,129 chaukidārs. The cost of the regular force in 1911 was Rs. 2,53,518 and there was one policeman to every 3,059 persons, while the cost of the village watch was Rs. 3,65,274 and there was one watchman to every 444 persons.

In 1818 there were only 182 foot constables and 48 police officers, although there was in addition a river patrol of 14 boats and 182 oarsmen. In 1860 the police force had not increased in numbers at all, but chaukidārs had been introduced. The police were reorganised in 1861 and in 1871 the regular police consisted of 3 European officers, 102 subordinate officers, 478 foot constables with a river patrol of 5 boats manned by a crew of 35 men. The total cost of the regular police force including office, allowances and contingencies was in 1871 Rs. 1,11,860. The village watch in the same year consisted of 5,135 men and cost Rs. 1,84,860. The cost of the regular police in 1914 was Rs. 3,00,266 and of the village watch Rs. 3,65,444. The cost of the regular police in 1805 was only Rs. 33,360.

JAILS.

There is a district jail at Barisāl and a subsidiary jail at each of the three subdivisions, Pirozpur, Patuākhāli and Bholā.

Accommodation is provided in the district jail for 754 persons, 732 males and 22 females, in the Pirozpur jail for 49 persons including 3 females, in the Patuākhāli jail for 32 persons including 4 females and in the Bholā jail for 18 persons including 2 females. The average daily number of prisoners in each of these jails in 1911 was 613, 26, 34 and 9, respectively. In Patuākhāli it will be seen that the average number of prisoners entertained daily was greater than the accommodation.

TELEGRAPH AND POST OFFICES.

There are 16 telegraph offices in the district, of which eight are in the Sadar subdivision, two in Pirozpur, three in Patuākhāli and three in the Sāhābāzpur island.

There are 157 post offices in the district, of which 89 are in the Sadar subdivision, 22 in the Patuākhāli subdivision, 30 in the Pirozpur subdivision and 16 in the Bholā subdivision. The extent to which the post is used has increased very greatly thus—

		1861-62.	1870-71.	1914.
Letters	received ...	67,903	173,803	2,293,226
Newspapers	do. ...	6,699	15,177	349.440
Parcels	do. ...	2,302	6,149	...
Books	do. ...	869	2,477	291,434
Letters	despatched ...	57,290	...	...
Newspapers	do. ...	503	...	...
Parcels	do. ...	645	...	41,186
Books	do. ...	86	...	...
Money-orders	Received ...	...	...	203,173
	Value ...	...	...	Rs. 31,80,208-13-4
	Despatched ...	...	...	317,015
	Value ...	...	...	Rs. 52,04,339-12-9

REVENUE AND EXPENDITURE.

The following is a comparison of the revenue and expenditure of the district at different periods :—

Revenue.	1818.	1850-51.	1870-71.	1892-93.	1913-14.
	Rs.	Rs.	Rs	Rs.	Rs.
Land Revenue	8,95,665	10,61,338	14,22,323	15,81,954	20,74,889
Stamps	25,950	87,471	2,15,154	6,37,655	11,59,600
Excise	27,127 (Excise and Opium)	50,556 (Excise and Opium)	63,811 (Excise and Opium)	85,742	1,47,990
Opium				34,989	80,995
Income-tax	...	...	1,23,529	58,129	1,06,300
Road and public works cesses	...	...	24,533	3,09,274	5,05,621
Dâk cess	...	...	21,902	16,955	...
Miscellaneous	2,776	6,405	1,41,251	420	12,183
Total ...	9,51,515	12,05,765	20,12,503	27,25,118	40,87,578

Expenditure.	1818.	1850-51.	1870-71.	1913-14.		
	Rs.	Rs.	Rs.	Rs.	A.	P.
Revenue charges, general.	32,984	74,679	97,033	5,36,300	0	0
Judicial charges, general.	87,901	120,834	99,479	2,01,258	0	0
Excise ...	4,426	15,511	6,969	11,383	0	0
Income-tax ...	...	...	6,895	4,300	0	0
Medical ...	...	...	11,521	33,300	0	0
Jails ...	...	...	14,971	73,100	0	0
Police ...	[included in judicial.]	[included in judicial.]	1,10,518	3,09,300	0	0
Roads and public works.	...	...	27,737	14,583	6	1
Post-office ...	108	1,866	12,006	...		
Education ...	..	360	34,164	5,91,069	0	0
Dâk funds ...	...	...	13,804	...		
Miscellaneous ...	...	...	13,827	...		
Total ...	1,25,719	2,23,207	4,49,024	17,74,593	6	1

CHAPTER XII.

LOCAL SELF-GOVERNMENT.

LOCAL BODIES.

THERE are five municipalities in the district, outside of which the administration of local affairs is vested in the District Board and in the Local Boards which have been constituted in each of the subdivisions. The District Board is responsible for the maintenance of roads, bridges and roadside rest-houses and has the general superintendence of primary and middle schools. It is also entrusted with the management of public ferries, the control over dispensaries, the provision of a proper water-supply and village sanitation. To the Local Boards, which work in subordination to it, have been delegated the management of pounds and the administration of the sums allotted for the construction and repair of village roads.

THE DISTRICT BOARD.

The District Board was created in 1887 and consists of 25 members. The District Officer is ex-officio Chairman, and besides him 6 officials are ex-officio members, viz., the Civil Surgeon, the Khas Mahal Deputy Collector, the Deputy Inspector of Schools and three Subdivisional Officers. Of the remaining members, 12 are elected by the Local Boards and 6 are nominated by Government from non-officials. Of the elected members 5 are pleaders, 6 landlords and 1 a muktear. Of the nominated members 6 are officials, 3 pleaders and 1 a landlord. The Vice-Chairman is nearly always chosen from amongst the elected members.

The Statistical Appendix shows the principal sources from which the District Board derives its income and the principal objects on which it spends it. Until 1914 only the road-cess belonged to the District Board; but subsequently the income from rates has been doubled by the surrender of the public works cess by Government to the District Board. In the period 1892—1901 the income averaged Rs. 2,71,000 and the expenditure Rs. 2,70,000, and in the period 1902—1911 the income averaged Rs. 3,92,000 and the expenditure Rs. 3,94,000. Since 1899 the income from rates has usually amounted to Rs. 2,20,000, while pounds have contribnted about Rs. 10,000, education about Rs. 3,000, medical about Rs. 3,000, civil works (the receipts from which vary very much from year to year) about Rs. 15,000, and miscellaneous about Rs. 4,000. Contributions by the Local Government until the first partition in 1905 averaged Rs. 34,000, whereas the Eastern Bengal and Assam Government made grants with an annual average of Rs. 1,22,000. No debt has been incurred by the District Board since its creation. The chief heads of expenditure are civil works, education and medical. Civil works include not only the construction and maintenance of roads and bridges, rest-houses and buildings, but the pay of the District Engineer and his staff, and the expenditure increased from an average of Rs. 1,35,000 in 1892—95 to an average of Rs. 2,31,000 in 1905—11. Medical expenditure (chiefly on dispensaries and medical stores) rose from Rs. 5,000 a year in 1892—95 to Rs. 30,000 in 1902-03 and Rs. 52,000 in 1908—11. The expenditure on education rose even more—from Rs. 39,000 in 1892—95 to Rs. 91,000 in 1908—11. In this case the increase was chiefly in the payment of an inspecting staff.

The immediate administration of the roads is vested in the District Engineer, who is responsible also for the management and repair of the dāk bungalows, inspection houses and other buildings belonging to the District Board. The mileage of the roads under maintenance by the District Board is 385, of which only 18 miles are metalled. As the country is low-lying, all roads require high embankments and the initial cost is very great. The District Board has, however, built practically all the roads in the district. The Board also controls 54 ferries and 190 pounds, which are generally leased out to the highest bidder.

For the assistance of education the Board maintains a staff of 10 Assistant Sub-Inspectors of Schools. It maintains and aids 32 middle English schools, besides aiding 1 industrial school, 156 upper primary and maintaining 231 lower primary schools and aiding 2,050 lower primary schools. Its grants-in-aid amount altogether to Rs. 89,156 annually. It also awards the following scholarships :—

60 lower primary scholarships at Rs. 2 per month each.

2 scholarships tenable at Dacca School of Engineering at Rs. 10 each.

1 scholarship tenable at the Calcutta Blind School at Rs. 10 per month.

2 scholarships tenable at the Bengal Veterinary College at Rs. 12 per month each.

For the relief of sickness, the District Board maintains 30 charitable dispensaries, of which, except those situated within municipalities, its grants are practically the sole income. When cholera and other epidemic diseases break out in the interior, it despatches doctors with medicines to the affected villages. The sanitary work done by the District Board is of a somewhat varied character. It includes preventive measures against epidemics, the excavation, clearing and preservation of tanks, the clearance of jungle, excavation of drains, and excavation of small streams. Well water is not popular with the population and the construction of wells is not undertaken. It also maintains, for the benefit of the rural population, a staff of 4 Veterinary Assistants, who are deputed, when necessary, to cope with outbreaks of epidemic disease amongst cattle in the interior.

It is reported that the District Board administers its duties satisfactorily and without friction, although there have been complaints that the southern thanas are neglected.

LOCAL BOARDS.

Subject to the control of the District Board, the Local Boards have jurisdiction in each subdivision. The Subdivisional Officer is ex-officio Chairman and the members, who number 18 in Sadar, 10 in Patuākhāli, 16 in Pirozpur and 10 in Bholā, are elected. At the subdivisional headquarters' the number of pleaders who are members is in each case large. The duties of the Local Boards are confined to the management of village roads and pounds, and their chief task is to maintain in an efficient state the roads made over to them. The average expenditure is in Sadar Rs. 12,500, in Patuākhali Rs. 8,000, in Pirozpur Rs. 10,500, and in Bholā Rs. 11,000 per annum.

CHAUKIDARI UNIONS AND PANCHAYATS.

There are altogether 488 unions in the district for the management of the village watch. There are ordinarily five members in each panchayat, but the collecting panchayat is the principal member, who does most of the work. In addition to the assessment of the chaukidāri tax, he is in general charge of the dafadar and chaukidārs, although they have still to report to the thana each week and are generally considered rather as members of the police force than as village servants. The collecting panchayat obtains 15 per cent. of the collections of chaukidāri tax as payment of his trouble and expenses; the assistant panchayats are not paid. A great deal of miscellaneous work is entrusted to panchayats, especially in connection with crops and agricultural statistics. They are also expected to give information and assistance to the police in the prevention and detection of crime. The Magistrates send a certain number of trivial quarrels and criminal cases to the panchayats for compromise or report. The superintendence of panchayats and the chaukidāri tax is at present entrusted to a Deputy Magistrate at headquarters and to the Subdivisional Officers, but the dafadars and chaukidārs are under the control of the Superintendent of Police. The whole system is at present under consideration in connection with the proposed establishment of the circle system.

MUNICIPALITIES.

There are five municipalities in the district, viz., Barisāl, Nalchhiti, Jhālakāti, Pirozpur and Patuākhāli. In 1914 the total number of rate-payers was 8,047, or 16·65 per cent. of the total municipal population. In all the municipalities taxation assumes the form of a tax on persons, but in Barisāl there is also a latrine-tax and a water-rate. Statistics of the receipts and expenditure in each municipality will be found in the B volume or Statistical Appendix of the Gazetteer. The maintenance of roads, the improvement of drainage and the provision of an adequate system of conservancy are the chief demands on the municipal income, but grants-in-aid are also made to dispensaries and schools. None of the municipalities has any elaborate system of drainage, as the rivers are tidal and sweep out the drains twice a day.

Barisāl.

The Barisāl Municipality, which was established in 1876, is administered by a Municipal Board consisting of 15 Commissioners, of whom 10 are elected, 4 are nominated and 1 is ex-officio. The Chairman and Vice-Chairman are elected. The area within municipal limits is 7½ square miles and the number of rate-payers in 1914 was 3,382, or 15 per cent. of the population. The average annual income in 1891—1900, excluding loans, was Rs. 22,676 and in 1901—1910 Rs. 27,735. In 1914 the income was Rs. 60,324, the expenditure Rs. 56,232. The chief source of income is a tax on persons, which brought in Rs. 14,174 in 1914. The latrine tax accounted for Rs. 13,793, and the water-rate for Rs. 16,167. The incidence of the rates per head of population was Rs. 2-4-11. Of the expenditure in 1914, 35·6 per cent. was spent on conservancy, 1·7 per cent. on education, 23·2 per cent. on public works, 16·4 per cent. on water-supply and 2·6 per cent. on medical relief. Establishment charges amounted to 5·8 per cent. of the expenditure. The water-supply is obtained by pipes from the river at Amanatganj and is distributed by standard pipes in the streets. The water-works were constructed in 1911-12 and cost Rs. 1,60,000, o which Rs. 60,000 was given by Government and Rs. 30,000 was obtained from private subscription. The District Board gave a donation of Rs. 35,000.

The Nalchhiti Municipality was established in 1875. It is administered by a Municipal Board consisting of 9 nominated members. The area within municipal limits is about ½ square mile and the number of rate-payers in 1914 was 306, or 15·6 per cent. of the population. The average annual income in 1891—1900 was Rs. 1,752 and Rs. 2,532 in 1901-10. In 1914 the income was Rs. 3,140 and the expenditure Rs. 2,175. The chief source of income is a tax on persons, which brought in Rs. 2,254 in 1914. The incidence of rate per head was Re. 1-4-5. Of the expenditure in 1914, 12·2 per cent. was spent on conservancy, 4·1 per cent. on education, 14·7 per cent. on public works, 2·7 per cent. on water-supply, 11·5 per cent. on medical relief. Establishment charges amounted to 26·2 per cent.

Jhālākāti. The Jhālakāti Municipality was established in 1875. It is administered by a Municipal Board of 9 elected members. The area within the municipal limits is 1·12 square miles and in 1914 the number of rate-payers was 963, or 16·3 per cent. of the population. The average annual income in 1891—1900, including loans, was Rs. 4,235 and in 1901—10 Rs. 7,676. The chief source of income is a tax on persons, which brought in Rs. 6,387 in 1914. The incidence of taxation per head of population was Re. 1-2-1. In 1914 the income was Rs. 14,662, the expenditure Rs. 11,391. Of the expenditure in 1914, 30·3 per cent. was spent on conservancy, 7·8 per cent. on education, 20·3 on public works, ·7 per cent. on water-supply, 8·7 per cent. on medical relief. Establishment charges amounted to 6·1 per cent.

Pirozpur. The Pirozpur Municipality was established in 1885. It is administered by a Municipal Board of 11 elected members. The area within the municipal limit is 11 square miles and the number of rate-payers 2,361, or 19·6 per cent. of the population. The average annual income in 1891—1900 was Rs. 5,516 and in 1901—10 Rs. 6,681. In 1914 the income was Rs. 10,090 and the expenditure Rs. 9,630. The chief source of income is a tax on persons, which brought in Rs. 5,115 in 1914. The latrine-tax accounted for Rs. 1,939. The incidence of rate per head of population was Re. 0-11-5. Of the expenditure in 1914, 18·5 per cent. was spent on conservancy, 3·06 per cent. on education, 23·09 per cent. on public works, 6·8 per cent. on water-supply, 13·5 per cent. on medical relief. Establishment charges amounted to 9·9 per cent.

Patuākhāli.

The Patuākhāli Municipality, which was established in 1892, is administered by a Municipal Board consisting of 10 elected members. The area within the municipality is 3½ square miles, and in 1914 the number of rate-payers was 1,035, or 16·55 per cent. of the population. The average annual income in 1891—1900 was Rs. 2,633 and in 1901—10 Rs. 3,634. In 1914 the income was Rs. 6,068 and the expenditure Rs. 6,279. The chief source of income is a tax on persons, which brought in Rs. 3,860 in 1914. The incidence of taxation per head of population was 13 annas 2 pies. Of the expenditure in 1914, 3·12 per cent. was spent on conservancy, 2·96 per cent. on education, 28·49 per cent. on public works, 8·92 per cent. on water-supply, 9·56 per cent. on medical relief. Establishment charges amounted to 13·36 per cent.

CHAPTER XIII.

EDUCATION.

PROGRESS OF EDUCATION.

THE advance of education amongst the people has been very rapid, and since the Partition of 1905 it has been particularly noticeable amongst the Muhammadan community, which had formerly been very backward. Only a few tols and a few maktabs were in existence during the Muhammadan administration, and it was not until sixty years after the British had assumed the administration of the country that education began to be encouraged. The first school in the modern sense was established by the Magistrate, Mr. Garrett, in Barisāl on the 31st of March 1828. A missionary school was established in Barisāl by the Serampore missionaries in 1829. The early state of education in Bengal is described in Mr. Adam's report on Education in Bengal, 1835. Both English education and primary education advanced much during the next 40 years. The Barisāl Zilla School was founded in 1842 and made a Government School shortly afterwards. A high English school was also started at Basanda near Jhālakati, and middle English schools were maintained in each of the subdivisions. But the English education was still an exotic and was described by Mr. Beveridge as being mainly sought "by the children of professional men, who are only temporary residents in the neighbourhood." Female education had in 1873 hardly begun. There was a girls' school in Barisāl and in some of the primary schools boys and girls were taught together. The movement in favour of primary education began about 1860 and was chiefly due to the Government and the missionaries. It was prosecuted with vigour. In March 1874, there were in the district 2 higher English schools with 437 students, of whom only 26 were Muhammadans, 18 middle English schools with 1,304 students, of whom only 86 were Muhammadans. For primary education there were 37 middle vernacular schools with 1,737 students, of whom 211 were Muhammadans, and 304 lower vernacular schools with 8,530 students, of whom 4,269 were Muhammadans. Even in the primary schools, the students were chiefly of the respectable classes and the attempt to introduce primary education amongst the Muhammadan cultivators in the south of the district was a failure. As Mr. Beveridge remarks :—"The peasants do not care for education ; and besides they need their children to gather their betelnuts, to row their boats, and above all to herd their cattle." Of the schools 280 were aided institutions, nearly all of which were in the triangular tract of country between the Barisāl, Swarupkāti and Ariāl Khān rivers, which the Educational Inspector described in 1870 as "one of the most forward educational tracts in East Bengal, both in the number of boys at school and in the number of minor and vernacular scholarships which it carries off. It supplies an unusually large number of pupils to the medical profession." There were only 6 girls' schools in the district with 80 students, all Hindus. Only 7 children in every thousand of the population were at school, but amongst boys only there were 14, 9 being the proportion amongst Muhammadans and 32 amongst Hindus. The amount spent on education was apparently about Rs. 34,000. The great interest which has subsequently been taken in education reflected in the figures, the total number of students being 75,859 in 1892 and 103,421 in 1911. During this period the percentage of male scholars to the male population of a school-going age had risen from 43 to 50 and of female scholars to the female population of a school-going age from 2 to 8. In 1911 in every thousand of the population 43 were at school, the proportion among the Muhammadans being 35 and among the Hindus 60. The number of institutions in 1911 was 3,088, of which all but 978 were aided by the public funds. The number of secondary institutions was 78 and the number of students pursuing an English education 9,738.

LITERACY.

At the census of 1911, 204,736 persons were returned as literate or 8·3 per cent. of the population. Only 12,831 were females. The percentage of literates amongst Hindus was 16 (males 29 per cent. and females 3 per cent.) and amongst Muhammadans 5 (males 10 per cent. and females ·2 per cent.). Literacy is much more widely prevalent in the Sadar subdivision and in the Pirozpur and Swarupkāti thanas than in the south of the district ; this is largely due to the number of *bhadralok* resident in the former area. The largest proportion of Muhammadan literates is to be found in the Pirozpur subdivision, the smallest proportion in the Sāhābāzpur island, where only 17 amongst Hindu males and only 6 amongst Muhammadan males are literate, while there are only 330 literate females in the whole island. Literacy in English is confined to 13,381 persons, of whom only 218 are females and only 14 of these Muhammadans. Amongst Hindu males 3·2 per cent. and amongst Muhammadans only ·1 per cent. are literate in English. In the Sāhābāzpur subdivision only 694 males and 10 females are literate in English; in Patuākhāli subdivision 1,200 males and 12 females. More than half of those literate in English are to be found in Barisāl, Gaurnadi and Jhālakāti thanas and more than one quarter in the Barisāl thana alone. In the census of 1901, ten years previously, the number of literates was returned as 181,453, so that there was an increase of 13 per cent. in literacy in the decade. Curiously enough this increase was almost entirely amongst Hindus (22 per cent.) and very slight amongst Muhammadans (4 per cent.). As might be expected, there are more literates in the north of the district than the south. The north contains all the Hindu higher castes, the district headquarters and the bulk of the professional and industrial classes, while the south is entirely agricultural. But the disproportion is not so great as might have been anticipated, as the literates are only twice as numerous in the north, while even in the south one male in every nine can read and write. The Hindu cultivator in the south is practically uneducated, and amongst the Namasudras of the north and west it is only in the last ten years that any desire for education has been displayed. The Hindu of the higher castes is not always educated, and in unprogressive tracts, such as Nalchhiti, he is curiously content to remain illiterate. Of the smaller communities all Magh males can read and write, while amongst Christians the men are mostly literate and there has been a great advance in literacy amongst the women.

NEWS-PAPERS.

Despite the comparative high level of literacy, newspapers and books are not published in any quantity in the district. In 1914 only 12 books were published, mostly school-books or books and pamphlets of an elementary nature, while there were only 4 newspapers in existence, the oldest being the "Kasipur Nibashi" established in 1881, which has a circulation of about 800 and is chiefly supported by Civil Court advertisements. The other newspapers are the "Barisāl Hitaishi" with a circulation of 600, the "Brahmobadi" published by a Brahmo missionary with a circulation of 500, and the "Senapati" published by the Barisāl Baptist Mission with a circulation of 220.

In 1870 only one newspaper was published in the district, the "Barisal Barttabaha." This was a monthly print with 150 subscribers.

There were at one time two colleges in Barisāl; but one, the Raj Chandra, was disaffiliated in 1902 for mismanagement. In 1901 there were 570 college students reading in Barisāl, but in 1911, owing to the disaffiliation of the Raj Chandra College and the general stiffening of the Matriculation and later examinations which took effect in 1901, the number had been reduced to 163, all at the Braja Mohan College which was founded in 1884 as a higher class English school and raised to the status of a first grade college in 1898. It is named after its founder, the late Babu Braja Mohan Dutt, Small Cause Court Judge, Nadia, who was an inhabitant of this district, and was carried on by his son Babu Aswini Kumar Dutt, the foremost man in the district in his time. The College has recently passed through troubles and has been near disaffiliation. There are 17 Professors in the College, but its buildings are inadequate and it has no grounds. The students live in messes throughout the town, as there is no hostel attached to the College. COLLEGES.

The Barisāl Zilla School was founded in 1842 and soon became a Government institution. By 1856 there were three more high schools which were all aided by Government, but these had been reduced to one in 1874. Altogether in 1874 there were 437 students in high schools, of whom 26 were Muhammadans; by 1892 the number of high schools had increased to 8 and the students to 2,076, while in 1911 there were 16 with 4,954 students including 706 Muhammadans. Four of these schools were Government institutions and one aided. The Barisāl Zilla School has a high reputation in Bengal. There is a class for teaching Elementary Survey and Engineering, to which, for the practical training of the students, the Barisāl Technical School has been affiliated. There are no hostels attached to the school as yet, although they have long been talked of. The number of students in the zilla school is 574 and the expenditure Rs. 18,196 or Rs. 31·7 per head. Of the income 57·08 per cent. is provided by fees and 42·92 per cent. by grants from Government and the District Board. The other high schools are as follows :— HIGH SCHOOLS.

In the Sadar subdivision—

		Pupils
(1)	B. M. Institution	866
(2)	Jhālakāti	368
(3)	Kirtipāsā	513
(4)	Gābhā	394
(5)	Uzirpur	475

	Pupils.
(6) Gailā	768
(7) Lakshankāti	475
(8) Village Union Naldeira	277
(9) Rahmatpur	348
(10) Siddhakāti	347
(11) Kalashkāti	295
(12) Uttar Sāhābāzpur	350
(13) Ulania	174
In the Pirozpur subdivision—	
(1) Pirozpur	501
(2) Baisari	512
(3) Banaripara	338
(4) Kadamtola	311
In the Patuākhāli subdivision—	
(1) Patuākhāli	483
In the Sāhābāzpur subdidision—	
(1) Bholā	505

The total expenditure is Rs. 1,62,932 or Rs. 18·3 per head. The income is obtained by fees (87·3 per cent.), grants (9·3 per cent.) and subscriptions and other sources (3·4 per cent.).

Middle English Schools

In 1874 there were 18 of these institutions with 1,304 pupils, of whom only 86 were Muhammadans. These had increased to 38 with 2,698 pupils in 1,892 and to 53 with 4,438 pupils in 1910. Of these schools 34 are in the Sadar subdivision (3,487 pupils), 31 in the Pirozpur subdivision (3,305 pupils), 5 in the Patuākhāli subdivision (455 pupils) and 9 in the Sāhābāzpur subdivision (911 pupils). The total expenditure is Rs. 99,341 or Rs. 12 per head. The income is obtained from fees (66·8 per cent.), grants (13·8 per cent.), and subscriptions and other sources (19·4 per cent.). Thirty-six of the total number were aided out of the public funds.

Middle Vernacular Schools.

There were 34 of these in 1874 with 1,737 pupils. In 1892 they numbered 46 with 2,171 pupils, but in 1910 they had been reduced to 31 with 1,669 pupils. Middle Schools are schools which teach up to the Middle Scholarship Examination, but in which the vernacular is the only recognised medium of instruction and forms the only course of studies. The decline in these schools illustrates the growing preference for English education among the people, not so much due to its intrinsic worth as to its superior market value. There are seven middle scholarships allotted to the district, of which one is reserved for Muhammadans. The cost of education of each pupil in these schools is Rs. 7·3 and 29 are aided out of the public funds.

PRIMARY EDUCATION.

Primary Schools have received a great extension of recent years. In 1856 only one such school with 26 pupils was aided, and in 1870 only 35 with 1,500 pupils. In 1874 they had increased to 235 with 6,678 pupils, while there were altogether in that year 304 schools with 8,530 pupils. In 1892 there were 127 upper primary schools with 4,597 pupils and 2,727 lower primary schools with 60,111 pupils. In 1910 the number of upper primary schools had increased to 239 and the number of their pupils to 11,845, while the number of lower primary schools had slightly decreased to 2,623, but the number of pupils had increased to 77,468. To these schools grants are given as follows :—by Government Rs. 9,286, by the District Board Rs. 78,784, by Municipalities Rs. 1,110. The total expenditure was Rs. 2,60,967, of which Rs. 1,17,599 is met by fees and Rs. 54,188 by subscription. The cost of educating each child is Rs. 3, of which Rs. 1·01 is provided by the public funds. There are 11 upper primary and 62 lower primary scholarships for boys. Education is still very much at the mercy of the parents. A proportion of the boys in most villages learn to read and write, but too many become fools and idlers from an idea that it is unbecoming a man who can read and write to work with his hands.

SPECIAL SCHOOLS.

There is only one technical school at Barisāl with 51 students and one commercial school at Barisāl with 6 students only. The latter is unaided, but a recognised institution ; the former is managed by Government. There are 4 training schools all managed by Government, with 72 pupils, and there are altogether 24 other public institutions with 673 pupils. Of private institutions one with 6 pupils (Kavindra College at Gailā) is classed as advanced and 39 with 924 pupils as elementary. These are mainly Sanskrit tols. There are also 29 schools teaching the Koran only with 565 pupils. Besides these there are 51 elementary schools with 1,077 pupils teaching only or mainly vernacular, and 26 schools with 2,996 pupils not conforming to departmental standards. In the marshes of Gaurnadi, several excellent missionary schools are maintained, while in the Sundarbans there are several Magh schools with about 200 pupils. In Barisāl itself both the Oxford Mission and the Baptist maintain special boys' and girls' schools. The object of the Baptist Mission is to train the boys who come from the villages in a trade ; but the Oxford Mission send their boys back to their villages, a few as preachers, but most as ordinary cultivators.

Hostels and boarding houses. A very little progress has been made in this direction. Altogether there are only 33 boarding houses in the district, one attached to Barisāl Zanana Mission School. The Bell Islamia Hostel, which was founded in 1895 by public subscription and the generosity of the Nawab of Dacca and has subsequently been aided by Government, is a very good institution and has accommodation for 52 students, who must be Muhammadans. It is an independent institution and not attached to any college or school.

Muhammadan education. The figures for Muhammadan education have already been given. The number of Muhammadan pupils in 1910 was 59,460 as compared with 41,412 in 1892; this is nearly 50 per cent. of the Muhammadan boys of a school-going age, and has much increased of late years. The number of Muhammadans in high schools was only 26 in 1874, but 588 in 1910 and of Muhammadans in middle schools 1,760 in 1910. The number of Muhammadans in the college is only 35. Secondary education has much increased of late years, as there were only 151 Muhammadan scholars in high schools and 492 in middle schools in 1892.

Female education. In 1874 there were only 6 girls' schools with 80 pupils in Bākarganj and in 1892 only 2·2 per cent. of girls of a school-going age were at school. In 1910 the percentage had increased to 8·4, the expansion being very great since the first partition in 1905. At first girls were taught in boys' schools and rewards were given to teachers for teaching girls. In 1885 4,294 girls were returned as reading in boys' schools; but between 1885 and 1895 the rules regarding grants-in-aid to *pāthsālās* were more strictly enforced and the number of girls under education soon dropped. In 1895, 4,209 girls were reading in boys' schools, while there were 113 girls' schools with 2,308 students. In 1911 the number of girls reading in boys' schools was 4,886 and the number of girls' schools 539 with 9,885 pupils. During the same period, the expenditure from public sources upon female education had risen from Rs. 2,418 to Rs. 9,202. Of the 14,771 girls receiving instruction in public schools, 34 were in the upper primary stage, 11 in the higher and 14,726 in the lower section of the lower primary stage. There is no prejudice against male teachers being employed in girls' schools, provided that they belong to the same school, nor is there any objection to boys and girls of tender years reading together. The best girls' schools in the district are the Barisāl School and the schools attached to the Oxford and the Baptist Mission. The Barisāl School proceeds on the ordinary lines and does not attempt to take girls beyond the upper primary stage. The two others, however, educate some of their girls far beyond that standard, chiefly to take their place as teachers in later years.

PUBLIC EXPENDITURE ON EDUCATION.

In 1850-51 the expenditure on education by Government was only Rs. 360 and in 1870-71 only Rs. 34,164. By 1901-02 the total expenditure had become Rs. 3,32,458, of which Rs. 19,119 were obtained from Government, Rs. 42,928 from the District Board and Rs. 1,158 from Municipalities. Rs. 1,75,036 was supplied by fees and Rs. 94,217 by other private sources. In 1914 the expenditure had grown to Rs. 6,44,049, of which Rs. 1,18,966 was obtained from Government, Rs. 96,038 from the District Board and Rs. 1,700 from the Municipalities. Fees accounted for Rs. 3,35,520 and other private sources, chiefly subscriptions, for Rs. 91,825. Of the total expenditure Rs. 52,980 was incurred in colleges, Rs. 1,62,932 in high schools, Rs. 1,03,248 in middle English schools, Rs. 11,227 in middle vernacular schools, Rs. 45,271 in upper primary schools, Rs. 2,38,463 in lower primary schools, and Rs. 6,024 in scholarships and Rs. 23,904 in special schools.

CHAPTER XIV.

GAZETTEER.

ĀILĀ-PHULJHURI.—These are two large villages in the Amtali thana. Both the villages were full of jungle when they were first settled in perpetuity in 1805 with an area of 44,000 acres at a small revenue of Rs. 372. The Collector of Dacca wrote that from the information which he had been able to gather through his officers, the land did not appear to be capable, when brought into cultivation, of bearing a higher assessment. The "officer" who gave the information was the real applicant for the lease, the Naib of Buzrugumedpur. He subsequently absconded and was prosecuted for the embezzlement of Rs. 70,000. Seven years after the grant was made, his family sold it to the ancestor of the present Nawab of Dacca for Rs. 21,000. The boundaries in the patta were vague. The owner sued Government, without success, for a further sixty thousand acres. The long litigation which began in 1830 ended in 1870.

The estate brings in about a lakh of rupees to the Nawab of Dacca.

There is a prosperous *hāt* in Phuljhuri.

ĀLIPUR—Is in thana Galāchipā and belongs to the Bāuphal zamindars, who made a survey of the mauza in 1896-97 and took kabuliats in 1897-98 from the tenants for amounts double and in some cases more than double of the rents previously paid by the tenants. The grounds of increase set forth in the kabuliats comprise almost all the grounds on which the Tenancy Act allows an enhancement of rent, but it is evident from the kabuliats that the landlords relied on an alleged increase in the area of the holdings as the rents shown in the kabuliats purported to be calculated on the prevailing rates of the village. At the time of attestation the Assistant Settlement Officer submitted to the Settlement Officer a note for orders with the remark that the enhancements were so excessive that the tenants were scarcely able to bear them. The Settlement Officer ordered the old rents to be recorded unless the landlords could prove by evidence that the alleged increase in area had actually taken place. Moreover, it was found on enquiry that the kabuliats were obtained by intimidation, that the increase in area of the different holdings was much less than alleged and that the prevailing rates mentioned in the kabuliats were not the true prevailing rates. It was found also by an examination of the *jama-wasil-baki* papers of the landlords that very few tenants had paid the enhanced rent and most of them were in arrears. The landlords brought an objection under section 103A, which was decided by the Settlement Officer, Mr. Beatson Bell, who refused to record enhanced rent on the ground that the increase in area alleged in the kabuliats had not been proved. The landlords then went to the Civil Courts, filing 24 suits for arrears of rent, which were decided together on the 25th April 1905. The Munsiff decreed the suits in full. He held that intimidation had not been proved and that, in view of the kabuliats executed, the burden of proof in the matter of area now rested in the tenants. The tenants appealed against this decree, but all the appeals were dismissed in default because their legal adviser did not appear on the day fixed for hearing owing to some misunderstanding with his clients. In due course the holdings were sold up in execution of the decree and purchased by the landlords through their agent and other *benamdars*. Khas possession was then taken of the land. The tenants were evicted in a body and their houses were burnt down and destroyed, together with such of their property as was found in them. Complete disorder reigned in the village, and for several years the land was never properly cultivated. New tenants could not be found to replace the evicted tenants, and the landlords were untimately compelled to take back the tenants whom they had ejected.

Āmtali Thana.—One of the four thanas in the subdivision of Patuākhāli. It comprises an area of 337 square miles. The police-station is situated at Chāwrā, a Government estate about 25 miles to the south of Patuākhāli. Formerly the station was at Gulishakhāli from which it was removed to Āmtali in 1902. The total population of the thana is 144,952 consisting of 16,890 Hindus, 120,449 Muhammadans and 7,613 others. The latter are chiefly Magh settlers, who are Buddhists by religion. The police-station of Bargunā, now an independent thana, was formerly an outpost under this thana. There are two charitable dispensaries, seven post offices, one registration office, one Muhammadan marriage registration office and two khas mahal Circle offices in this thana. There is also the colonization office at Khepupārā. The most important of the Sundarbans estates are under the jurisdiction of this thana.

BAGĀ.—This is an important rice mart for the Calcutta trade. It is situated on the Lohāliā river in thana Bāuphal, Patuākhāli subdivision. Rice merchants purchase rice in January and February and store it here in big granaries called *golās*. The rice is exported to Calcutta, generally during the rains, in the long and low bālām boats of Chittagong and the high and roomy *marua* (up-country) boats. The Bārisāl-Patuākhāli steamer service calls here daily, and there is a good road to Bāuphal and Kālāiā. It has also a combined post and telegraph office.

BĀKARGANJ.—A village with a big mart in the Sadar subdivision, situated about 13 miles to the south-east of Barisāl near the junction of the Krishnakāti and Khairabad rivers. The name is derived from Āgā Bākar, who was a servant of the Nawab of Murshidabad and was the proprietor of parganā Buzrugumedpur and 11½ annas of Selimābād. He had his tahsil cutchari in this village. It was formerly the headquarters town of the district. Since 1801 the headquarters have been transferred to Barisāl. All that remains of the old town is a side wall of what was once the Magistrate's Court and another wall which probably belonged to the Jail. The police-station of Bākarganj is now located within the site of the old town. The market here is largely attended, the principal commodity being rice, the best that can be obtained in the district. The Portuguese settlement of Sibpur is situated three miles to the south of this village. The road between the two places is one of the oldest in the district.

BĀKARGANJ THANA.—This thana is in the Sadar subdivision. The police-station is at Bākarganj, the former headquarters of the district. It was established in 1874 and comprised an area of 153 square miles. It has a population of 43,111 Hindus, 98,533 Muhammadans and 843 Christians, making a total of 142,487. There are some places containing interesting old relics in this thana, the most important of them being Bibichini, Nyamati, Sibpur and Bākarganj. This thana is famous for its rice, the best grown in this district. There are one registration office, thirteen post offices, one combined post and telegraph office and two charitable dispensaries in this thana.

BĀKLĀ.—The ancient name for the tract of country which is now Bākarganj. Bāklā (Ismailpur) was a Sirkar in Todar Mull's assessment of 1582 A.D. and is described by Abul Fazl in the "Ain-i-Akbari" as being overwhelmed by an inundation, apparently a cyclone, in 1584 A.D. It was visited and briefly described by Ralph Fitch in 1586. It is also mentioned in the Missionary report of the Portuguese priest Nicolas Pimenta (see "Purchas's Pilgrimage", V, p. 513) as having been visited by another priest, Malchior De Fonseca, who was well received by the boy-king. Du Jarric says that the kingdom of Bacola was shortly afterwards destroyed by the king of Arracan, apparently in revenge for aid given to the Portuguese adventurer Gonzales, as related by Faria of Sousa in his "Asia Portuguesa" (published in 1666). Later the name occurs in a story told of one of the more recent Rajas of Chandradwip, Udai Narain, who was deprived forcibly of his zamindari by the Mazumdars of Chakhār, whose beautiful sister was married to the Nawab at Dacca. Udai Narain pleaded his cause before the Nawab at Dacca and was asked to exhibit his prowess in a fight in the arena with a tiger, which he killed. He craved a boon and the Nawab's wife (the Mazumdar's sister) scornfully threw him the rind of a plantain (Bengali bāklā) which she was eating. Picking it up, he gracefully thanked the Nawab for restoring his zamindari of Bāklā to him. The name Bāklā has now disappeared, and if there was ever a town of that name, it has "left not a rack behind." The compound Bāklā-Chandrawip is still, however, employed to indicate the pargana.

Bamna.—Joar Bamna Bāmnā in thana Matbaria is the largest of the shikmi mahals which appertained to pargana Buzrugumedpur. The joar covers an area of about 33 square miles, lying on the west bank of the river Biskhali. It contains 45 villages and is now possessed by a Muhammadan family, the Bāmnā Chaudhuris. It was originally entered in the name of an Armenian named Khajat Michael and is described in the partition papers of Mr. Thompson as "Mudafat Khajat Michael." After the purchase of the pargana by Government one Muhammad Safi got settlement of this joar from the Board in 1809 at the very low revenue of Rs. 1,165 for seven years. The tradition is that he was originally a salt peon and this is supported by the fact of his appearing in the official papers as Muhammad Safi jamadar. The estate continued to be under temporary settlement up to 1844, when it was sold for arrears of revenue and was settled as a taluk in perpetuity at an annual revenue of Rs. 19,488. The Nawab of Dacca now owns by purchase a share in the taluki right; the remaining shares, as well as most of the patnis which cover the joar, are still in possession of the descendants of Muhammad Safi. The newly created thana of Bāmnā, formerly an outpost under the Matbaria thana, has its headquarters at Bāmnā. It is served by a feeder line of steamers from Jhālakāti to Bargunā.

BĀNARIPĀRĀ.—A village in thana Swarupkāti, subdivision Pirozpur, about 17 miles south-west of Barisāl. There is a District Board road running from Barisāl to the village. It is one of the most thickly populated villages in the district. The area of the village is 248 acres or less than half a square mile with a population of 2,238. The special feature of the village is that there is no paddy land and that the houses cluster together so closely that there is hardly any space between one homestead and another. There are a high English school, charitable dispensary and a combined post and telegraph office at Bānaripārā. The Kayasthas (Guha Thakurtas) of the village are Kulins of the highest class.

The weavers of the village weave *dhotis* of the Dacca pattern, which still command a sale. A fair is held here in the month of December. It lasts for about a month and is attended by thousands of persons.

BĀRAIKARAN.—A village in thana Nalchhiti, Sadar subdivision. The local tradition points to this village as the old headquarters of the district and this is supported by a reference, in the decree for the resumption of the Bāraikaran char, to a piece of land which had originally been the cutchari of Mr. Christophêr Keating, who was Civil Judge of Bākarganj in 1785. The district headquarters were removed from this place to Bākarganj in 17-3, and in 1801 they were removed to Barisāl. The ancient importance of Bāraikaran is also shown by the fact that it was the site of the police-station which was not removed from here to Nalchhiti until 1824.

BARGUNĀ.—Chak Bargunā is a resumed Sundarbans estate almost entirely reclaimed from forest. It was resumed by an order of the Presidency Commissioner dated the 25th July 1856. It was claimed by the Nawab of Dacca as belonging to Āilā-Phuljhuri, but was ultimately decreed to Government by the Privy Council in 1870. It is the key to the Bākarganj Sundarbans and is the healthiest of the Sundarbans estates.

There is a Khas Mahal Tashil cutchari under the supervision of a Sub-Deputy Collector (Circle Officer), a charitable dispensary, a middle madrasa school and a post office. There is also a police-station. The *hāt* (market) is largely attended and fairly prosperous, the principal export being rice and the principal imports corrugated-iron, sugar, timber, oil, etc. Bargunā is served by a feeder steamer service connected with Jhālakāti.

BARHĀNUDDIN THANA.—This thana is in the subdivision of Dakhin Sāhābāzpur and comprises the southern half of the subdivision. The headquarters station of the thana is at Barhānuddin *hāt*. It comprises an area of 402 square miles with a population of 27,698 Hindus and 123,542 Muhammadans. The police-station at Tazumuddin, now an independent thana, was formerly an outpost under this thana. There are one registration office and 10 post offices including two combined post and telegraph offices in this thana. It has three charitable dispensaries, one at Barhānuddin, one at Tazumaddin and a third at Lalmohan. The South Bhola Khas Tahsil circle with headquarters at Lalmohan is comprised in this thana.

BĀRISAL SUBDIVISION.—Headquarters subdivision of the district, extending over 1,073 square miles in the north of the district. It is bounded on the north by the Madaripur subdivision of the Faridpur district, on the south by the subdivision of Patuākhāli, on the east by the river Ilsha or the Tetulia and on the west by the subdivision of Pirozpur. Its length from north to south is almost equal to its breadth from east to west. A considerable part of the subdivision consists of lowlying marshes in thanas Gaurnadi and Jhālakāti. It is intersected by various streams and rivers, the principal of which are the Tarki, Sabipur, Āriāl Khān and the Nayā Noābhāngāni. The river Āriāl Khān enters the district from Faridpur in two main channels, the western is called the Tarki and the eastern the Ārial Khān, which falls into the Ilsā, pursuing a south-easterly course. The southern portion of this river is called the Kālābadar. Nayā Noābhāngani issuing from the Meghnā flows almost due west for some miles and then separates into two channels which flow southwards; the eastern is called the Nayā Noābhāngani and the western the Safipur river. The upper part of the river Bishkāli, which is fed by many streams in the subdivision, lies in the south of the subdivision.

The subdivision comprises the thanas of Barisāl, Mehendiganj, Gaurnadi, Jhālakāti, Nalchhiti and Bākarganj. Its population, according to the census of 1911, is 985,184, the density being 918 to a square mile. It contains the towns of Barisāl, Jhālakāti and Nalchhiti and its headquarters are at Barisāl. The headquarters are connected by raised roads with Gaurnadi, Mādhabpāsā, Nabagram, Jhālakāti, Nalchhiti and Patuākhāli.

BARISĀL THANA—In the Sadar subdivision. It comprises the east central part of the subdivision. It extends over an area of 160 square miles and has a population of 153,397 persons, consisting of 103,607 Muhammadans, 48,750 Hindus and 1,040 others. The density is 958 to a square mile. The thana is intersected by many streams and there are some District Board roads, the principal of which are the Barisāl-Gaurnadi road, the Barisāl-Bānaripārā road and the Barisāl Jhālakāti road. The police-station is at Barisāl, the headquarters of the district. A new thana with a police-station at Babuganj has been created out of a portion of this thana in the north. Besides the post office at Barisāl there are 17 post offices including 2 combined post and telegraph offices in the thana. There are also a Special Sub-Registrar's office, a marriage registrar's office, and a charitable dispensary in the thana.

BARISĀL TOWN.—The headquarters station and the chief town of the district of Bākarganj. Geographically it is situated in 22° 41′ north latitude and 90° 24′ east longitude. It stands on the western bank of a river locally known as Kirtan Khola, which is an off-shoot of the Āriāl Khān river. By the river route it is about 183 miles due east from Calcutta, 75 miles from Dacca and rather more than 100 miles from the sea.

The first headquarters station was at Baraikaran, a village to the west of the present Nalchhiti police-station. Early records describe the district as "Zilla Baraikaran" under Dacca Jalalpur. Subsequently the headquarters station was transferred to Bākarganj, a place close to Sibpur, the old Portuguese settlement, where there is still a Portuguese Church. The transfer to Barisāl took place in 1801 under the magistracy of Mr. Wintle. In 1801 Barisāl was a small village consisting of a few acres of land owned by a Muhammadan family. This village is a distinct pargana called the "Gird Bandar," which appears to have been formed out of pargana Chandradwip. Gird Bandar changed hands several times. In 1831 it was the property of Babu Ram Kanai Roy, the Government Pleader. From him Government took a permanent lease of the land on which all the present offices have been built.

A feature of Barisāl is the "Strand Road," which runs along the bank of the river. It was probably constructed by Mr. Wintle. One of the bridges on the Strand Road contains a tablet stating that the bridge was rebuilt in 1811 by Mr. John Battye, the then Magistrate. A gentleman named Chapman incidentally mentions in a letter dated 22nd May 1819 that he rode along this road.

As the town expanded it became necessary to include other villages. In addition to Barisāl proper the town now extends to Bagura-Alekanda, Amanatganj and Kaunia.

Before the Municipal Act of 1876 the affairs of the town were managed by the Town Committee under Act VI of 1868 (B.C.) with the District Magistrate as its Chairman. The Municipal area is now about 7½ square miles. In point of population Barisāl stands third among the towns of the Dacca Division. The population of Barisāl was 12,501 in 1872, 13,186 in 1881, 15,482 in 1891 and 18,978 in 1901. The census of 1911 recorded the population as 22,473, consisting of 12,614 Hindus, 8,952 Muhammadans, 71 Brahmos, 6 Buddhists, 829 Christians and 1 Animist. The Municipality has an income which in 1914 amounted to Rs. 60,324 from all sources. It maintains 16 miles of road, of which 15 miles are metalled. The town has water-works which were inaugurated during the magistracy of Mr. Weston and were opened in 1912. The town has a good system of natural drainage, the khals being flushed by the tides. The charitable dispensary was originally established in 1847. It was rebuilt on a new site in 1912 with many modern improvements. In 1915 the out-patients numbered 20,986 and the in-patients 834. As regards religious buildings, Barisāl has 8 Hindu temples, 7 Muhammadan mosques and a *mandir* of the Brahmo Samaj. The town is also a centre of missionary effort on the part of Oxford Anglicans, Roman Catholics and Baptists. The station church was built in 1845, the Roman Catholic Church about 1845, the Baptist Church in 1829 and the Oxford Mission Church in 1904. Barisāl had formerly two private colleges affiliated to Calcutta University, the Raj Chandra College and the Braja Mohan College. The former disappeared in 1904. The latter still continues. It was founded by Babu Aswini Kumar Dutta and is named after his father. It is now managed by a Committee, of which the District Magistrate is President, and is aided by Government with establishment grants. Barisāl has two high schools, namely, the Zilla School, which was founded during the magistracy of Mr. R. C. Dutta, and the Braja Mohan School, which is connected with the College of the same name. There are also many other educational institutions in Barisāl, among which may be mentioned the excellent schools attached to the Oxford and Baptist Missions, the Girls' School, the Deaf and Dumb School, and the Bell Islamia Boarding House for

Muhammadan boys. Although Barisāl is not a trading centre, it is an important point in the steamer system of Eastern Bengal. There are no railways in the district. For long Barisāl could only be reached by country boats or *budgerows*. In 1884 a steamer service between Barisāl and Khulna (the nearest railway town) was opened by the Bengal Central Flotilla Company. In 1896 the steamer service was taken over by the "Joint Companies," namely, the "India General" and the "Rivers Steam." These companies have now an agency and a workshop at Barisāl, in charge of one of their senior officers. They maintain lines with branch in every direction from Barisāl as the central point.

Barisāl has a public library, which was founded by Mr. Kemp, the District Judge, in 1855. It has also a public park which was constructed by subscriptions during the magistracy of Mr. Beatson Bell to celebrate the visit of Sir Alexander Mackenzie, Lieutenant-Governor of Bengal, in 1896.

BARSĀKĀTI.—A village in thana Swarupkāti. The village is the residence of timber merchants who principally deal in *sundari* logs. Large cargo boats are made here.

BĀSANDĀ.—A village in thana Jhālakāti, Sadar subdivision, about two miles from Jhālakāti. The Mohalanabises of the village are among the principal taluqdars in the pargana of Selimābād. There is a High English School in the village.

BĀTĀJOR.—A village in thana Gaurnadi, Sadar subdivision. It is 17 miles from Barisāl. The road leading to Madaripur from Barisāl passes through this village. The village Harhar which is locally known as Bātājor is the native village of two famous cousins and rivals, namely, Dwarka Nath Datta, for six years Vice-Chairman of the District Board, and Babu Aswini Kumar Dutt, a political leader in Bengal and founder of the "Brajamohan Institution." During the Jagatdhatri Pujas a fair meets here. It lasts for seven days and is attended by thousands of persons. There is an old tank in the village said to have been dug by the Maghs in 1657. It is locally known by the name of *Magher Aski*. The village has a charitable dispensary and a combined post and telegraph office. There is a daily market at Bātājor.

BĀUPHAL THANA.—This thana in the subdivision of Patuākhāli is situated to the south-east of Barisāl. The police-station is at Bāuphal on the bank of the Kālāiā river. It is found to have been in existence before 1812 and comprises an area of 161 square miles. The total population is 120,255, consisting of 21,324 Hindus, 98,918 Muhammadans and 13 others

There are one registration office, a combined post and telegraph office and a charitable dispensary at Pāuphal and a charitable dispensary and a post office at Kanakdia in this thana. The total number of post offices in the thana is six. The great storm of 1822 was most felt in this thana where 10,984 lives are said to have been lost. Kachuā, which according to tradition was the former seat of the Rajas of Chandradwip or Bāklā, is in this thana.

The land in this thana is fertile and well cultivated, the pulses being particularly good.

BĀUKĀTI—A village in thana Jhālakāti, Sadar subdivision. It is three miles off Jhālakāti and stands on the District Board road from Jhālakāti to Kowkhali. The village has a reputation as the residence of thieves.

BHĀNDĀRIĀ THANA.—This thana is in the subdivision of Pirozpur and comprises a large tract between the Biskhali and the Baleswar rivers. The police-station is located at Bhāndāriā *hāt* on the bank of a small river, which is an offshoot of the Kāchā river. The thana was established in the year 1882. It comprises an area of 122 square miles with a population of 29,433 Hindus and 70,360 Muhammadans. The thana has one charitable dispensary and one registration office, both at Bhāndāriā. It has four post offices including one combined post and telegraph office. It contains many *bils* (marshes), which are gradually drying up and being brought under cultivation. *Pani kachu* (water arum) is grown in abundance in this thana.

BHOLĀ THANA.—In the subdivision of Dakhin Sāhābāzpur. It comprises the northern half of the island of Sāhābāzpur. The police-station was formerly at Daulatkhān, which was also the headquarters station of the subdivision. After the flood of 1876 the station along with the subdivisional headquarters was transferred to Bholā, an outpost being left at Daulatkhān. This outpost has recently been converted into an independent thana. The area of the thana including that of the outpost is 252 square miles with a population of 20,119 Hindus and 14,177 Muhammadans. There are two charitable dispensaries, one at Bholā and the other at Daulatkhān, two registration offices and seven post offices including two combined post and telegraph offices. There are also two khas tahsil offices, one at Jaynagar and the other at Bairagia under a Sub-Deputy Collector (Circle Officer of North Bholā).

BHOLĀ VILLAGE.—The village of Bholā, the headquarters of the subdivision Dakhin Sāhābāzpur, was established in the year 1877, immediately after the great cyclone of 1876. The site was selected by the late Mr. R. C. Dutt, the then Subdivisional Officer. At the time of acquisition, the village consisted of paddy fields by the side of a big khal. The village is gradually increasing on all sides both in area and population, and has extended on the other side of the khal. There is a rectangular embankment round the headquarters. The place is of some importance on account of its trade in betelnuts, chillies, cocoanuts, jute and betel leaves. Besides the subdivisional office, there are two Munsiffs' courts, a sub-registry office, jail, thana, high school, charitable dispensary and a combined post and telegraph office. There is a Local Board office in the town with the Subdivisional Officer as Chairman. There is no Municipality at Bholā.

BIBICHINI.—A small village in Bakārganj thana in which there is an old mosque raised upon an artificial mound of considerable size. The mosque is said to have been built by Bibichini, sister of Niamatulla, who founded the large neighbouring village of Niamati (population 4,741), a flourishing mart with a commanding position on the Biskhali river.

BUZRUGUMEDPUR PARGANA.—This is an old pargana and was formerly included in Sarkar Bazuhā. It is said to derive its name from Buzrugumed Khan, son of Shaista Khan, who governed Bengal in the latter half of the seventeenth century. Subsequently it passed into the hands of Agā Bākar. On Agā Bākar's death, it became the property of Raja Raj Ballabh.

The pargana was partitioned into five shares during the time of the grandchildren of Raja Raj Ballabh. In 1792 an engagement was made for eight years ending in 1799. The pargana was sold for arrears of revenue and purchased by Government in 1799. In 1801 all the dependent tāluks were sold and thereafter treated as practically independent, though Government never formally parted with the proprietary right. The chakran (service) lands were resumed by Government and became a scattered khas mahal known as "Chakran Bazyafti." The tāluks are 407 in number. The largest is called Joar Ramna-Bamna, but the most interesting as regards its origin is the tāluk Padrian or mission tāluk of Sibpur. It was originally granted by Raj Ballabh Sen to some Christians from Bandel. It is still managed by a resident priest, whose flock inhabit the tāluk.

CHANDRADWIP PARGANA.—Chandradwip was one of the four parganas into which Sarkar Bāklā was divided at the time of Todar Mull's settlement. At that time it seems to have been known by the name of Ismailpur or Bāklā, and it appears that Abul Fazl used the term Bāklā as synonymous with Chandradwip. Chandradwip belonged from early time to a Hindu family of the Kayastha caste who bore the title of Raja. The name Chandradwip means *island of Chandra* and possibly dates back to a time when a great part of the district was covered by the sea. Many stories are told in connection with the name Chandradwip. According to one story it was founded by a Brahman of the name of Chandra, who came from the Bikrampur pargana, obtained the pargana from the goddess Bhagabati and called it after his own name. According to another story, the pargana was founded by one Ram Nath Danuj Mardan De, disciple of a great ascetic of the name of Chandra Sekhar Chakravartti. One night, when the ascetic was asleep in his boat, he was told in a dream by the goddess Kali that there was some images lying under water near his boat and that he should secure them. Next morning he made his disciple dive twice into the water. Each time a stone image was brought up. The two images he brought up were those of Katyayani and Madan Gopal. Images of these deities sculptured in black stone are still worshiped at Madhabpasa, the present capital of the pargana. Chandra Sekhar predicted to his disciple that the sea would one day be dry land and that he would be the Raja of it. He also bade him call it after the name of his preceptor.

The old seat of the family was at Kachuā, a village on the west bank of the river Tetulia, in thana Bāuphal, subdivision Patuākhāli. According to one tradition the family was forced to leave Kachuā on account of the incursions of the Maghs, and according to another tradition they left it owing to the encroachment of the river. There are still to be found some remains of the old Rajbari. Raja Ram Nath Danuj Mardan De was succeeded by his son Ram Ballabh. Ram Ballabh was followed by Sri Ballabh, Hari Ballabh and finally by Krishna Ballabh. Krishna Ballabh had no sons and with him therefore the direct male line became extinct. Krishna Ballabh was succeeded by Sib Nanda, son of his daughter Kamala. The "Basu dynasty" thus began. Kandarpa Narayan, third in descent from Sib Nanda, removed from Kachuā and settled at Madhabpasa, the modern seat of the Chandradwip family, about the year 1590. Kandarpa Narayan was succeeded by his son Ram Chandra, who married a daughter of the famous Raja Pratapaditya of Jessore. This Ram Chandra is in all probability the boy-king whom the Jesuit Fonseca speaks of as mild, amiable and intelligent though only nine years old.

Tradition says that owing to a hitch with his father-in-law, Ram Chandra abandoned his first wife, who landed at a place since called "Bau Thakurani's Hat", when the festivities of Ram Chandra's second marriage were being celebrated. This forms the theme of a novel called "Bau Thakurani's Hat" by Sir Rabindra Nath Tagore. Ram Chandra was succeeded by Kirti Narayan, who, like several other Hindus in history, is said to have lost his caste by smelling a Musalman's dinner. He was succeeded by his brother Basudeb, who in his turn was succeeded by Kirti Narayan's son Pratap Narayan. With Prem Narayan, who succeeded Pratap Narayan, the Basu family became extinct and was replaced by the Mitra family. Prem Narayan was succeeded by his son-in-law Gouri Charan Mitra, whose son Uday Narayan was expelled by Mendi Mazumdar and Sharfuddin Mazumdar of Chakhar. Uday Narayan, however, succeeded in recovering his zamindari by a clever feat (see Bāklā). Jay Narayan, third in descent from Uday Narayan, was dispossessed by a servant, Sankar Baksi. Jay Narayan's mother recovered the zamindari with the help of the famous Ganga Gobinda Singh of Kandi. The cost of recovering the zamindari was very heavy, and this and the digging of a large tank near Madhabpasa, which is called Durga Sagar after the Rani, are said to have impoverished the estate. Jay Narayan *alias* Durga Kumar Narayan was the last zamindar, as in his time, in 1799, the Chandradwip pargana was sold by the Collector for arrears of revenue. Thus the famous pargana of Chandradwip or Bāklā, which once comprised the greater portion of the modern district of Bākarganj and consisted of 22 dependent parganas, ultimately passed away from the Kayasth Raj family. The pargana was sold in shares, the largest share falling to the grocer (mudi) of the Raja. The descendants of the grocer still retain their purchase. They reside at Mādhabpāsā, some of them in prosperous circumstances. The descendants of the Raja also reside there in great poverty, retaining nothing but a little rent-free land.

In the settlement of Todar Mull, the revenue of Sarkar Bāklā is put down at Rs. 1,08,699. In 1728 the revenue of the pargana Chandradwip was only Rs. 6,608. This represents the khalsa or exchequer revenue, the greater portion of the pargana having been held rent free as jāigir on condition of the zamindar's supplying boats and crew to the Dacca flotilla. In 1758 the revenue was Rs. 68,509, of which only Rs. 1,170 was khalsa. In 1790 the Board directed the Collector,

Mr. Douglas, to make the decennial settlement of Chandradwip at a revenue of Rs. 89,725. Three years after, Mr. Douglas proposed that the revenue for the remaining period of the decennial settlement, viz., from 1793 to 1799 should be Rs. 87,652-1-8, and this was approved by the Board and the Governor General. The Raja Jay Narayan did not engage for the revenue. The zamindari having fallen into arrears was sold as already stated in 1799. Apart from the grocer, the purchasers were two Armenians named Panioty and one Dal Singh of Dacca. The share of the Panioty brothers has passed to other hands, but the share of Dal Singh (like the share of the grocer) is still in the family. The present revenue of the zamindari is Rs. 82,495.

CHARĀMUDDIN.—A village in thana Bākarganj, subdivision Sadar. It is about 8 miles to the south-east of Barisāl. The finest Bākarganj *bālām* rice is grown in the places round about Charāmuddin and sold in the local market. Asmat Ali Khan Chaudhuri of Charāmuddin was a famous landholder, more feared than loved by his tenantry. His son Ismail Khan Chaudhari became a member of the Provincial Legislative Council.

CHAR BHUTĀ AND CHAR FASSON.—These are Government estates situated in the south of the Dakhin Sāhābāzpur subdivision. Char Bhutā was resumed in 1839. Shortly after resumption an ābādkāri tāluk was granted for the purpose of reclaiming thousand bighas, under pain of forfeiture if the conditions of clearance were not fulfilled. They were not fulfilled and the lease was forfeited; but on appeal the Board of Revenue "as an act of grace" continued the lease to the ābādkār. Subsequently the ābādkār sued Government for the large accretions on the south as land which had been gained from the sea since the creation of the tāluk and won his suit, although Kelso's map prepared before the grant of the lease shows that the accretion was then already in existence. The case was mismanaged in the Collectorate and no appeal was lodged against the decree. A second char formed further south in the Bay of Bengal, of which Government took possession as an island. The island was named Char Fasson after the then Collector. For this the talukdar again sued in 1895 in suit No. 28 of 1895 claiming it as an accretion to the taluk and again won his suit, as the witnesses upon whom the State relied were all tenants of the talukdar. A third island, Char Madras, again formed during the course of the settlement proceedings, of which, after a careful enquiry into the fordability of the channel, Government took possession as an island. The talukdar claimed it as an accretion and attempted to take forcible possession of it, compelling the Collector to send down a force of Gurkha Military Police to maintain the possession of Government. The talukdar has subsequently sued Government for this island also as an accretion to his taluk. As a result of these proceedings the little lease of 330 acres has swollen into a huge estate of nearly 28,000 acres and has opened out like a fan at the southern end of Sāhābāzpur, shutting out the Government estates from access to the Bay of Bengal and thus swallowing all of the enormous accretions which are annually gained from the sea. Since 1878 the land thus gained from the sea has measured 1 square mile a year. In the last revision, the estate has been divided into two parts—Char Bhutā with an area of 8,157 acres representing the land which was in existence at the time of the last settlement, and Char Fasson with an area of 19,726 acres representing the subsequent accretion. The old portion of Char Bhutā is under Hāolādāri Settlement and has been brought completely under cultivation. Of the 51 hāolās in the estate four were found to be fictitious and were merged in the taluk. Six more belong to the talukdar's aged mother or minor son. The purpose of the creation of these hāolās was to obtain for the talukdar the additional profits allowed to hāolādārs. Many of the other hāolādārs were reclaimers of the land and they have granted a large number of nim hāolās, whose holders are resident in the estate. The allowances given to hāolādārs and divisible as usual with nim hāolādārs were 20 per cent. if not resident and 25 per cent. if resident; but when the hāolādār was the talukdar himself in his various disguises as his aged mother or his minor son, the allowance was reduced to 5 per cent. The talukdar was granted 15 per cent. on his own collection as the profits of his taluki right, but on appeal this was converted into a rate of 14 annas per bigha of cultivated and culturable land. The existing rents, of all the raiyats in the estate which were leased on contract were maintained without alteration. The cultivators for the most part do not suffer from overwork. It is true that they plough their own lands, but they hire men from Noākhāli to transplant, weed, reap and thresh. The revenue of Char Bhutā was increased from Rs. 4,509 to Rs. 20,474 by this assessment. The previous assessment took place immediately after the destruction wrought by the great wave of 1876 and was on that account very generous in its terms. Moreover, three-fourths of the whole area was uncultivated in 1878, and though it has since been brought under cultivation, no part of the rental had hitherto come into the treasury. It should be added that the talukdar by his own conduct deserved no consideration. At a second and unexpected survey made in 1910, it was found that the talukdar has deliberately kept a large amount of cultivated land fallow during the original survey of 1905 in order to reduce his assessment. The talukdar claimed to hold at a fixed rate of rent (7¾ annas per bigha) on a construction of the terms of the kabuliat which he gave in 1880. The claim was rejected. Whatever the legal construction of the terms of the documents may be it is clear that the State at no time intended to give the talukdar a lease at a fixed rate of rent. The terms of the kabuliat were drawn out in English by the Commissioner of the Dacca Division and were subsequently translated into the Bengali edition, which the talukdar signed. It is significant that there is a mistranslation in the Bengali, and that it is upon the clause containing the mistranslation that the talukdar relies in claiming to hold at a fixed rate of rent.

Char Fasson contains 3,830 acres of cultivation and 12,762 acres of culturable jungle and grass besides 1,500 acres of river and stream and 905 acres of sand and mud. There were two fictitious hāolās covering a large area in the estate, but after careful proceedings they were cancelled. In the cultivated area there are a large number of nim hāolādārs and osat nim hāolādārs who cultivate most of their lands and sublet a part to raiyats at Rs. 3 per acre. The tenure-holders were allowed 25 per cent. if resident and 20 per cent. if non-resident as profit, and were assessed at Rs. 2-4 and Rs. 2-6¾ per acre on land which they themselves cultivated. During the course of assessment it was found that talukdar had deliberately refrained from granting leases in the char for several years, although there was a great demand for land from cultivators whose holdings had been diluviated on the eastern side of Sāhābāzpur. In order to test the truth of the information, applications were invited at short notice from *bonâ fide* cultivators who were prepared to take up land in the char paying rent at Rs. 3 per acre for 1910. In two days 636 cultivators applied for 9,300 acres, prepared to pay a year's rent in advance and to bring the land under cultivation forthwith. The lists were then closed, although applications were still coming in. The lease of the talukdar is an ābādkāri lease, that is, a lease for the purpose of reclaiming waste. In face of such clear evidence as to the demand for the land and refusal of the talukdar to grant leases, it was obvious that the whole purpose of the lease was defeated by his conduct. It was, therefore, decided to assess the whole of the culturable waste at 12 annas a bigha or 75 per cent. of its letting value, a period of three years' grace for the discovery of tenants being granted in half the area and a period of six years in the other half. The talukdar was assessed at the same rate in the cultivated area also. The revenue of the char under these arrangements became Rs. 10,059 in 1910, Rs. 24,536 in 1913 and Rs. 39,013 in 1916. The talukdar has instituted a suit in the Civil Court to substantiate his claim to hold the char at a fixed rate of rent and for possession of Char Madras as accretion to his taluk. The talukdar is now anxious to settle the matter amicably and in order to avoid costly litigation he has thrown himself upon the mercy of Government with a prayer that he may be allowed a permanent settlement of the area which was settled with him in 1878-79 as Char Bhutā at an annual revenue of Rs. 4,000 and that he is ready to give up Char Fasson as well as his claim on Char Madras. The whole matter is now under consideration of the Government.

CHĀWRĀ.—It originally consisted of two estates, the smaller (T. No. 4802) measuring only 220 acres and comprising the land which some Maghs had brought under cultivation before resumption, the larger estate consisting of virgin forest which was after resumption reclaimed by the D'Silva family, who also purchased the smaller estate from the Maghs. The Maghs then abandoned the estate. The reclamation was not made under any authorized forest grant, but the Sundarbans Officer also treated the D'Silvas as talukdars of a resumed mahal. At the last settlement made in 1869, the whole of the forest had been reclaimed and all but 6 per cent. of the land was classified as *hasil*. At the present time, of 7,727 acres of land, 6,279 acres are under cultivation, 657 acres homestead and garden, 473 acres pasture and only 264 culturable fallow. The D'Silva talukdars had sublet the estate to 24 tenure-holders and they in turn to many smaller middlemen, who were mostly absentees and money-lenders. The tenure-holders were not only very troublesome, but paid rent most irregularly to the talukdar. At the last settlement the tenure-holders were at first excluded, but on appeal they were admitted for the term of the settlement on condition that they should have no claim to resettlement and that they should not increase the rent of the cultivators. They protested against these terms to the local Government, but without success. In the present settlement it was found that the rents of the cultivators had not merely been increased, but had often been doubled or trebled. With the sanction of the Board of Revenue the tenures were terminated in 1909 and such of the tenure-holders as cultivated any part of their lands were recognized and assessed as raiyats. The board of Revenue had granted the tálukdars on the termination of their old lease a farming lease for 30 years from 1902. The allowance of the farmer was fixed by the Board of Revenue at 25 per cent. Subsequently on the application of the farmers this arrangement was changed to one under which farmers received an annual subsidy of Rs. 8,000, Government assuming, as the cultivators desired, the management of the estate. The total land revenue of the estate is Rs. 35,370. The D'Silvas' interest will disappear in 1931-32. The two estates have now been amalgamated. The total area of the estate is 12·63 square miles. It is surrounded on all sides by rivers and khals. There are low lands in the interior.

The Amtoli thana, the sub-registry office and the khas mahal circle office are in the mauza.

DAKHIN SĀHĀBĀZPUR PARGANA.—This pargana belonged to Sarkār Khalifābād also called Sarkar Fathābād. It formed part of the district of Bākarganj up to the year 1822, when it was transferred to the newly created district of Noākhāli. In 1869 it was re-transferred to this district. The pargana formerly belonged to Mirza Jan of Dacca. In 1780, seven annas of it were sold for arrears of revenue and purchased by Khaja Michael, an Armenian merchant in Dacca. In 1786 the remaining nine annas were also sold and purchased by the same Khaja Michael. In 1788 Mr. Douglas, Collector of Dacca, restored 3 annas 1¼ gandas and 1 kranti share to Mirza Jan. This share is now in possession of Babu Ananda Chandra Roy and others of Dacca by purchase. It is a distinct estate from the 12 annas 18¼ gandas and 2 krantis share which is held by many proprietors, some of whom are descendants of Khaja Michael. This pargana was bounded on the west by a large river called Betua. To the west of this river were lands of several parganas which were formerly dependent on Chandradwip, and to the west of them was the Ilsha or the Tetulia river, which was then a small stream. The Betua has dried up and much of the land situated in its old bed was resumed by Government, while the Tetulia has become a very large river. The river Meghnā (also called the Sāhābāzpur river) between Sāhābāzpur and Hatia was also a small stream and there is still a portion of the Sāhābāzpur pargana in Hatia.

The revenue of this pargana, at the time of the Permanent Settlement, was fixed at Rs. 54,000 (sicca) and a deduction of Rs. 12,208 (sicca) was made as compensation for land occupied for salt manufacture by Government officers.* When this manufacture was abandoned there was a proposal to raise the revenue to what it would have been if the manufacture had never been in existence. The proposal was ultimately abandoned, but in the course of the process "Kelso's Survey" (1847-48) of the island was carried out. As a result of serious agrarian disturbances the Court of Wards assumed management of this pargana in 1886 under section 95 of the Bengal Tenancy Act. The management is still in the hands of the Court of Wards. A survey and record-of-rights of this pargana was carried out by Babu Pyari Mohan Basu in 1890-92. Full particulars of the pargana will be found in his final report.

DAKHIN SĀHĀBĀZPUR SUBDIVISION.—Dakhin Sāhābāzpur is the oldest of the four subdivisions in the district and indeed one of the oldest in Bengal, having been formed in 1845. The islands of Hatia, Dakhin Sāhābāzpur, Manpura and some smaller adjacent islands were originally part of Bākarganj. In 1822, when the headquarters were transferred from Bākarganj to Barisāl, these islands were separated and annexed to Noakhali and so continued up to 1869. In that year, Dakhin Sāhābāzpur was re-transferred to Bākarganj in accordance with a petition from the inhabitants of the island. Manpura returned to Bākarganj along with Dakhin Sāhābāzpur, but Hatia remained in Noakhali. Dakhin Sāhābāzpur is bounded on the north and west by the Ilsha or Tetulia river, on the east by the Meghnā and on the south by the Bay of Bengal. This subdivision forms the highest portion of the district. There are few streams, but many roads in the interior of the island. There are already 121 miles of road in the subdivision. The roads radiate from Bholā, the subdivisional headquarters, two going south, one east, one west and two traversing the island from east to west.

The headquarters of the subdivision is situated at Bholā, to which it was transferred from Daulatkhan after the great tidal wave of 1876. The present area of the subdivision is 654 square miles. There is diluvion on the north and east and alluvion in south and west. It comprises the thanas of Bholā, Barhānuddin, Daulatkhan and Tazumuddin. The last two thanas were formerly outposts belonging to Barhānuddin and

Bholā, respectively. It has a total population of 318,337, of whom 46,305 are Hindus and 272,032 Muhammadans. The density is 487 to a square mile. There are five charitable dispensaries, 17 post offices including four combined offices, and four registration offices in the subdivision. The subdivision was once famous for the manufacture of salt. Betelnuts formed the principal item of export. The subdivision, once the most turbulent in the district, is now the quietest.

DAULATKHĀN.—The former headquarters station of the subdivision of Dakhin Sāhābāzpur. After the tidal wave of 1876, which devastated the whole subdivision, the headquarters were removed to Bholā. The village of Daulatkhan continued for nearly 40 years to be a place of importance as the headquarters of the Dakhin Sāhābāzpur zamindari. The village has recently been diluviated. The police station is now at Amani, as also the zamindari office (Court of Wards), the charitable dispensary, the combined post and telegraph office, and the steamer station. The local market is an important centre of the betelnut trade.

DEULBĀRI DOBRĀ BIL.—Deulbāri Dobrā is a mauza in thana Swarupkāti, subdivision Pirozpur. The entire mauza (18,278 acres) consists of a marsh, the level of which is gradually rising by the deposit of silt.

GĀBHĀ.—A village in thana Jhālakāti, subdivision Sadar. It is 17 miles to the west of Barisāl, with which it is connected by a District Board road. It is the seat of the Kulin Ghoses, of whom there are about 60 families, each of which is divided into 8 to 12 hissas (branches). The village is densely populated. The area of the village is 1⅓ square mile and it has a population of 3,423. The density is 2,567 to a square mile. There is a high English school in the village.

GAILĀ.—A big village spread over 7 mauzas, viz., Kālupurā, 3 Shibipāsās, Gailā, Murihār and Mānsi-Phulsri in thana Gaurnadi, subdivision Sadar. Its population of 10,450 consists largely of Brahmans and Baidyas. The area of the combined mauzas is 4⅓ square miles, the density being 2,411 to a square mile. Gailā is connected with the Barisāl-Mādāripur road by a branch road which takes off near Gaurnadi. Gailā has a high English school containing 768 pupils. It has also a Sanskrit institution, known as the Kavindra College, founded by the late Madan Mohan Kavindra, one of the most erudite Sanskrit scholars of his time. It is the birth place of Trilochan Kavikanthabharan, the author of the Panji, a commentary on the famous Sanskrit Grammar *Kalāp Byakaran*. Bijay Gupta, the author of *Manasha Mangal*, written in praise of Manasha, the goddess of snakes, was born here in the beginning of the fifteenth century. Gailā has a market which meets every day. There is a combined post and telegraph office in the village. The place is celebrated for the manufacture of molasses.

GALĀCHIPĀ THANA.—This thana is in the subdivision of Pātuākhāli, and comprises the south-eastern portion of the subdivision. It is bounded on the east by the Tetulia river and on the south by the Bay of Bengal. This thana, which was formerly located at Khalisakhāli, is found to have been in existence before 1812. The area of the thana is 337 square miles with a population of 13,398 Hindus, 86,828 Muhammadans and 1,069 others, chiefly Buddhist Maghs. A registration office, a charitable dispensary and a khas mahal office are situated at Galāchipā in addition to the police-station. The number of post offices in the thana is three, one at Galāchipā, one at Chhota Baisdia and one at Amkhola. A considerable portion of the thana consists of marshes.

GAURNADI THANA.—This thana was formerly in the district of Faridpur and belonged to the subdivision of Mādāripur. It was transferred to the district of Bākarganj in 1807. It comprises the northern and north-western portion of the Sadar subdivision. The police-station was at a village called Gaurnadi on the western bank of the Āriāl Khān river. This village has been washed away and the station is now at Palardi. The thana is found to have been in existence before 1812. The police outpost of Muladi, now an independent thana, was under this thana. A new thana with headquarters at Ujirpur has recently been created out of this thana. The area of the thana including that of Muladi and Ujirpur is 255 square miles. It has a population of 129,827 Hindus, 130,677 Muhammadans and 4,102 others, chiefly Christian converts. It consists mostly of low swampy lands and is one of the few thanas which grow to a considerable extent *aus* or early rice. There are three charitable dispensaries, one at Palardi, one at Muladi and a third at Lātājor, one registration office and twenty-four post offices. This is one of the most thickly populated thanas in the district and is the only thana where Hindus preponderate. There are some villages in this thana which are the seat of many educated Hindus, and the most notable of these are Gailā, Mahilara and Ujirpur. Gaurnadi contains many *bils* (marshes), the largest of which are Satla *bil*, Chanda *bil* and Ashkor *bil*. A considerable number of the Namasudras of the thana residing in the *bil* area have embraced Christianity. There are six principal churches—three Anglican at Dhamsar, Dhandoba and Jobarpar, two Baptist at Askor and Amboula and one Roman Catholic at Bijaypur near Palardi.

The roads locally known as *jangals*, which were made by the famous Sabikhān in the 17th century, are to be found in the northern and north-western parts of the district especially in this thana and Kotwalipar (transferred to Faridpur). One of the important roads constructed in Gaurnadi is the road from Palardi to Amboula in the heart of the *bils* in this thana. It has opened up the marshes to the cultivators and the colonists and has brought many fertile areas under the plough.

IDILPUR PARGANA.—This is one of the four parganas originally included in Sarkar Bāklā. Grant describes it as having belonged in 1764 to one Ram Ballav. He says it is situated at the confluence of the Ganges and the Meghna and consists of three zamindaries and *eight mahals* (Taluks). Perhaps no pargana gave more trouble to the early Collectors than Idilpur. The Chaudhuris of Idilpur were Hindus of the Kayastha caste and had the bad reputation of harbouring dacoits.

In 1777 the revenue of the pargana was fixed at Rs. 83,506. The proprietors, owing to mutual quarrels, submitted a petition to the Provincial Council of Revenue, praying that their estate might be divided. An Amin was accordingly deputed, and the estate having been divided, the proprietors entered into separate engagements for the payment of revenue at the rate of Rs. 81,115, on which terms they held it until the year 1781, when, on the refusal of the proprietors to continue the settlement, the estate was farmed out to one Manik Basu for seven years. In 1788 the estate was held khas and fell into an arrear of Rs. 30,541. In 1789 the revenue was reduced to Rs. 80,000 and the Chaudhuris again undertook the management, but finding that it could not pay such a high revenue, relinquished it at the close of the year. In 1790 the pargana was held khas and the collection amounted to Rs. 63,346 ; on deduction of the cost of collection, the nett revenue came to Rs. 54,769. In 1791 the dependent taluks were separated from the pargana at Rs. 13,547. The Chaudhuris declined to accept the terms offered to them at the Decennial Settlement. Afterwards when the estate was sold for arrears of revenue, they made this a ground of appeal. The pargana was held khas at various terms, but this did not mend matters very much. The Collector, Mr. Armstrong, in a long report, ascribes the arrears to the encroachment of the river Meghnā, the contumacy of the Chaudhris and the interference of the Civil Court. Another reason, perhaps more powerful than others, was that the raiyats deserted the oid and not very fertile mainland for the new *chars*, which formed in the Meghnā. In a subsequent report the Collector reported that there was a plague in the pargana which carried off hundreds of inhabitants daily.

Mr. Armstrong was superseded by Mr. Massier. At his instance the Board instituted a suit against the Chaudhuris for arrears due by them. In 1804, the Chaudhuris having agreed to pay up the arrears within ten years from the beginning of 1807, the Board ordered the Chaudhuris to be put in possession of their estate. This is an instance of the authorities trying to preserve an old family from extinction. The proprietors, however, again defaulted and the pargana was put up for sale in 1812, when it was purchased by Mohini Mohan Tagore, in whose family it still remains.

The revenue of the pargana is now Rs. 65,903-10 exclusive of the independent taluks, of which the revenue is Rs. 8,637. A considerable portion of the pargana lies in the district of Faridpur.

There is extensive betelnut cultivation in the pargana and it also produces a limited quantity of oranges. In the Asiatic Society's proceedings for January 1838 an account is given of a copper-plate inscription found in this pargana. The inscription records that three villages were given to a Brahman in the third year of Kesab Sen's reign in 1136 A. D., with a direction that the Brahman, Iswar Devasarma, should suppress the risings of the Chanda-Bharendas, an aboriginal tribe inhabiting the southern portion of the district, and should enjoy the villages as fief.

JABARĀMAL.—The term literally means possession by force. In the days of anarchy which preceded and followed the British occupation, the oppressed tenants of one landlord sought the protection of neighbouring and stronger landlords, who took possession of the properties of their weaker neighbours by sheer force. Raja Raj Ballabh is said to have obtained a great deal of property in this way. Three villages, viz., Babla, R. S. No. 229, Sikdar *Mallik*, R. S. No. 235 and Juzkhola, R. S. No. 238, in thana Pirozpur, all appertaining to pargana Selimābād, are still known as "the Jabarāmal villages".

JAYNAGAR.—A village in thana Bholā about 6 miles from Bholā, the headquarters of the Dakhin Sāhābāzpur subdivision. It is a big village comprising an area of about 13 square miles

It was originally formed as a *char* by the recess of the river Betua, which then constituted the western boundary of the Sāhābāzpur island. The river Betua was formerly wide and deep, but is now almost silted up. It appears from the old papers of pargana Dakhin Sāhābāzpur that Jaynagar originally belonged or was claimed to belong to a permanently-settled estate. It was, however, resumed as an alluvial accretion to Tāluk Degaldi under Regulation II of 1819 in the 10th September 1830, and was settled with Radha Madhab Bandopadhyay, the proprietor of the present taluk, at the time of the Decennial Settlement. He gave up the settlement in 1850-51 and the estate has been under direct management since 1853-54. The estate was last settled during the district settlement operations. The revenue according to the settlement is Rs. 28,896-10 including malikana.

The estate is fully developed and contains no jungle. It is well-cultivated and contains numerous homesteads and fine gardens of cocoanut and betelnut. A District Board road running from Bholā to Lalmohan passes through the estate, while another connects it with Daulatkhan. A tidal khal, navigable at all seasons of the year, runs parallel to the latter road.

The village contains the headquarters of the North Bholā Khas Mahal Tahsil Circle. Many improvements have been effected by Government. A market has been established at a cost of Rs. 1,200 and four reserved tanks and a pucca well have been dug.

JHĀLAKĀTI.—The town of Jhālakāti is an important centre of trade, situated at the junction of the Jhālkāti and Nalchhiti rivers in 20° north latitude and 90° east longitude in thana Jhālakāti, subdivision Sadar. Jhālakāti literally means a clearing of the Jhālas or fishermen. Raja Satya Saran Ghosal of the Bhukailas family, who owned 8 annas 12½ gandas and 2 krantis of pargana Selimābād, had his principal tahsil cutcheri at Gurudham near Jhālakāti. He flourished in the 19th century, built three houses here, laid out some gardens and made some roads through and near the bazar. Owing to these improvements, the place is also called Maharajganj.

Jhālakāti is one of the largest timber markets in Eastern Bengal. A considerable export trade is also carried on in rice, paddy, cocoanut and betelnut, the principal imports being salt, cloth and kerosine oil. An oil mill was established here by a German named Ziegler in the latter half of the 19th century. He was famous for his charity and hospitality. The mill is now owned by the Pal Chaudhuris of Bhojeswar and is in a prosperous condition.

The local municipality was established is 1875. It is administered by a body of 9 elected members. The area within the municipal limits is 1·12 square miles with a total population, according to the census of 1911, of 5,979 persons, consisting of 3,958 Hindus, 2,015 Muhammadans and 6 Christians. There is a high English school and a charitable dispensary in the station.

JHĀLAKĀTI THANA.—In the Sadar subdivision. It was established in 1874. The police outpost of Rajapur, now an independent thana, was under this thana. The area of the thana, including the outpost, is 149 square miles, and it has a population of 167,305, of which 75,952 are Hindus and 91,298 Muhammadans. The density is 1,121 to a square mile. It is thus one of the most densely populated thanas in the north. The police-station is on the western bank of the Jhālakāti khal. There are two charitable dispensaries, one at Jhālakāti and the other at Rajapur, the headquarters of the Rajapur thana. There are two registration offices in the thana. The number of post offices in the thana is 15. There is a dāk bungalow situated on the road from Kritipasha to Jhālakāti.

The thana contains some *bils* or marshes and has an extensive cultivation of *pani-kachus* (water arums). In this thana there are many small gardens of cocoanut trees separate from the homesteads. The thana contains some villages which are the seat of higher class Hindus, such as Gabha, Basanda, Kritipasa, Ramchandrapur and Nathulabad.

KACHUĀ.—A village on the right or west bank of the river Tetulia in thana Bāuphal of the Patuākhāli subdivision. According to tradition it was the old seat of the Chandradwip Rajas, who were forced to leave this place and who established themselves at Madhabpasa on account of the incursions of the Maghs. Another story is that they were forced to leave the place on account of the encroachment of the river.

Kamalā, a daughter of Raja Jaydev, fourth in descent from Raja Ramnath Danuj Mardan De, the founder of the family, made her name famous by excavating a very large tank near Kachuā. The tank was called *Kamalārdighi* after her name. There is an interesting tradition about this tank. According to the story, after the tank was dug, water would not come in. Kamalā was warned in a dream that unless she walked across the tank, the water would not come in. Kamalā proceeded to do so, but had hardly reached the middle of the tank when the waters rose up and closed round her and she remained in their midst in the guise of a water lily.

The tradition goes on to say that Kamalā had an infant child and that when her husband saw the waters closing round her, he called to her to come out. She replied that she could not, and when asked who would nurse her child, she answered that if the child were placed every morning on the steps of the ghat, she would come and nurse her. The child was accordingly set down on the ghat every morning and Kamalā rose out of the water and nursed it. The Raja, being disconsolate at her loss, resolved to bring her back. One day he hid himself near the ghat and attempted to seize Kamalā as she was suckling the child. She escaped from his embrace and disappeared in the water never to emerge again.

The tank is no longer full of water, but Kamalā's good work has not been unfruitful, for the bed of the tank now yields a rich harvest of rice and its high banks support about fifty homesteads.

KĀLĀIĀ.—Kālāiā is a big market in thana Bāufal. The country round Kālāiā grows *mung* (pulses) of a very superior quality. There is a good road from Baga to Kālāiā, passing through Bāuphal.

KALASGRĀM.—A village about 6 miles to the north-east of Barisāl, in thana Barisāl, subdivision Sadar. The village is the seat of some Baidya families notorious for their skill in forging documents and letters. They are professional forgers and are pronounced to be extraordinarily expert in their sinister profession. It is said that people from distant parts of Bengal place their orders for forged documents with the Baidyas of Kalasgrām.

KALASKĀTI.—A big village in thana Bākarganj, subdivision Patuākhāli. It is the seat of the zamindars of pargana Aurangpur, the principal representative of whom is now Bisweswar Rai Chaudhuri, who is reputed to be the wealthiest man in the district. He is a very orthodox Hindu, who spends most of his time in religious ceremonies. The affairs of his estate were found in great confusion by the settlement authorities notably in Marichbunia.

The village is the residence of many *Kulin* Brahmins brought down to marry into the family. These *Kulin* Brahmins are mostly dependent on the zamindar's family, receiving grants in money or land.

A local annual fair is held annually in the month of November, on the occasion of the Ganes Puja. It lasts for a fortnight and is attended by thousands of persons.

KĀLISURI FAIR.—The oldest of all the fairs in the district. It is held at Kālisuri, a small village in thana Bāuphal, subdivision Patuākhāli, in the month of December. It is said to have been established about 250 years ago by a Muhammadan saint named Syed-ul-Arafin, whose tomb is still shown at Kālisuri at the foot of a very old banyan tree. The tradition is that Syed-ul Arafin was a holy man who had the power of working miracles. One day as he was floating down the river on his magical carpet, he saw a Hindu girl coming down to the bank to wash rice. He asked her to cook some food for him, and on the girl's refusing to cook for a Muhammadan, he bade her look into the vessel in which she had been washing the rice. She did so and saw that the rice was already cooked. This miracle made her at once become a convert to the Syed's religion. She besought him to grant her a boon, and in reply he promised that the place where she was standing should become the site of a great annual gathering and that it should be called after her name. As the girl's name was Kali and she belonged to the Suri caste, the village and the fair got the name of Kālisuri.

The fair differs from most fairs in the absence of amusements. It is purely devoted to business.

KASBĀ.—An old village in thana Gaurnadi, which contains one of the three most ancient mosques in the district. According to tradition it was built by the famous Sabi Khan, who also made a road through the marshes in the 16th century.

KHEPUPĀRĀ.—A part of south Tea-khali, a resumed Sundarbans estate, the proprietary right of which belongs to Government. It is situated on the northern bank of the river Nilganj. The place derives its name from one Khepu Magh, who was the headman of the Magh residents in this locality. As the place is easily accessible from all parts of the Sundarbans it has been made the headquarters of the Sundarbans Colonization officer. There is a charitable dispensary and a post office.

KIRTIPĀSĀ.—A large village in thana Jhālakāti, subdivision Sadar. It is about 4 miles to the north-west of Jhālakāti. Benode Kumar Sen and others of this village are the principal talukdars in the pargana Selimābād. They have also a small share in the pargana. Their ancestor Krishna Ram Sen was the Dewan of Satrajit Roy. It is said that when at the time of Jay Narayan (*see* Bākla) the zamindari was confiscated for arrears, Krishna Ram rescued it at great personal sacrifice. There is a road connecting the village with Jhālakāti, constructed originally by Naba Krishna and Kala Chand, grandsons of Krishna Ram. It is now under the management of the District Board. There is a high English school in the village maintained by the local zamindars. An excellent library was established in the village by the late Babu Rohini Kumar Sen, an enlightened landlord, who wrote a number of Bengali novels and an interesting account of his ancestors. He died in 1904.

KUKRI-MUKRI.—An island measuring 12 square miles classed as a Sundarbans estate in thana Galāchipā, subdivision Patuākhāli. This island existed at the time of the Revenue survey and is now about 19 miles from the mainland. It is called Kukri-Mukri or properly Kukuriā Mekuriā, *i.e.*, Dog and Cat island, because the rats in the island are so large as to resemble dogs and cats. Several attempts have been made to colonize the island, but although the climate is healthy, all attempts have hitherto failed. The island is now used as a pasture for buffaloes.

On the eastern part of the island signs of the attempts to cultivate are still visible in the shape of mango trees, lemons, jack trees, tamarinds and flowers. From November to February fishermen from Chittagong come over to the island and catch chingri and small fish, which they sell to Muhammadan merchants coming out from the same district. The merchants dry the fish in the sun and export them to Chittagong in bālām boats.

The Crown Prince of Germany visited this island and shot wild buffaloes in 1912.

KUKUĀ.—It is one of the reclaimed estates in the Sundarbans. It is contiguous to mauza Chāwrā. It is bounded on all sides by khals with the exception of a small portion on the west, where there is no natural boundary. It was formerly under a osat talukdari settlement, but the osat talukdar defaulted and Government purchased the estate in 1890. Amtali is about 10 miles off from this mauza. According to the last census, the total population of Kukuā was 4,004 Muhammadans and 386 Hindus. Rice is the principal product of the estate.

LĀKHUTIĀ.—A village about 6 miles to the north-west of Barisāl. It is the seat of one of the principal families holding lands in the pargana of Chandradwip. They are the Rais of Lākhutiā. The founder of the family was Ram Chandra Khan. The ancestors of the family are said to have been the cooks of the Raja of Chandradwip. Whatever their origin, they can at least boast of one member who did great honour to the family. He was Raj Chandra Rai. He was a pleader as well as an enlightened zamindar. He constructed at his own cost a good road and khal from Lākhutiā to Barisāl. He had three sons, Rakhal Chandra, Behari Lal and Pyari Lal. They all became Brahmos, but Pyari Lal alone has remained in that faith. He is a leading barrister in Calcutta. Rakhal Chandra has died and is now represented by his son Debkumar, a minor poet of some celebrity. Behari Lal made a name by establishing a high school and a college in Barisāl. These, however, have ceased to exist.

A mela or fair is held annually in the village. It meets in November, on the occasion of the Rash Jatra, and lasts for seven days, being attended by thousands of persons.

MĀDHABPĀSĀ.—A village about 7 miles north-west of Barisal. It is the last seat of the Rajas of Chandradwip. It is connected with Barisāl by a road made many years ago by a Hindu lady named Parbati Chaudhurani belonging to the grocer family, who purchased a share of the estate. There are many old ruins in this village, but none of them is remarkable. There is, however, a fair large tank called Durga Sagar after Raja Jay Narayan's mother. There is a brass cannon lying near the bazar and there is a small tank in the neighbourhood called Kaman Tola. The weavers of the village weave mosquito-nets, which command a considerable sale among the middle classes.

MĀNPURĀ.—The island of Mānpurā lies in the extreme east of the district, beyond the island of Dakhin Sāhābāzpur. It was in existence before the Permanent Settlement and was resumed in 1833 apparently as an island or as a Sundarban forest, although it was never subsequently included within the jurisdiction of the Commissioner of the Sundarbans. It measured probably less than a thousand acres at the time of the Permanent Settlement, but it grew by alluvion to ten thousand acres in 1873 and to thirty-six thousand acres in 1910. The later accretions are still, to a great extent, uncultivated and uninhabited. The other part of the island, which measures 8,925 acres and supports a population of 5,000, was divided into 8 estates between 1845 and 1858, and these estates were settled with the original talukdars, who had obtained *ābādkāri* grants from the zamindars of Dakhin Sāhābāzpur in 1796 and 1808. In 1867 and 1869 it was proposed to settle these estates in perpetuity, but the proposal was not accepted by Government. One of the estates with an area of 745 bighas (242 acres) was, however, permanently settled before 1830 at a revenue of Rs. 55. It has subsequently suffered from diluvion and measured only 50 acres in 1910. In the 36 years which had elapsed since the last settlement, the cultivated area in the whole island had increased by 20 per cent., although the total area had decreased by 14 per cent. owing to diluvion.

The manufacture of salt was begun in 1812, and by 1818 the oppression of the salt contractors had compelled 350 families to leave the island. In 1822 and again in 1876 the island was swept by a storm-wave, in which all the cattle and many of the inhabitants perished. The island has been colonized from Noākhāli and chiefly by the Dasses of Sandwip, who, although Hindus, eat pork and marry widows.

The soil is fertile, the homesteads are substantial and surrounded by orchards.

In about 1870-71 a shark was stranded on the island and some of its bones were afterwards brought to Barisāl and placed in the Public Library.

MARICH-BUNIĀ.—This is a resumed Sundarbans estate entirely reclaimed from forest. It is situated on the east bank of the Marich-buniā river. It was first resumed in 1833-34. The tenure-holder of the estate is Babu Bisweswar Rai Chaudhuri of Kalaskāti. The local agents have consistently mismanaged the property and oppressed the tenants. A full account will be found in the District Settlement report of the attempts on the part of the Settlement Officer to bring about a better state of affairs.

The place is 6 miles from Gulishakhali steamer station. There is a *hāt* in the mauza.

MASJIDBĀRI.—A Sundarbans village in thana Patuākhāli (outpost Mirjaganj) on the bank of the Ayla, a tributary of the Bighai. There is a mosque in the place. According to an inscribed slab (now removed to the Asiatic Society's Museum) the mosque was erected in 1465. The inscription runs: "The Prophet of God (on whom be peace) said whoso buildeth a Mosque, God shall build for him seventy palaces. This mosque was built in the reign of the Sultan, the mighty pillar of the Church and State, Abooal-Mozaffar Barbek Shah, son of the Sultan Mohammed Shah, by Khan

Moazzam Ozyal Khan, year of Hijira 870 (A.D. 1465)". The question of preserving the mosque was at first mooted by Rai Sahib Hara Kisore Biswas, Assistant Settlement Officer, when he resettled the land revenue of the estate. It has been declared to be a protected monument under section 3 (3) of the Ancient Monuments Preservation Act, VII of 1764, *vide* Government Notification No. 3471, dated the 17th July 1913.

MATBĀRIĀ THANA.—Of the four thanas in the subdivision of Pirojpur, this is the largest. It is on the eastern bank of the river Baleswar. The police-station is at Ghatichorā. The registration office, the combined post and telegraph office and the charitable dispensary are at Matbāriā. The police-station of Bāmnā, now an independent thana, was formerly an outpost under this thana. The area of the thana including that of the outpost is 254 square miles. The total population is 123,005, consisting of 29,459 Hindus, 93,536 Muhammadans and 30 others. There are six post offices, one telegraph office, one registration office and a charitable dispensary in this thana. Abad Tushkhali, one of the largest Government estates, lies in this thana. The southern portion of the thana, extending to the Bay of Bengal, comprises some big Sundarbans estates. The important products of the thana are rice and cocoanut.

MEHENDIGANJ THANA.—The largest of the six thanas in the Sadar subdivision. It is bounded on the east by the Ilsa river, which separates the mainland from the Dakhin Sāhābāzpur island. The thana is found to have been in existence before 1812. The police-station is now situated at Pāterhāt. The police-station of Badartuni, now an independent thana, was an outpost under this thana. The area of the thana including that of the Badartuni is 266 square miles with a total population of 174,154, consisting of 33,815 Hindus, 140,281 Muhammadans and 58 others. There are 11 post offices, two charitable dispensaries and one registration office in this thana. The thana being bounded on the west by the Āriāl Khān river and on the east by the Tetulia contains many resumed estates. The important products of the thana are rice, cocoanuts and betelnuts. It also produces jute and sugarcane to a large extent.

The best *kosh* boats are built at Gobindapur in this thana.

NALCHIRĀ.—A village in thana Gaurnadi. It is the residence of the Nalchirā Mias, who were the proprietors of the pargana Tappe Nazirpur. According to the family papers Altaf Ghazi of Ghazipur was the founder of the family. He was Vizier of one of the Delhi Emperors and came to Dacca in the time of Jahangir. His son Syed Jan obtained the zamindari and settled at Tero Char. Ainuddin, the grandson of Syed Jan, removed the family residence to Nalchirā, where his descendants still live in straitened circumstances. The family has become degraded by misalliances, but it still enjoys some respect on account of its antiquity. The zamindari was sold for arrears of revenue and purchased by the Tagore family of Calcutta in 1819.

A fair is held here in the month of April and lasts for seven days. It is attended by thousands of people and is celebrated for its horse races.

NALCHHITI.—Formerly an important centre of trade in thana Nalchhiti, Sadar subdivision, situated on the south bank of the river of the same name. The chief exports are rice, paddy and betelnuts and the chief imports are salt, tobacco and sugar. There is a quarter in Nalchhiti called *Magh pārā*, because it is mainly occupied by Maghs, who come to Nalchhiti in the cold weather to trade in betelnuts. There is an oil mill for the manufacture of mustard oil. Cocoanut oil is also manufactured in the locality.

Nalchhiti was constituted a municipality in 1875. The present area of the municipality is only half a square mile. The population, according to the census of 1911, was 1,953, consisting of 1,123 Hindus, 819 Muhammadans and 11 Buddhists. The importance of the town is declining owing to diluvion.

NALCHHITI THANA.—It is a small thana on the west of Barisāl under the Sadar subdivision. Its establishment at Baraikaran appears to have preceded the year 1793. The station was transferred to Nalchhiti in 1824. The area of the thana is 90 square miles and it has a population of 82,335, consisting of 26,564 Hindus, 55,696 Muhammadans and 75 others. The police-station is at Nalchhiti. There are nine post offices, including one combined office, one registration office and one charitable dispensary in this thana. The important product of the thana is rice. There was a short but severe outbreak of plague in 1898, chiefly in the village of Siddhakati.

PĀDRI-SIBPUR.—A village in thana Bākarganj, about 5 miles from Bākarganj. The Portuguese were the first Europeans or quasi-Europeans who engaged in the Bākarganj trade. They settled at Sibpur towards the middle of the eighteenth century. According to tradition Raja Raj Ballav, the zamindar of the pargana Buzrugumedpur, wanted to coerce his tenantry, who were inclined to be refractory, and thinking that these foreigners would be suitable for the purpose, applied to the Portuguese Mission at Bandel for some settlers. These were accordingly sent to him. A priest was afterwards brought to perform their religious ceremonies and four pieces of land or hawalas were assigned to the priest for his maintenance These hawalas were subsequently formed into a taluk called the Padrian or Mission Taluk. The first priest was Fra Raphaeldas Anjos and the patta or lease for the taluk granted to him is dated the 9th Falgun 1171 B.S. or 1764 A. D. The first church at Sibpur is said to have been built by one Pedro Gonsalves. In 1823, in accordance with the will of Domingo D'Silva, his son Marel pulled down the old church and built the present larger edifice. The taluk yields a profit of about Rs. 800, which is spent in supporting the mission. The Priest also receives fees on baptisms, marriages and funerals. Sibpur was once a flourishing place and there are remains of many large houses in it. It is connected with Bākarganj by a road in which there are several masonry bridges. The prosperity of the place was due to the rice and betelnut trade. The most conspicuous resident of Sibpur was Domingo D'Silva, who made his fortune in the rice trade. By his will, he left money for the building of the church and also ordered that Rs. 500 should be distributed in charity every year on the anniversary of his death alike to Christians, Muhammadans and Hindus. This charity is still continued. A few of the leading families are treated as Europeans, *e.g.*, are exempted under the Arms Act. The zamindars speak Bengali and are hardly distinguishable from their Bengali neighbours except in the matter of religion. Many of these people are professional shikaris, killing boars for those who hire them. Their priests endeavour to improve their education, and the village has a minor school and a girls' school, as well as a charitable dispensary. The parish is in the diocese of the Bishop of Mylapur, near Madras.

PATUĀKHĀLI SUBDIVISION.—This is the largest of the subdivisions in the district, comprising an area of 1,334 square miles in the south of the district extending down to the Bay of Bengal. It is bounded on the north by the Sadar subdivision, on the south by the Bay of Bengal, on the east by the Ilsa or Tetulia river and on the west by the river Bishkhali. The subdivision is intersected by innumerable streams and rivers of which the most important are the Bighāi and the Lohāliā fed by many small streams in the north and north-east of the subdivision.

The subdivision comprises the thanas of Patuākhāli, Bāuphal, Āmtali and Galāchipā, and has, according to the census of 1911, a population of 574,972 persons, the density being 431 to a square mile. It contains only one town, viz., Patuākhāli, the headquarters of the subdivision. There are eight charitable dispensaries, six registration offices and 22 post offices in the subdivision. Most of the Sundarbans estates lie in this subdivision.

PATUĀKHĀLI THANA.—This thana in the subdivision of Patuākhāli comprises the northern portion of the subdivision. The area of the thana is 278 square miles with a total population of 208,470, of whom 37,132 are Hindus, and 171,130 Muhammadans. The police-station is situated at Patuākhāli, which is also the headquarters of the subdivision. There are six post offices, three charitable dispensaries and one registration office in this thana. The police outposts of Mirzaganj and Betāgi, now independent thanas, were under this thana. The principal product of the thana is rice.

PATUĀKHĀLI TOWN.—Patuākhāli town, the headquarters of the subdivision of Patuākhāli, on the southern bank of the Patuākhāli river. A civil court with one Munsiff was set up here in 1868. The present town was then full of jungle and along the river-side a small market used to meet once a week. On the northern bank of the river, in the village Lāukāti, were the tahsil cutcheries of the principal landlords of the subdivision. The criminal court was established in the year 1871. With the influx of population from the districts of Dacca and Faridpur, a good market, a middle English school and a charitable dispensary were gradually established and trading firms opened up business. The supply of filtered water dates from 1899-1900.

The high school and the Begum Hospital are probably the most important public institution in the town. The school was established in 1887 and a hostel attached to the school in 1904. The hospital was established in 1872, and was provided with a new building in 1904, the entire cost being borne by the late Nawab Sir Khajah Ahsanulla Bahadur of Dacca. The hospital is called the "Begum Hospital" after the Nawab's wife. Rice, firewood, coarse cloth made by the local weavers and hogla mats made by the Namasudras are the chief items of trade. A hosiery factory was established in 1911-12, and is doing fair business.

Patuākhāli was constituted a municipality in 1892. The Commissioners were at first nominated, but the elective system has recently been sanctioned. The Local Board was established in 1871. The area within the municipal limits is about 3 square miles with a population, according to the census of 1911, of 6,217 persons, consisting of 3,028 Hindus and 3,189 Muhammadans. The density is 2,072 per square mile.

PIROZPUR SUBDIVISION.—This subdivision, which comprises a large tract on the west of the district, was established in 1859 with a view to checking river dacoities. It extends over an area of 729 square miles and is bounded on the north partly by the Mādāripur subdivision of the district of Faridpur and partly by the Sadar subdivision, on the south by the Bay of Bengal, on the east by the river Bishkhali and the Sadar subdivision and on the west by the river Baleswar, which separates Bākarganj from Khulna. A considerable portion of the subdivision consists of marshes, chief among which are the Rāmpur Chechri bil in Bhāndāriā thana and the Sātlā Deulbāri Dobrā and Jhanjhaniā bils in Sarupkāti thana. The subdivision is intersected by many streams and rivers, the largest being the Kāchā, which carries the waters of many streams in the north and finally feeds the Baleswar.

The subdivision comprises the thanas of Pirozpur, Swarupkāti, Bhāndāriā and Matbāriā. The population, according to the census of 1911, is 550,418, the density being 758 to a square mile. The subdivision has only one town, viz., Pirozpur, the headquarters of the subdivision. There are seven charitable dispensaries, seven registration offices and twenty-eight post offices in the subdivision. The principal products of the subdivision are rice, cocoanuts and betelnuts. The marshes referred to above are gradually drying up and yielding excellent rice.

PIROZPUR THANA.—This thana in the subdivision of Pirozpur is bounded on the west and south by the Baleswar river and on the east by the river Kāchā. The area of the thana is 127 square miles and it has a population of 122,935, of whom 52,718 are Hindus and 70,158 Muhammadans. The police-station is at Pirojpur, which is also the headquarters of the subdivision. There are six post offices, including two combined offices, two charitable dispensaries and two registration offices in the thana.

PIROZPUR TOWN.—The headquarters station of the Pirozpur subdivision on the southern bank of the river Damodar. This river was gradually drying up, but has recently been re-excavated. The subdivision of Pirozpur was established in 1859, but the town of Pirozpur was not established till 1866. During the interval there were no headquarters for the subdivision. Pirozpur was constituted a municipality in 1885. The area within Municipal limits is 11 square miles including a tract on the north bank of the Damodar. The Municipality consists of 10 Commissioners. They were formerly nominated by Government, the Subdivisional Officer being the Chairman. The elective system has recently been sanctioned. A Local Board was established here in 1887.

The town proper is not a centre of any commercial importance, but the Rajganj *hāt* on the north bank is an important market for rice and betelnut. Tiles and earthen pots are manufactured here. Salt, sugar, clothes and piece-goods are the principal imports. The health of the town was formerly very good, but some 15 years ago it became malarious. Some improvement has, however, been effected by the establishment of filtered water-works and the clearing of jungle.

According to the census of 1911, the town has a population of 11,996 persons, consisting of 7,850 Hindus, 4,092 Muhammadans, 41 Christians, 6 Buddhists, 6 Brahmos and 1 Animist. The density is 1,090 to a square mile. The town has a Government high English school and a charitable dispensary. The steamers from Barisāl to Khulna touch at Hularhat, from which the town is 4 miles distant.

PONĀBĀLIĀ.—An old village in thana Jhālakāti. It was formerly the headquarters of the zamindars of the pargana of Tappe Havili Selimābād. The Sugandha or Sunda river is said to have flowed past it in old times, when the village Sikarpur in thana Gaurnadi was on its opposite bank. There is an ancient image of *Siva* at *Shamrail* near this village. According to tradition the image was not established by anybody, but rose from underneath the ground of its own accord. Shamrail is regarded as a place of pilgrimage by the Hindus, thousands of whom flock here to worship the image on the *Siva Chaturdahsi* day. It is regarded by the Hindus as a *Pitha-Sthan*, *i.e.*, one of the places where a portion of the body of *Sati*, the wife of the god *Mahadeva*, fell severed by the discus of *Vishnu* when *Mahadeva* was carrying her dead body. The Ponābāliā Chaudhuries belong to an old Baidya family. They are now in impoverished circumstances and the greater portion of their zamindari is in possession of the Nawab of Dacca.

THE RĀBNĀBĀD ISLANDS.—The Rābnābād islands were originally one island which was afterwards cut into two by the Dārchira Channel. These islands appear in old maps under the name of Don Manic Island. They were apparently first colonised by Maghs from Arakan under the leadership of Angu Magh, whose descendants are still in the islands, in reduced circumstances. Apart from these Maghs who settled in the island under the authority of the Magistrate (of Dacca), there appear to have been no other inhabitants at the time of of the Permanent Settlement, although collusive leases were granted by the Chandradwip zamindars in the year preceding it. At the time of resumption (1831) considerable reclamation had been made and the usual malguzari settlement was made with talukdars, ignoring the prior claims of the Maghs. The islands are exposed to cyclones and to annual fluvial action. At the present time diluvion is most destructive on three sides and has not been compensated by alluvion on the south. The area at resumption was 40,000 acres in 1840, and in 1880 48,000 acres, whereas in 1910 it had been reduced to 45,000 acres. There are, however, extensive mud chars on the south, which are only visible at low tide, but will shortly add considerably to the area of the islands. The area of Bara Bāisdiā, the larger island, is 22,142 acres. That of the smaller island, which contains two tāluks Chhota Bāisdiā and Rāngābali, is 19,313 acres. In the larger island 70 per cent. of the land, and in the smaller island 60 per cent., consists of cultivation and homesteads. There are gardens of cocoanut and betelnut, but the soil is not very suitable. The population has increased from 11,899 in 1891 to 14,601 in 1901, the inhabitants being chiefly Muhammadans with 673 Hindus and 1,060 Maghs. The Hindus are Halia Dasses from Noākhāli, and many of the Muhammadans have migrated from that district.

Paddy is the principal product of the islands. They are accessible by dāk boats which ply every day from Galāchipā.

Of the three islands Chhota Bāisdiyā, Bara Bāisdyā and Rāngābāli, the last two have been declared proprietary estates by the Civil Court.

RAHMATPUR.—A village about 8 miles to the north-west of Barisāl with which it is connected by a road. The village derives its name from Rahmat Ali and Pūr Ali, two brothers who lived on plunder. They were caught and put to death during the time of Raja Kandarpa Nārāyan. The Chakravartis of the village are among the largest talukdārs in the pargana of Chandradwip. They are said to have been descended from one Narayan Chakravarty, who was a dewan of the Rajas of Chandradwip.

There is a khal in the village called Rājār Ber, so called because of a tradition that the Raja of Chandradwip had it excavated as a moat to his palace at Mādhabpāsā.

RĀMPUR CHECHRI BIL.—Rāmpur Chechri is a mauza in thana Bhāndāriā, subdivision Pirozpur. A considerable portion of this mauza consists of swamp, which is gradually being silted up and brought under cultivation. (*See* Deulbāri Dobrā Bil.) The centre of the *bil* is full of dense kachia grass, the home of wild buffaloes and swamp deer.

RĀMSIDHI.—A village in thana Gaurnadi. There is an old mosque in this village which is said to have been built by the famous Sabikhan. It is a more imposing building than that at Bibi Chini and has four stone pillars. Two of the pillars are slender and are said to have been worn away by the embraces of devotees. A man named Kangali, a resident of this village, is said to have been the first Christian convert in the district.

RANGASRI.—A village in thana Bākarganj, famous for the production of sitalpati mats.

RĀYERKĀTI.—A village in thana Pirozpur, about 4 miles from the subdivisional headquarters. The name Rāyerkāti literally means the clearing of the Rays. According to tradition the Nawab of Dacca presented Madan Mohan Rai with the pargana of Selimābād and some other parganas as a reward for good service. Madan Mohan came from Diganga near Calcutta and established himself at Nathullabad. One of his successors named Rudra Narayan made his home at Rayerkāti. The family is one of the oldest in this district and the Sanskrit inscription on the temple of *Kali* shows that the image was set up by Rudra Narayan Ray in 1050 B.S. (1643 A.D.), that the temple for it was erected in 1144 B.S. and that Jay Narayan, third in descent from Rudra Narayan, inaugurated it on the 30th Paus 1162 B.S. (1755 A.D.). The Rais of Rāyerkāti are Dakhin Rarhi Kayasthas.

SĀTLĀ BIL.—The village Sātlā is situated in thana Gaurnadi, subdivision Sadar. It is a vast expanse of swamp and joins with the Deulbāri Dobrā and other *bils* in thana Swarupkāti. (*See* Deulbāri Dobrā Bil.)

SELIMĀBĀD PARGANA.—This pargana is the largest in the district. It comprises most of the lands in the subdivision of Pirozpur and extends across the Baleswar into the Bagherhat subdivision of the Khulna district. According to Professor Blockman, this pargana was originally called Sulaimanabad, after Sulaiman Shah of Bengal. This author suggests that the name may have been changed to Selimābād in honour of

Prince Selim, afterwards known as the Emperor Jahangir. There is, however, no proof in support of this suggestion. The pargana belonged to Sarkar Fatehabad. It has been partitioned into 17 estates. There are many independent taluks in the pargana. According to an account, given Mr. Collector Thompson, Aga Bakar took possession of the pargana when he was *wudadar* or farmer of it. In 1156 B.S. (1749 A.D.) the dispossessed proprietors complained to the Subah and 4½ annas of it were restored to them. Aga Bakar remained in possession of 11½ annas till 1160 B.S. (1753 A.D.), when he was put to death for rebellion, and Raja Raj Ballav was appointed to attach his property. Raja Raj Ballav managed to retain possession till 1164 B. S. (1757 A. D.), when Siv Narayan, a son of Jay Narayan, one of the original proprietors, recovered the estate through the influence of Gokul Chandra Ghosal, Dewan of the Provincial Council of Chittagong, to whom, as a reward, Siv Narayan gave half of the recovered property, *i.e.*, 5 annas and 15 gandas. This share was entered in the name of Bhawani Charan, which is said to have been the astrological name of Gokul Chandra Ghosal. Siv Narayan and Gokul Chandra Ghosal held this 11½ annas jointly till 1172 B.S. (1772 A.D.), when at their request a partition was made by Mr. Barwell, who was then the Chief of Dacca. Gokul Chandra Ghosal died in 1779, and in 1789 his share was sold for a private debt under a decree of Court and was bought by Kasinath Chaudhuri for Rs. 29,100. Kasinath was, however, merely the *benamdar*, the real buyers being the Ghosal family. A few years before this Siv Narain fell into arrears and half of his share, namely, 2 annas 17½ gandas, was bought by Jay Narayan Ghosal in the name of his son Kali Sankar. In 1796 Kasinath's share was sold by a decree of the Supreme Court to Raja Raj Krishna, and ten years afterwards his son, Naba Krishna, resold it to Kali Sankar Ghosal. Thus the Ghosal family became possessed of 8 annas 12½ gandas and 2 krantis of the whole pargana and these shares they still retain. They reside at Bhukailash near Calcutta and have enjoyed the title of Raja from the time of Kali Sankar Ghosal, who was made a Raja Bahadur in 1825. Their head cutchari is at Jhālakāti, about 12 miles west of Barisāl.

The descendents of Jay Narayan reside at Rāyerkāti, in thana Pirozpur (*see* Rāyerkāti).

The pargana was once the centre of salt manufacture, and on this account much of it lay waste. In the ninth report of the Committee of the House of Commons, dated the 25th June

1783, it is stated that an Armenian merchant, named Khaja Kaworke, was in possession of the salt farm of Selimābād in 1773. In 1774 Mr. Barwell, the Chief of Dacca, held the salt estates of Selimābād. He relet them to Khaja Kaworke in consideration of a present, for which he was censured by the Court of Directors.

SHĀMRĀIL.—Shāmrāil is regarded as a place of pilgrimage by the Hindus, thousands of whom flock here to worship the image on the *Siva Chaturdashi* day (*see* Ponābāliā).

SIĀL GHUNI.—A village in thana Bākarganj. There is an old mosque in this village, said to have been built by one Nasarat Ghazi. It appears to have been at one time richly ornamented and still has some carved flowers and arabesques. The villagers say that there was an inscription which fell down and disappeared.

SIKARPUR.—A village 13 miles north of Barisāl which is said to have been at one time on the east bank of the wide river Sugandha when Ponābāliā-Shāmrāil was on the west bank. There is a temple here, dedicated to the goddess *Tara* or *Ugra-tara*, a manifestation of the goddess *Sati*. The temple, which was long in ruins, has recently been repaired and the broken image of the goddess has been replaced by a new image.

SOHĀGDAL.—A village in thana Swarupkāti. Good *panshi* boats and large cargo boats are made here.

SUJĀBĀD.—A small village in thana Nalchhiti, about 5 miles south-west of Barisāl, on the north bank of the Nalchhiti river. It derives its name from Shah Suja, the ill-fated brother of Aurangzeb. In this village there are remains of an old fort which appears to have been erected by Shah Suja when he was Viceroy of Bengal and had to defend the country against the incursions of Burmese Maghs. The fort was rectangular and surrounded by an earthen wall with a mound at each corner. Inside were four small tanks and in the centre of the inner space where the four roads met, was the prince's dwelling house. The greater part of the wall has fallen into the river, the tanks are nearly dried up and the greater portion of the grounds are covered with jungle. The area of the whole village is only 77 acres and there is a document in the Collectorate record-room showing that it was given rent-free by Shah Suja to the families of some Pathans who had fallen in battle against the Maghs. It is also said that the fight lasted for two days and that Shah Suja's force was victorious. In 1845 it was proposed to resume the grant and an amin was deputed to make a map of the locality. The land was then in possession of the descendants of the Pathans, who succeeded in obtaining its release. None of them now resides here and their rights have passed into other hands by purchase. There is a tragical story about Asman Singh, one of the last Pathan residents of the village. The story is the subject of a popular ballad. Asman's wife was unfaithful to him. News was brought to him, while he was away at Nalchhiti, that his wife's Muhammadan paramour was in his house. Arming himself with a sword Asman rushed home to take vengence. On the pretext of illness his wife delayed to open the door and thereby gave her lover time to escape. At last Asman Singh burst open the door and aimed a blow at his wife. The blow missed her and fell upon her child, who died in her arms. Asman Singh was tried for murder, and having been found guilty was hanged in chains on the river bank near the scene of his crime. The ballad adds that his brother in Calcutta succeeded in obtaining a pardon for him. He hurried with it to Barisāl, but arrived too late to stay the execution.

THE SUNDARBANS.—The Sundarbans are the southern portion of the Ganges delta, extending from the Hughli on the west to the Meghna on the east through the 24-Parganas, Khulna and Bākarganj. Their limits on the north are the permanently-settled lands of those districts. The Bākarganj portion of the Sundarbans now lies on the seacoast in the southern part of the district, but at the time of the British occupation the Sundarbans extended far into the centre of the district and covered 610 square miles. A full account of the Bākarganj Sundarbans will be found in the District Settlement report.

The derivation of the word Sundarbans is undecided. Several derivations have been suggested. According to one of them (and it is perhaps the most probable) the name is derived from the *Sundari* trees with which the Sundarbans are said to have been covered at one time. It is, however, a singular fact that the *Sundari* tree is by no means common in the Bākarganj portion of the Sundarbans. The prevailing trees in the Sundarbans are *Kewrā*, *Gomā* and *Bāin*. In Latā Chāpli *Jām* trees are found in abundance. The present scarcity of *Sundari* tree is probably due to the fact that they have been cut down by the wood-cutters owing to their value in the market.

Were the Sundarbans inhabited in ancient times? This is a question which has excited a great deal of attention. It is said that there were formerly large cities in the Sundarbans, that the present desolate condition of the Sundarbans may be due to the subsidence of the land, and that this may have been contemporaneous with the formation of the submarine hollow in front of Khulna and Bākarganj known as the "Swatch of No Ground." It is, however, very doubtful that the Sundarbans were ever largely peopled and that their inhabitants lived in cities or were otherwise civilised. As regards the eastern portion of the Sundarbans including the islands in the Meghna estuary, the fact that so much salt had been manufactured there in old times militates against the view of extensive cultivation, for salt could not have been made without a great consumption of fuel and this implies the existence of a large tract of forest. Another fact which is against the supposition is the terrible suffering of the crew of the Dutch Ship *Jar Schelling* which was wrecked off the coast of Bengal in 1661. An account of the wreck was first published in Amsterdam and afterwards in London under the title of "A Relation of an Unfortunate Voyage to the Kingdom of Bāngālā." The ship-wrecked men seem to have landed on an island near Sundwip and their sufferings from hunger were terrible. Their only drink was salt water. They saw very few inhabitants and those whom they did come across were in almost as wretched a plight as themselves. They looked like people driven from more civilised regions. The copper plate inscription found at Idilpur and described in the Asiatic Society's Journal (1838) seems also to indicate that the Sundarbans were not inhabited by a high caste population at an early period. By far the most interesting account of the Sundarbans is contained in the letters of the Jesuit priests who visited Bākarganj and Jessore in 1599 and 1600. The description of the route from Bāklā to Chandecan (Jessore) by the Priest Forseca is by no means suggestive of the Sundarbans having been populated at that time; it rather shows that the Sundarbans were in much the same condition in 1599 as they are now.

As the forest was the property of the State, the Sundarbans were not included in the Permanent Settlement. It was not, however, till about the year 1838 that the claims put forth by the zamindars to the forest were decided and the confusion removed. By successive Regulations XXIII of 1817, II of 1819 and III of 1828, it was affirmed that "the uninhabited tract known by the name of the Sundarbans has ever been and is hereby declared to be the property of the State", while

Regulation IX of 1816 established the office of Commissioner in the Sundarbans for the management of the property thus acquired. The survey of the Sundarbans boundary, ordered by Regulation III of 1828, was made in 1830 in Bākarganj by Mr. William Dampier as Commissioner in the Sundarbans and Lieutenant Alexandar Hodges as Surveyor. The boundary then laid down was marked by a line of bamboos and has always been known as "the Dampier-Hodges line".

The area of the Sundarbans belonging to Bākarganj is less than that belonging to Khulna or the 24-Parganas, but is more cultivated owing to its higher level and the large quantity of fresh water brought in by the Meghnā. The reclamation would have been much more and the revenue greater, had the Commissioner in the Sundarbans been able to pay more attention to Bākarganj. He had his headquarters at Alipore near Calcutta. His office was abolished in 1904 and the Bākarganj forest area came under the control of the Collector of Bākarganj, who soon proposed a scheme for colonization by cultivators. A Colonization officer was appointed in 1907 with headquarters at Khepupārā.

The Bākarganj Sundarbans lie in thanas Amtali, Galāchipā, Pirozpur, Mathāriā, Bhāndāriā and Patuākhāli, the major portion lying in the first thana. The present area of the tract including the islands in the Meghna estuary is 697 square miles. There are 120 estates of which 13 are permanently-settled, two are revenue free grants, where 105 are temporarily-settled. The revenue obtained from the permanently-settled estates is Rs. 99,856, and the present revenue of the temporarily settled estates, excluding the rents of the area colonised since the establishment of the Colonization office and the wood-cutting and grazing fees, is Rs. 3,83,101.

The Muhammadans and the Maghs are the principal settlers of the Sundarbans. According to the census of 1911, the number of Maghs in the Sundarbans was 8,600. They are chiefly found at Bargunā, Nishanbaria, South Teakhāli, Char Chapli, Lata Chapli, Bara Bagi, Chhota Bagi, Lalua, Baliatali, Dhulashar, Bara Baishdia, Rangabali, Khapra-bhanga and Chakamaia. The Maghs are interesting people. They are excellent reclaimers of forest, but are somewhat indifferent as permanent raiyats, partly because they have a rooted objection to paying rent. They live in huts raised on piles and form communities under their own headmen. They are unfortunately addicted to the use of opium. They dress in home-spun coloured cloths, the elder men affecting stripes and the younger men checks. The wealthy among the Maghs are found at Bara Baishdia and Chhota Bagi. Tigers and deer are plentiful in the Sundarbans, and wild buffaloes in some places. The rivers swarm with crocodiles.

The general aspect of the Sundarbans is that of a lonely forest traversed by streams of brackish water. Many works of improvement have, however, been made in the Sundarbans since the establishment of the Colonisation office. Previously there were only 15 tanks in the Government estates. To this number 30 more have been added, besides many small tanks excavated by the Maghs, which supply good drinking water. A good dāk-bungalow has been built at Latā Chapli on a mound of sand near the seashore. There are two charitable dispensaries and five post offices in the Sundarbans.

SUTĀLARI.—This is a village situate on the bank of the Nalchhiti river, a mile east of the famous mart at Jhālakāti. It was so named owing to a large number of weavers that inhabited it in former times. In the seventeenth and eighteenth centuries it was a famous centre of trade, which subsequently shifted itself to Jhālakāti, owing to the erosion of the river. There were a large number of Dacca merchants settled here, who gave it the name of "Nārayanganj." A stone slab attached to a mosque very recently swallowed up by the river, contains inscriptions in Persian which indicate that in 1732—the date of construction of the mosque—the place was a flourishing one. The slab is deposited at the Dacca Museum. The following is the English translation of the inscription contained in it: "In the reign of Mohamed Shah, the Protector of Religion, under whose justice the world got relief, Gholam Muhammed, out of loyalty to God, under God's mercy, this place of worship did build." [To give date of construction of his mosque, Wisdom wrote: 'Approved by the grace of God.'] It was also the headquarters of a salt manufacturer, Durgagati Rai, who held a license for the manufacture of salt nearly 200 years ago from the Nawab Nazim of Dacca. There is a very big monument, erected over the ashes of Durgagati Rai, which exists up to this day.

SWARUPKĀTI THANA.—One of the four old thanas in the subdivision of Pirozpur, comprising the northern portion of the subdivision. The police outpost of Nazirpur, now an independent thana, and the new thana of Banaripārā were under the jurisdiction of this thana. The police-station is at Swarupkāti on the east bank of the Swarupkāti river. The area of the thana, including that of Nazirpur and Banaripārā, is 223 square miles, and it has a population of 204,669, consisting of 115,654 Hindus, 88,814 Muhammadans and 201 others. There are twelve post offices, one registration office and three charitable dispensaries in the thana. The villages of Panaripārā and Narottampur in this thana are the homes of many Kulin Kayasthas. Cocoanuts are the most important product of the thana and the *bil* portion of it, which is gradually drying up, produces excellent rice.

TUSHKHĀLI.—Ābād Tushkhāli is situated in thana Matbāriā. It is a resumed Sundarbans estate entirely reclaimed from forest. The estate comprises 23 villages containing an area of about 36 square miles.

The estate was originally a jungle tract belonging to the Sundarbans; the zamindars of the adjoining pargana Saidpur encroached upon the lands and granted leases for its reclamation. This fact was discovered in March 1830 by Mr. William Dampier, then Commissioner of the Sundarbans, and a suit under Regulation II of 1819 and Regulation III of 1828 was instituted for the resumption of the lands. The case was decreed in favour of Government, and the lands were attached on the 25th November 1833. On an appeal being preferred against this decision by the zamindars of Saidpur, the resumption decree was confirmed by the Special Commissioner on 5th September 1836. The estate was accordingly surveyed by Captain Hodges and held under direct management for about five years, but owing to the persistency with which rents were withheld, and the continued opposition offered by tenants of all classes, it was resolved to farm out the estate.

Mr. F. B. Kemp, then Commissioner of the Sundarbans, farmed out the estate to one Devanath Roy, zamindar of Taki, for 20 years from 1839-40 to 1859-50 at a net revenue of Rs. 39,149-15-5.

The term of the aforesaid farming settlement having expired, Mr. Reily, then Commissioner of the Sundarbans, was entrusted with the settlement of the estate. He found that it then contained 34,252 acres.

When the estate was being resurveyed, several petitions were filed by the tenants against the Government farmer. It was found, on enquiry, that the farmer was very high-handed and oppressive. The estate was, therefore, taken over for direct management. The total revenue according to this settlement was Rs. 1,17,663.

The area of the estate as ascertained by Mr. Reily did not, however, remain intact. The estate was after a time transferred to the jurisdiction of the Collector of Bākarganj, who, on the 2nd February 1866, sold as a separate estate a mauza called Halta with an area of 17,065 bighas. Besides this a civil suit (suit No. 47 of 1863) having been instituted against Government, 19,472 bighas of land were by a decree of the High Court, dated 30th April 1864, excluded from the Tushkhāli estate and given to the adjoining Sundarbans estate of Debnathpur. Moreover, five scattered plots comprising a total area of 549 bighas within the general boundaries of the jungle grant of Debnathpur, which according to Mr. Reily's settlement belonged to Tushkhāli, were settled by the Collector of Bākarganj as a separate estate (No. 5328 of the Bakarganj Tauzi) in 1871.

The total area thus excluded from Mr. Reily's settlement of Tushkhāli amounted to 37,086 bighas. The remaining area was let in farm for 20 years to Messrs. Morrell and Lightfoot on the 30th January 1871 by the Collector of Bākarganj.

The settlement of the estate was completed by Mr. Gomes, who settled the estate khas for 20 years from 1876-77 to 1895-96. The revenue of the estate according to this settlement was Rs. 1,02,352. The term of the settlement having expired, the estate was resettled khas for 15 years from 1898-99 with a revenue of Rs. 1,11,361, and an area of 21,356 acres. The Settlement Officer on this occasion was Babu Pyari Mohan Basu, Deputy Collector.

There are four markets in the estate situated in mauzas Matbāriā, Tushkhāli, Bara-masua and Dhanisafa. They are all well attended ; the principal articles of export are rice, cocoanuts and betelnuts and the chief imports are salt, tobacco, sugar, oil, piece-goods, corrugated-iron and timber.

There are good District Board and Local Board roads and also khals either natural or excavated at the expense of Government, which serve the purpose of irrigation.

There are a combined post and telegraph office, one sub-registry office, a police-station, a charitable dispensary and a Government tahsil cutchery in Matbāriā.

The people are prosperous but litigious.

The estate has been recently settled by Babu Ramesh Chandra Sen, Assistant Settlement Officer, and the revenue has been fixed at Rs. 1,21,740-8-9.

UZIRPUR.—A village in thana Gaurnadi. It is the residence of the old zamindars of the pargana Ratnadi Kālikāpur, which was given by the Nawāb Alivardi Khān in 1149 B.S. (1742 A. D.) to Ratneswar, who gave his own name to the pargana. Ratneswar was descended from Ram Mohan Māl, a servant of one of the Chandradwip Rajas. The family is one of the four old Hindu families in the district, the other three being the Chandradwip Rajas, the Rāyerkāti and Kalaskāti families. Ratneswar's descendents are now in reduced circumstances and the greater part of the pargana has passed into the hands of other persons. It is said that one Fakir Muhammed, who was a vizier of the Nawabs, resided in this village, and hence the village is called Vazirpur or locally Uzirpur. The village and its neighbourhood is famous for the manufacture of *dāos* and cutlery. It has been made the police-station of the newly created thana of Uzirpur and has a high English school. It is noteworthy that though Bākarganj is pre eminently a Muhammadan district there is not a single Muhammadan resident in this village. Another special feature of the village is that it is divided into separate *pārās* (hamlets), each inhabited by families belonging to a single caste The weavers of the village make *dhotis* of the Dacca pattern which are still appreciated.

INDEX.

A

B

C

D

E

O

P

Q

R

S

T

U

V

W

Z

B. S. Press—18-5-1916—759J—400—R. F.